Herman Melville

Nashville
Public Library
Foundation

*Books and other materials
on Poetry, Drama, and Classics
made possible
through the generosity of*
Judy and Steve Turner

Blackwell Introductions to Literature

This series sets out to provide concise and stimulating introductions to literary subjects. It offers books on major authors (from John Milton to James Joyce), as well as key periods and movements (from Old English literature to the contemporary). Coverage is also afforded to such specific topics as 'Arthurian Romance'. All are written by outstanding scholars as texts to inspire newcomers and others: non-specialists wishing to revisit a topic, or general readers. The prospective overall aim is to ground and prepare students and readers of whatever kind in their pursuit of wider reading.

Published

1. *John Milton*	Roy Flannagan
2. *Chaucer and the Canterbury Tales*	John Hirsh
3. *Arthurian Romance*	Derek Pearsall
4. *James Joyce*	Michael Seidel
5. *Mark Twain*	Stephen Railton
6. *The Modern Novel*	Jesse Matz
7. *Old Norse-Icelandic Literature*	Heather O'Donoghue
8. *Old English Literature*	Daniel Donoghue
9. *Modernism*	David Ayers
10. *Latin American Fiction*	Philip Swanson
11. *Re-Scripting Walt Whitman*	Ed Folsom and Kenneth M. Price
12. *Renaissance and Reformations*	Michael Hattaway
13. *The Art of Twentieth-Century American Poetry*	Charles Altieri
14. *American Drama 1945–2000*	David Krasner
15. *Reading Middle English Literature*	Thorlac Turville-Petre
16. *American Literature and Culture 1900–1960*	Gail McDonald
17. *Shakespeare's Sonnets*	Dympna Callaghan
18. *Tragedy*	Rebecca Bushnell
19. *Herman Melville*	Wyn Kelley

Herman Melville

An Introduction

Wyn Kelley

Blackwell
Publishing

BLACKWELL PUBLISHING
350 Main Street, Malden, MA 02148-5020, USA
9600 Garsington Road, Oxford OX4 2DQ, UK
550 Swanston Street, Carlton, Victoria 3053, Australia

The right of Wyn Kelley to be identified as the author of this work has been asserted in accordance with the UK Copyright, Designs, and Patents Act 1988.

Designations used by companies to distinguish their products are often claimed as trademarks. All brand names and product names used in this book are trade names, service marks, trademarks, or registered trademarks of their respective owners. The publisher is not associated with any product or vendor mentioned in this book.

This publication is designed to provide accurate and authoritative information in regard to the subject matter covered. It is sold on the understanding that the publisher is not engaged in rendering professional services. If professional advice or other expert assistance is required, the services of a competent professional should be sought.

First published 2008 by Blackwell Publishing Ltd

1   2008

Library of Congress Cataloging-in-Publication Data
Kelley, Wyn.
Herman Melville : an introduction / Wyn Kelley.
p. cm.—(Blackwell introductions to literature)
Includes bibliographical references (p.) and index.
ISBN 978-1-4051-3157-5 (hardcover : alk. paper)—ISBN 978-1-4051-3158-2 (pbk. : alk. paper) 1. Melville, Herman, 1819–1891—Criticism and interpretation. I. Title.
PS2387.K45 2008
813′.3—dc22
2007015879

A catalogue record for this title is available from the British Library.

Set in 10 on 13pt Meridian
by SNP Best-set Typesetter Ltd, Hong Kong
Printed and bound in Singapore
by Utopia Press Pte Ltd

The publisher's policy is to use permanent paper from mills that operate a sustainable forestry policy, and which has been manufactured from pulp processed using acid-free and elementary chlorine-free practices. Furthermore, the publisher ensures that the text paper and cover board used have met acceptable environmental accreditation standards.

For further information on
Blackwell Publishing, visit our website at
www.blackwellpublishing.com

Desk and writing implements used by Herman Melville. Photo courtesy of staff, Berkshire Athenaeum, Pittsfield, Massachusetts

To
Britt Kelley Peterson
and
Bayne William Peterson
with love

Contents

Texts and Abbreviations

Unless otherwise noted, references to Melville's works come from Harrison Hayford, Hershel Parker, and G. Thomas Tanselle, eds., *The Writings of Herman Melville*, 14 vols. (Evanston and Chicago: Northwestern University Press and the Newberry Library, 1968–).

The exceptions are:

Douglas Robillard, ed., *The Poems of Herman Melville* (Kent, OH: Kent State University Press, 2000) for all published poems (*Battle-Pieces and Aspects of the War*, *John Marr and Other Sailors*, and *Timoleon, Etc*).

Howard P. Vincent, ed., *Collected Poems of Herman Melville* (Chicago: Hendricks House, 1947) for unpublished poems ("Weeds and Wildings, Chiefly; With a Rose or Two").

Harrison Hayford and Merton M. Sealts, Jr., eds., *Billy Budd, Sailor* (Chicago: University of Chicago Press, 1962).

The "Agatha" correspondence, reprinted in the appendix to this book, comes from volume 14 in *The Writings of Herman Melville*.

Abbreviations for Melville's works are as follows:

BB	*Billy Budd*
C	*Clarel*
IP	*Israel Potter*
J	*Journals*
L	*Correspondence*
PT	*Piazza Tales and Uncollected Prose*
R	*Redburn*

Illustrations

Acknowledgments

When Ahab grasps Pip's hand in Chapter 125 ("The Log and Line") of *Moby-Dick*, he wonders at the cabin-boy's bottomless capacity for "the sweet things of love and gratitude." Although I cannot claim to resemble Pip in his wisdom (or his reverence for Ahab), I share his feelings for those who have extended their hands so generously.

Deepest gratitude goes to Andrew McNeillie, Emma Bennett, Karen Wilson, and Janet Moth at Blackwell Publishing, who initiated, steered, and shaped this book; to my superb readers Mary K. Bercaw Edwards, John Bryant, Anthony Lioi, Dale Peterson, and Ellen Weinauer; and to Dennis Marnon and Kathleen Reilly for special help with the illustrations.

I have had the very best teachers: George Dekker, Jay Fliegelman, and Albert Gelpi – mentors for life. The Melville Society Cultural Project team have nurtured everything I do; warmest thanks to Jennifer Baker, Jill Barnum, Mary K. Bercaw Edwards, Elizabeth Schultz, Christopher Sten, and Robert K. Wallace.

To the many people who encouraged and inspired me at critical points I owe an immense and unending debt: Jana Argersinger, Charlene Avallone, Dennis Berthold, Walter Bezanson, Hester Blum, Alex Calder, Christopher Castiglia, Gail Coffler, Carol Colatrella, Wai Chee Dimock, Edgar A. Dryden, Marvin Fisher, Peter Gibian, Robin Grey, Bruce Harvey, Diana Henderson, Henry Hughes, Pawel Jedrzejko, Henry Jenkins, Carolyn Karcher, A. Robert Lee, Maurice S. Lee, Caroline Levander, Robert S. Levine, Tia Lombardi, Paul Lyons, Robert D. Madison, Sanford E. Marovitz, Timothy Marr, Robert Milder, Lea Newman, Hilton Obenzinger, Samuel Otter, Rachela Permenter, Leland

S. Person, Ricardo and Bernadet Pitts-Wiley, Basem Ra'ad, Milton Reigelman, Elizabeth Renker, Arthur Riss, Laurie Robertson-Lorant, Douglas Robillard, Nancy Ruttenburg, Geoffrey Sanborn, Robert J. Scholnick, Bryan Short, Haskell Springer, John Stauffer, Gale Temple, Joaquin Terrones, Rosanna Warren, Margaret Weigel, Cindy Weinstein, John Wenke, and Dorothy Wheeler.

The people who supported me throughout the decades I have been thinking about Melville know, I hope, how deeply I rely on them. Bayne Kelley and Millicent Kelley have sustained me lovingly. Britt Peterson and Bayne Peterson, to whom I dedicate this book, give me reasons to keep on writing. Dale Peterson holds the other end of the monkey-rope and keeps the sharks away.

Preface

In his 1849 novel *Redburn*, Herman Melville writes of the dockmasters' lively calls to ships as they jostle together within the confines of Prince's Dock in Liverpool: " *'Highlander ahoy! Cast off your bow-line, and sheer alongside the Neptune!' – 'Neptune ahoy! get out a stern-line, and sheer alongside the Trident!' – 'Trident ahoy! Get out a bow-line, and drop astern of the Undaunted!'* And so it runs round like a shock of electricity; touch one, and you touch all" (p. 164). Melville's picture of a busy, noisy port crowded with ships from all parts of the globe, yet brought into electric contact with one another, evokes the current state of Melville studies. Globalizing economies and digital technology have transported Melville's works into a wider world than ever before, opening up to expanding audiences a broad range of issues: from the diverse literary influences on his texts to the politics of a burgeoning nation spreading its colonial power into the Pacific, from the impact of American slavery and capitalism to the emergence of new science, changing gender roles and sexual identities, and a growing literary market. As these themes jostle for readers' attention, and as his works compete with those of other authors in ever-enlarging anthologies and websites, readers may feel themselves in the midst of an almost intolerable din. On the one hand, they have the freedom of almost unlimited access to Melville's wide-ranging ideas: "touch one, and you touch all." On the other hand, they may seek the "shock" – and pleasure – of more intimate contact with the texts and their writer.

Herman Melville: An Introduction addresses the first generation of readers who might have grown up reading his works in online rather than print editions, readers for whom the "shock of electricity" might serve as a literal medium of communication rather than a dynamic metaphor. Reading Melville in a digital environment evokes certain assumptions about texts. Most significantly, for anyone with access to the internet, they are there for the taking. In Melville's day, depending on questions of wealth, education, or class, readers could find his books in a more limited variety of venues: in a library, a club reading room, perhaps, or a private collection. (Melville borrowed many books from his friend Evert Duyckinck, checking them out as if from a public library and returning them.) They could buy or subscribe to a journal and find long sections of a book quoted in reviews; they might buy the book as part of a subscription program organized by the publisher; or they could purchase it in a shop. If so, they might spend as much as a working person's weekly salary.

The fact that texts are now "there for the taking" has created a reading environment of tremendous opportunity. Readers can not only find a book but they can also search it, import text into their own writing, and remix what they read into "albums" of their own. Copyright law has struggled to maintain the protections of literary property it used to ensure. Nevertheless, in a digital universe, literary and artistic production has come to seem less the property of the maker and more raw material for future users. While the academic world levies harsh penalties for plagiarism, in a fluid online market of information, ideas, images, and stories the appropriation of other people's work seems as natural as breathing.

In spite of his very different historical context, Melville might have felt very much at home in a digital age. He was a voracious reader of all kinds of texts, from revered literary works to popular encyclopedias. And he was a tireless sampler of his culture, borrowing freely from a wide range of sources to produce new combinations of his own. The opening section of *Moby-Dick*, "Extracts," with its pastiche of quotations from all the known authorities, ancient and modern, on whaling, shows him mixing cultural materials in very contemporary ways. Like Dante, Shakespeare, Milton, and many other authors he admired, Melville often exhibits a proprietary attitude to the books and ideas of the past. They become his, he seems to say, and then, in a fluid interchange, they become ours.

Melville's fluid habits of literary appropriation show him being *inventive*, in a peculiarly late eighteenth- and early nineteenth-century way. In his period the US was in the process of creating a national identity rooted in ideas of self-making and self-marketing in a rapidly expanding environment. The word "invention" at that time included an older sense of a discovery of or coming upon knowledge (*OED*); it meant not only the making of something wholly new but also the ingenious recombining of previously existing elements. So too, Melville in many of his books seems to invent a literature, a voice, and an identity, by taking up the literary materials of his culture. In a period of extraordinary inventiveness – Benjamin Franklin's lightning rod, Robert Fulton's steam engine, Eli Whitney's cotton gin come to mind – Melville combined classical literary traditions with fresh items from his sensational travels to capture a vividly recognizable American spirit. His concern with invention itself – of a text, a narrative, a character or self – seems emblematic of the larger project with which the American nation and its people were centrally engaged in the nineteenth century.

In this book we will study some of the characteristic methods and tools of Melville's invention, beginning with a series of letters, the so-called "Agatha" correspondence, in which he described to his friend and fellow-author Nathaniel Hawthorne how he might construct a story from raw materials Melville had collected during a trip to Nantucket in 1852. As we will see, these letters reveal an author fascinated by the processes of literary invention, and by the literary inventors – many of them knaves, tricksters, and confidence men – who populate the worlds of fiction and poetry. We will find that in his distinctive habits of invention, Melville is a writer very much of his time – but also, strikingly, of our own.

PART I

Introduction

CHAPTER 1

Melville's Life

Melville's life and career, which spanned nearly three-quarters of the nineteenth century, display many of the patterns of self-making and literary invention he explored in his writing. The son of a man who reinvented himself a number of times as he launched one unsuccessful business venture after another, Melville similarly made himself up as he went along: as sailor, novelist, civil servant, poet. He may seem to readers today the man who represents one. nation, one novel, one thematic obsession – whaling – but it might be safer to take him at his word in *Billy Budd* when he ruefully called himself "a writer whom few know" (p. 114).

Born in Manhattan, New York on August 1, 1819, in the same year as Queen Victoria and Walt Whitman, Melville was reared in the Dutch Reform Church and middle-class propriety of his mother, Maria Gansevoort, and her Albany Dutch forebears. His father, Allan Melvill (the family added the final "e" after Allan's death in 1832), also came from an established family; Allan's father, Thomas Melvill, participated in the Boston Tea Party and reminisced about the American Revolution for the rest of his life. Committed to upholding the status of two such respectable clans, Maria and Allan Melvill nevertheless suffered serious reversals in their generation. Allan, an importer of dress goods and fashionable accessories from Europe, managed to ride out a period of tremendous financial volatility in US markets after the War of 1812, long enough for Maria to bear eight children with clockwork regularity: Gansevoort (1815), Helen (1817), Herman (1819), Augusta (1821), Allan (1823), Catherine (1825), Frances (1827), and Thomas (1830). But in numerous dubious financial schemes, Allan Melvill borrowed until he could borrow no more. The family was forced to leave New York in 1830 and move to Albany, closer to Maria's relatives. In 1832, massively indebted and raving with a fever, Allan died, leaving his family dependent on the powerful Gansevoorts.

Herman had probably been educated for a career in business or commerce, since the family could not have afforded to send its sons to college. He and his brother Gansevoort attended the Albany Classical School and later the Albany Academy. Although his father had early considered him a bit slow, even backward compared to the glib and polished Gansevoort, Melville proved an apt pupil.[1] As a teenager in the village of Lansingburgh (now incorporated into Troy, New York, near Albany), where the family moved in 1838, he also joined a debating society, wrote scathing letters to the local newspaper deriding his rivals, and penned various love poems. Two early sketches, called "Fragments from a Writing-Desk" and published in the *Democratic Press and Lansingburgh Advertiser* in 1839, suggest that he saw himself potentially as an author, although they imitated styles that he would eventually renovate: the anecdotal pose of the urban spectator, and the Gothic mode of Poe's tales of mystery.

Although he experimented with literary pursuits in his late teens, Melville needed more secure employment. Having worked in 1835 in Gansevoort's fur store, in 1837 he began teaching in the Sikes District School in the Berkshires, near his Uncle Thomas Melvill's farm. The following year he studied surveying at Lansingburgh Academy, hoping to get work on the Erie Canal, but with his chances for engineering jobs looking dim, he shipped out in the summer of 1839 on the *St. Lawrence*, a packet, to Liverpool. Melville's first voyage lasted only four months but gave him a taste of adventure that he would never forget. When he returned he taught at the Greenbush and Schodack Academy in Greenbush, New York, and then in Brunswick, New York. In 1840, with his friend E. J. M. Fly, he journeyed to Galena, Illinois, where Uncle Thomas had moved his family. The trip exposed him to the rough and adventuresome waterways of the Great Lakes region and the Mississippi and Ohio rivers; but the two men returned to Manhattan without prospects.

In New York City Melville took some time to ponder his next move: he decided on whaling. Factory work, farming, or mining would have been no less monotonous, brutish, or poorly paid, and the fact that he chose whaling, one of the most dangerous of the maritime trades, speaks as much to his economic desperation as to his spirit of adventure. It may have been with a free heart, however, that in late 1840 he packed a small bag, betook himself to New Bedford, Massachusetts, and shipped on the whaler *Acushnet*, which sailed from nearby Fairhaven on January 3, 1841, bound via Cape Horn for the Pacific whaling grounds. Most of his nautical novels record the joy of setting sail, even when that joy proves to be short-lived.

For Melville scholars and biographers, the significant events of Melville's voyages are the ones that ended up in his books. Most sensational was his desertion in the Marquesas. In July 1842, while anchored in Nuku Hiva Bay, he and a friend, Richard Tobias Greene, jumped ship and fled inland to escape discovery. From this point on, the primary evidence we have of his movements appears in *Typee*, a fictional account. Most scholars have assumed that Melville made his way to the Taipi Valley and stayed several weeks.[2] According to what he wrote in *Typee*, because of a leg injury, or perhaps because the Taipis saw the two white sailors as valuable hostages, or even, as he may have imagined, because they intended to eat him, Melville was held in an extended but pleasant captivity. Toby journeyed back to the coast to get help for his friend, who waited anxiously, and vainly, for news of his return. Thinking himself abandoned, Melville plotted his escape, but not before sampling the island's many delights. Although the Taipis treated him hospitably, he eventually made his way to the beach and signed on another whaler, the *Lucy Ann*, beating a hasty retreat from this island Eden. His experiences shaped his first book, *Typee* (1846). When news of its publication reached Toby Greene, who had returned to the US having been frustrated in his efforts to retrieve Melville, Toby wrote to his friend, who added "The Story of Toby" to his next edition.

From the Marquesas, Melville's journey took him to Tahiti. On the *Lucy Ann* he encountered a crew dissatisfied with its ailing captain and drunken first mate; eventually they mutinied, and were jailed in Papeete. Melville may have supported the revolt reluctantly, for the crew were, he said in his second book *Omoo* (1847), "villains of all nations and dyes; picked up in the lawless ports of the Spanish Main, and among the savages of the islands" (p. 14). But he seized the opportunity to abandon an unlucky vessel and, with the implicit permission of his lenient Tahitian jailers, wandered the islands with a friend from the ship, John Troy. After a period of beachcombing, Melville and Troy made their way to a neighboring island, Moorea (or Eimeo), where in November 1842 Melville shipped on the *Charles and Henry* for further whaling. The early sections of his third novel, *Mardi* (1849), take place on a ship much like this one.

His whaling came to an end in May 1843 in the Sandwich Islands (Hawai'i), where Melville was discharged in Lahaina, Maui, and worked in Honolulu at various jobs, including setting pins in a bowling alley. After three months, he tired of onshore labor, and shipped out once again, this time on the US naval frigate, the *United States*. Melville may have had little taste for naval life, but he knew that he could be seized and prosecuted for desertion if he signed on a whaler. The navy, as he would make clear much later in *Billy Budd* (published post-humously in 1924), gladly accepted even the "promiscuous lame ducks of morality" (p. 65).

Life aboard the *United States*, where numerous public floggings schooled the men to perform their tasks unquestioningly, was hard. The experiences chronicled in his fifth book, *White-Jacket* (1850), pub-lished shortly after *Redburn*, appear a grueling round of duties that nevertheless exposed him to a new class of men. Jack Chase in par-ticular, the captain of the foretop, struck Melville as a romantic figure of revolt and leadership. Not only did he picture him in *White-Jacket* as a charismatic hero, but he also dedicated one of his last works, *Billy Budd*, to his memory.

Melville returned to Boston in October 1844 an experienced seaman, though by no means a wealthy one. He was encouraged to write, however, by family and friends who relished his stirring tales, and urged on as well by necessity to make a living, as he contemplated marriage with Elizabeth Shaw. She was the daughter of his father's old friend Lemuel Shaw, chief justice of the Massachusetts Supreme Court. Hoping to succeed as other educated maritime authors like Richard Henry Dana had done in his *Two Years Before the Mast* (1840), Melville turned to writing to make his name. His first effort, *Typee*, dedicated to Lemuel Shaw, won him remarkable success, and on the strength of that public acclaim and the equally enthusiastic reception of his second novel, *Omoo*, he and Lizzie married in the summer of 1847 and moved to the city of New York, where Melville took up authorship in earnest.

The rapid succession of his first novels – *Typee* (1846), *Omoo* (1847), *Mardi* (1849), *Redburn* (1849), and *White-Jacket* (1850) – bespeaks

Melville's creative energy, the quick flowering of his reputation, and his considerable professional anxiety as well. For he soon found the demands of writing for an aggressively expanding commercial literary market more onerous than he might have expected. The births of four children – Malcolm (1849), Stanwix (1851), Elizabeth (1853), and Frances (1855) – during the years of his most intense literary output strained his financial and emotional resources.

At the same time, he undertook a furious process of self-education, reading avidly in a range of authors, from writers of travel and maritime literature to the great poets and playwrights of the past: Dante, Rabelais, Montaigne, Browne, Milton, Shakespeare, Jonson, to name just a few. Traveling to Europe in 1849, ostensibly to negotiate contracts for his books in London, Melville soaked up literary and artistic culture with the wonderment of the self-taught provincial he may still have considered himself to be. The persona of sailor-author or democratic naïf at first served him well as proponent of the Young America literary movement, among whose members Melville found a kindred interest in carving out a new literary world, apart from the superannuated models of Europe. In time, as he implied in his essay "Hawthorne and His Mosses" (1850), he came to consider himself an American Shakespeare and began to feel confined by the genres and limited expectations of maritime adventure.

Yet those early books, which he later thought of as apprentice or experimental work, prepared him well for a period of concentrated literary experimentation and achievement that began with his metaphysical novel *Moby-Dick* (1851). Drawn to the Berkshires region of western Massachusetts by family connections, Melville decided to settle in 1850 on the farm he called Arrowhead, hoping to enjoy a growing literary community that included Nathaniel Hawthorne, Catherine Maria Sedgwick, and Oliver Wendell Holmes, among others. Meeting Hawthorne at a point well along in the writing of *Moby-Dick*, Melville recast his novel along more ambitious lines, inspired by Hawthorne's example to believe that he could reach the full potential of literary genius. Their extraordinary friendship encouraged Melville to explore new latitudes of thought and invention, as he had done in his earlier philosophical novel, *Mardi*, and to pour his febrile excitement into long letters to Hawthorne. Although their period of proximity did not last long – Hawthorne moved his family back to the Boston area in 1852 and to England in 1853 – Melville's tide of enthusiasm carried him through an astonishing range and variety of literary endeavors for nearly a decade: his sensational romance *Pierre* (1852); a series of magazine stories of the mid-1850s, some of them eventually collected in *The Piazza Tales* (1856); his picaresque historical fiction, *Israel Potter* (1855); and a dark comedy, *The Confidence-Man* (1857), his last published work of prose fiction. These works did not garner for him the success of his earlier adventure narratives, but they did sustain his considerable reputation.

The effort of supporting his family on dwindling earnings and increasingly burdensome loans exhausted Melville. By the time he finished *The Confidence-Man* in 1856, his health was failing, and his alarmed family, particularly the perennially supportive Lemuel Shaw, sent him to Europe and the Levant for a six-months' journey. During that time he visited Hawthorne, then American consul in Liverpool; toured the pyramids of Egypt, the Greek isles, and the city and environs of Jerusalem; came back through Italy and Europe; and throughout his travels reveled in ancient and European art, architecture, and culture, storing up impressions for later works.

Back in the US, Melville began composing not stories but poems based on his travels; but no published volumes emerged until after the Civil War. Instead he attempted a brief career on the lyceum circuit, writing and delivering lectures on topics he thought might prove popular: "Statues in Rome" (1857–8), "The South Seas" (1858–9), and "Travel" (1859–60). Receiving mixed to tepid reviews, he made scarcely enough money to consider prolonging his efforts. Another journey, this time a restorative global sea voyage with younger brother and sea captain Thomas Melville in 1860, turned out to be similarly abortive. His manuscript, *Poems*, which he had left with his brother Allan while he went off to sail around the world, was not accepted for publication; feeling ill and homesick, Melville ended the journey in San Francisco and returned home.

Little is known of Melville's literary activities during the Civil War except that he appears to have actively pursued writing poems during a time when he also sought civil service employment, as Hawthorne and other authors had successfully done. His family had long wished to leave Arrowhead and return to Manhattan, and in 1862, after a painful accident when his carriage overturned on the road, Melville finally found farm work too hard to maintain. In 1863 he and his family, including his mother and some of his sisters, moved to 104 East

26th Street, where he lived for the rest of his life. Although he was not as active in New York literary circles as he had been over ten years earlier, Melville took a keen interest in political and cultural issues of the day, reading newspapers and following the course of the war with close attention. Hoping for a post in President Lincoln's civil service, he traveled to Washington, DC, in 1864 and visited army units and battlefields in Virginia. These experiences and his intensive reading of the *Rebellion Record* culminated in a collection of poems, *Battle-Pieces and Aspects of the War*, published in 1866. Although the volume won him only modest attention, it announced Melville's emergence as a poet concerned with patriotic themes. Rather than reaching the status of national bard that Walt Whitman enjoyed, Melville gained a political appointment after the war, as District Inspector of Customs in the New York Custom House, where he began employment in December 1866.

Here Melville maintained a steady, mainly uneventful (as far as we know) career for nineteen years, traveling each day from his house to the office, inspecting cargoes for contraband, and engaging with sailors and captains on very different terms from those he had experienced as a seaman before the mast. Still plagued by the ill health that had beset him since the 1850s, he endured and indeed caused considerable family tension as well. These tensions erupted in 1867, when Elizabeth Melville sought advice from her pastor about her marital problems, which had gone so far that she and her brothers considered a plan to kidnap her to get her away from Melville's heavy drinking and black moods. She decided against such a sensational proposal, continuing in a situation that clearly strained her devotion and, according to family letters, Melville's sanity. Conflicts with his eldest son Malcolm escalated in September 1867, when the boy returned late from an evening out, locked himself in his room, perhaps to avoid a harsh paternal scolding, and was found the next day dead with his pistol at his side.

In spite of these considerable shocks, Melville embarked on his most ambitious poetical work, *Clarel: A Poem and a Pilgrimage to the Holy Land*, published in 1876 in a limited printing financed, in an act of characteristic generosity, by his uncle Peter Gansevoort. Melville did not expect a large readership for this long, often knotty poetic narrative of a young theological student's exploration of the rigorous geographies and faiths of the ancient world. Nevertheless, in his profound engagement with the period's most pressing religious questions, as well as its vexing political debates and cultural conflicts, Melville produced one of his era's most complex expressions of doubt and faith. Almost completely ignored in his lifetime and little valued for a century or more, *Clarel* has emerged among many readers as one of Melville's most challenging yet rewarding works.

After his retirement from the Custom House in 1885, Melville embarked on a period of revising and consolidating earlier poems, publishing two collections, *John Marr and Other Sailors* (1888) and *Timoleon, Etc.* (1891) in private printings and leaving a third collection, "Weeds and Wildings, Chiefly: With a Rose or Two," unpublished at his death. He also wrote sketches and narrative poems on topics related to art, aesthetics, and politics. As part of his twin concerns with sailors from voyages long gone (explored in *John Marr*) and questions of art and aesthetics (*Timoleon*), he wrote a ballad, "Billy in the Darbies," that eventually grew into a longer prose work, now titled *Billy Budd, Sailor: An Inside Narrative*, which consumed him in multiple revisions until his death on September 28, 1891. Although the work exists only as a loosely shaped and never finished narrative, twentieth-century editors saw it as a late masterpiece and constructed Melville's presumed intentions into the print editions we have today.

Melville earned his greatest success and reputation from the early works he regarded least (*Typee* and *Omoo*) and lived long enough to understand that he would never win recognition for the achievements, especially in poetry, he valued most. That reputation changed in remarkable ways after his death. The so-called Melville Revival, beginning in the 1920s with the discovery and publication of *Billy Budd*, along with his collected works and the first full biography by Raymond Weaver, culminated in the mid-twentieth century with major scholarship by such leading critics as D. H. Lawrence, Lewis Mumford, Charles Roberts Anderson, Stanley Williams, F. O. Matthiesson, Charles Olson, Nathalia Wright, Elizabeth Foster, Walter Bezanson, Harrison Hayford, Wilson Heflin, Merrell Davis, Merton M. Sealts, Jr., Leo Marx, Howard Vincent, Eleanor Metcalf, Jay Leyda, Leon Howard, William Gilman, and Hershel Parker, among many others. This large body of critical and scholarly work established Melville as central to the so-called American Renaissance, a literary canon of texts in which *Moby-Dick* stood squarely at the center, along with Dickinson's poems, Emerson's essays, Hawthorne's *The Scarlet Letter*, Thoreau's *Walden*, and Twain's *The Adventures of Huckleberry Finn*.

Succeeding generations of critics discovered his short fiction and less highly appreciated works, especially *Pierre* and *The Confidence-Man*. Beginning in the 1960s, with heightened interest in issues of race, gender, class, and religion, stories like "Benito Cereno," "Bartleby, the Scrivener," and "The Paradise of Bachelors and the Tartarus of Maids" became newly relevant, and questions about Melville's attitudes to slavery and abolition more pressing. Burgeoning scholarly attention to American territorial expansion and colonial adventurism renewed debate over Melville's politics in *Typee* and other works set in the contested islands of the Pacific. Among other recent developments, growing interest in Melville's poetry and in the output of his later, seemingly private, career has raised new questions about this complex body of work and about texts and textuality in an author who seems to travel across generic boundaries with bold abandon.

In a long career, Melville wrote many works of fiction and poetry but relatively little about *how* he wrote. We turn now to an instance, one of few, in which he speaks directly about his own creative process in ways that illuminate the entire body of his writing: the story of "Agatha" in his correspondence with Nathaniel Hawthorne. While Melville changed the subjects of his fiction and poems many times over a long lifetime, he remained consistently fascinated by the problem of literary invention itself. As we will see, that process often grew out of chance encounters, lucky accidents, like his meeting with a New Bedford lawyer; and it worked because he knew a good find when he saw it.

CHAPTER 2

"Agatha" and the Invention of Narrative

Surely Herman Melville, author of *Moby-Dick*, needs no introduction.

But what if he did? Suppose we stumbled upon a previously unknown text, something that had escaped our notice? How would we know it to be his? What could it tell us about his writing methods, themes, characteristic practices, and thoughts?

Such a work might be the "Agatha" story that Melville heard from a lawyer in 1852 and, in an extraordinary series of letters, offered to Nathaniel Hawthorne to write; then, when Hawthorne eventually declined, Melville declared he would write the story himself. (The lawyer's narrative and Melville's letters to Hawthorne appear in the appendix to this volume.) The "Agatha" story, as carefully sketched in Melville's correspondence, shows Melville thinking out loud about the creative process, and it gives a superb view of the writer at work.

Beyond his manifesto on artistic genius – "Hawthorne and His Mosses" (1850) – some letters, a few travel journals, and sections of his published works, Melville left little evidence of how he wrote. He discarded most of his manuscripts and letters. He did not keep a personal diary, apart from the travel journals. The remaining manuscripts – a few chapters of *Typee*, fragments from *White-Jacket*, "Bartleby," and *The Confidence-Man*, his late lyrics, and the unfinished *Billy Budd* – offer only fugitive glimpses of the stages of his composition. The "Agatha" correspondence, on the other hand, revealing a story hardly known and certainly not published, shows in abundant detail how Melville thought about literary invention. It began with literary appropriation, the seizing on a good story and making it his own.

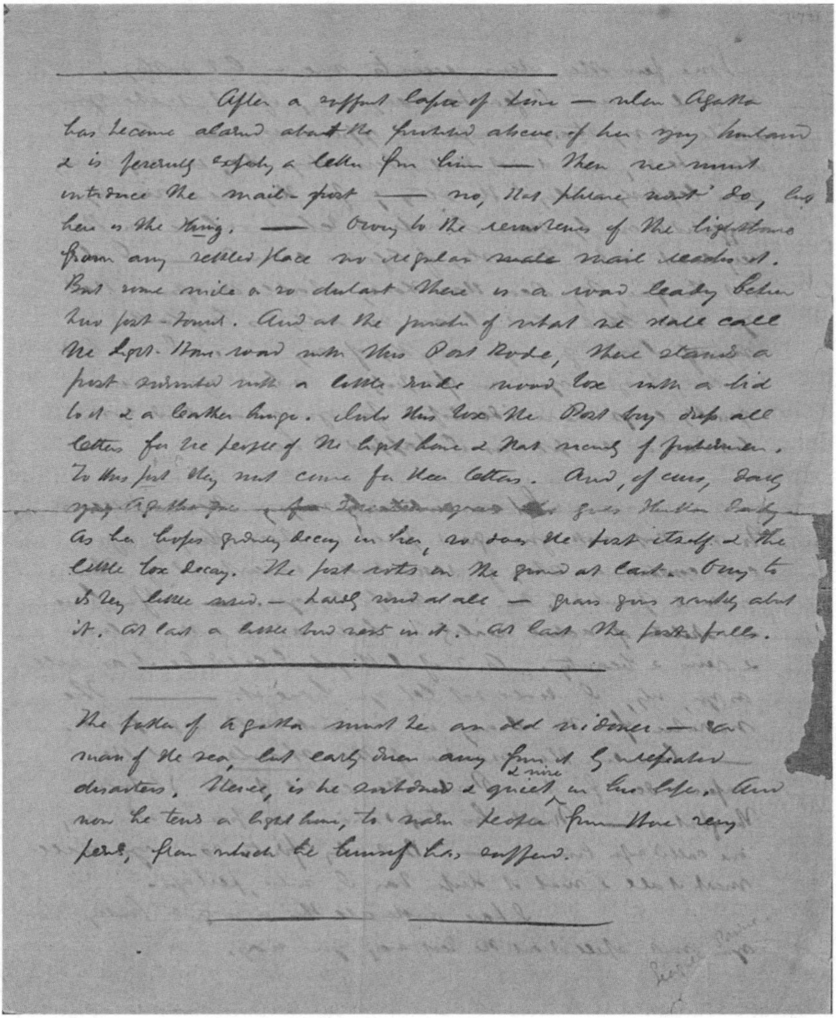

FIGURE 1 Page from Melville's letter of August 13, 1852 to Nathaniel Hawthorne, the first in the so-called "Agatha" correspondence. Courtesy of the Houghton Library, Harvard University, Cambridge, Massachusetts

While vacationing on Nantucket Island with his father-in-law, Judge Lemuel Shaw, in 1852, Melville heard Agatha's story from John Henry Clifford, a friend of Shaw and an eminent New Bedford lawyer. Ten years before, Clifford had encountered the case of a young woman, Agatha Hatch, who had rescued and married a shipwrecked sailor named Robertson. The sailor abandoned her before the birth of their daughter and disappeared for seventeen years; eventually he re-appeared, bearing gifts and money that seemed suspiciously to have come from his marriage to another woman, now dead. After renewing ties with Agatha and her family, Robertson disappeared again, married a third time, and then died. The case involved this wandering confidence man's complicated legacy to his multiple heirs.

Melville wrote to Hawthorne that the story fascinated Clifford because of "the great patience, & endurance, & resignedness of the women of the island in submitting so uncomplainingly to the long, long abscences [*sic*] of their sailor husbands." Melville saw something equally mysterious in the narrative: the predicament of a sailor whose "sin stole upon him insensibly – so that it would perhaps have been hard for him to settle upon the exact day when he could say to himself, '*Now* I have deserted my wife.'" How to tell such a story, replete with mysteries and metaphysical implications?

Reminded of Hawthorne's tale of a runaway husband, "Wakefield," Melville sent him the "Agatha" narrative. He then proceeded to explain how Hawthorne should compose it. In an extraordinary series of letters, a set of performances, really, of the act of writing, Melville gave Hawthorne the plot, symbols, characters, setting, and plenty of advice. If Melville then completed the story himself after Hawthorne's refusal, and if it was the manuscript, called *Isle of the Cross*, which some of his biographers claim was later rejected by the Harpers Brothers publishing firm in 1853, we have no idea what it eventually looked like. To the best of our knowledge, the story appears only in the form of the letters Melville wrote about it and the account he received from Clifford.

The text exists in four separate documents: Clifford's legal diary; the letter Melville wrote to Hawthorne on August 13, 1852, accompanying the diary, summarizing the story, and suggesting how he write it; a second letter, dated October 25, elaborating on the character of the wandering sailor-husband Robertson; and a final letter, written in December, in which Melville, having met with Hawthorne in Concord,

Massachusetts, concludes that since Hawthorne "expressed uncertainty," Melville will go ahead himself. He requests Hawthorne's permission to use the title they discussed – "Isle [*sic*] of Shoals" (based on Hawthorne's September vacation at Isles of Shoals, off New Hampshire and Maine) – and asks him to return the diary and letters. No materials from Hawthorne's side of the correspondence survive.

If we were to use the "Agatha" story as a frame for viewing Melville's writing, we might perceive in it several characteristic habits of mind: (1) Melville drew his inspiration from a wide range of *sources* that one might identify as actual, factual, and imaginary; (2) Melville adopted *symbols* to express the big ideas that engaged him deeply; (3) as a social writer, Melville expressed *sympathy* for people marginalized, misunderstood, or maligned; (4) Melville had an elegiac sensibility, a tendency to represent *memorials* of the past, meditating on death in richly poetic language; and (5) Melville saw reading and writing as parts of a process of engaging, often collaboratively, with a reader, a process he called finding the *suggestiveness* in things. The details of the "Agatha" story show him playing with these different tools of literary invention.

Sources

What kind of sources did Melville use for "Agatha"? He claims that the story interested him first because it contained "matters concerning which I was curious": the real lives of women on the islands from which sailors launched their voyages and the adventures of the sailors themselves. Various "accidental circumstances" surrounding the occasion of his hearing the story on Nantucket further aroused his excitement. After turning over the ideas for a bit, he thought of Hawthorne's "Wakefield," in which a London man leaves his wife, moves into a house just a few streets away, and spends years in her neighborhood, essentially spying on her, before unexpectedly moving back long after she had given him up for dead. Furthermore the emotion of the teller, John Henry Clifford, increased the story's meaning for him: "The very great interest I felt in this story while [he was] narrating to me, was heightened by the emotion of the gentleman who told it, who evinced the most unaffected sympathy in it, tho' now a matter of his past." "Agatha" thus had a range of sources that intrigued Melville: the actual (what really happened), the factual (the information he collected around it), and the imaginary (related fictional works, emotional responses, speculation). It is fascinating to watch Melville develop other narratives throughout his career from similarly various sources.

Actual experiences supplied the bedrock of most of his novels and stories and many of his poems. His first books, through *Moby-Dick*, were based on events drawn from his own life or from the yarns he had heard sailors spin at sea. *Pierre* represented a radical turning away from his maritime subject matter, taking place in rural and urban New York and concerning genteel lovers and starving artists, but many of its details arise from Melville's background; scholars have speculated that even the story's most sensational features, including an illegitimate sister for the hero, may have had their origins in Melville's family. His short fiction tends to grow out of his own exact observations: of London lawyers, for example, in "The Paradise of Bachelors," whom he met on his trip to Europe in 1849; or of the factory workers in "The Tartarus of Maids," whom he encountered in a paper mill near his home in the Berkshires; or of the scrivener of "Bartleby," whom he might have seen in his brother's Wall Street law office. "The Encantadas," a collection of ten sketches about the Galápagos Islands, emerged from his own travels. At times he draws on historical accounts, like Amasa Delano's *Narrative* of his voyages, which provides the story and many of the details of "Benito Cereno," or the autobiographical chronicle of an American Revolutionary War soldier that furnished the plot of Melville's short novel, *Israel Potter*. But generally he starts with events in his own life. An early trip to the Mississippi River when he was young probably provided strong impressions that he drew on for his novel *The Confidence-Man*, which takes place on a Mississippi steamboat. For one of his poems in *Battle-Pieces*, he depended on memories of his visit behind enemy lines during the war. His long poem *Clarel* took up his trip to Jerusalem. *John Marr and Other Sailors* contained portraits of sailors he could have known, and *Billy Budd*, dedicated to his shipmate Jack Chase, owed some of its conception to his cousin, Guert Gansevoort, and his role in the *Somers* mutiny of 1842. It would be hard to find a purely original work in Melville's *oeuvre*. He was perpetually drawn to any tale that seemed to him "so interesting a story of reality," as he called "Agatha." Indeed, in many cases the fact that the story could be verified by a sober lawyer, historian, or other chronicler served his purposes handily, for he could play off their reports against his own imaginative reconstructions and ironic subversions of actual events.

And thus we see how naturally Melville also turned to factual sources to bolster what he knew from actual experience. With the "Agatha" story he collected information about Nantucket – although Agatha lived in Pembroke, Massachusetts – which he offered to Hawthorne as "tributary items." In his October letter he spoke of introducing an "old Nantucket seaman," who may have been a version of George Pollard, the unfortunate captain of the *Essex*, a man whom Melville saw on Nantucket and whose story of shipwreck he had used in *Moby-Dick*. The rest of his "Agatha" research involved gathering scenic descriptions and information about maritime life in and around Nantucket, material "visably [*sic*] suggested to me by scenes I actually beheld while on the very coast where the story of Agatha occurred." These included observations of natural history and environmental forces at work, such as in the erosion of the cliffs near the Sankaty Head lighthouse, where Agatha lived and walked along a receding shoreline.[1]

Often in his writing Melville borrowed creatively from a range of print sources. Beginning with *Typee*, when he found himself running out of direct impressions, he turned to historical narratives, in this case, to accounts of the Marquesas like Captain David Porter's *Journal of a Cruise Made to the Pacific* (1815), or Charles S. Stewart's *A Visit to the South Seas* (1831). What we might now, in an era of strict intellectual property laws, condemn as plagiarism or at least call liberal paraphrasing was a widely tolerated practice in a period when authors' works were not protected by international copyright laws. Melville drew from the work of missionaries like William Ellis in his *Polynesian Researches* (1833) in *Omoo*; on scientists like Robert Chambers in his *Vestiges of the Natural History of Creation* (1844) in *Mardi*; and on the *Penny Cyclopedia* and popular scientific works in *Moby-Dick*. Ishmael claims in *Moby-Dick* to provide "naught but substantiated facts" (p. 113); no matter how far Melville strayed from his factual sources, he seldom published a fiction without them. They were too useful, not only for "substantiating" his flights of imagination and fancy, but also for providing foils to his own playful manipulations of information.

Melville's sensitive response to sources went well beyond the factual, historical, and encyclopedic sources he loved. He also depended on works of fiction, drama, and poetry. Along with the bizarre husband Wakefield, for example, he may also have had in mind certain memorable female characters in Hawthorne's novels: Hester Prynne, Zenobia, and Hepzibah, all of whom, like Agatha, exhibit extraordinary devotion to weak and errant men. Melville's delight in literature developed early in his life and sustained his writing in greater measure as he aged. *Mardi* shows the impact of his encounters with Sir Thomas Browne, Swift, Montaigne, and Rabelais, as well as ancient and Romantic philosophers. *Moby-Dick* and *Pierre* owe much of their language to Melville's deep knowledge of the Bible and his discovery of Shakespeare in the late 1840s, but he also read other Renaissance playwrights, as well as Milton and Dante, Wordsworth and Coleridge, Kant and Emerson, Carlyle and Goethe, de Staël and Hawthorne, and a host of other poets and philosophers. His short stories indicate close attention to authors like Cicero, Cervantes, Spenser, Byron, Poe, Dickens, Catherine Maria Sedgwick, and Mary Shelley; and *The Confidence-Man* assumes the reader's knowledge of classical philosophers as well as popular outlaw tales and westerns. Melville's imagination was as much visual as literary, and throughout his life and especially in his poems his works show confident knowledge of artists like J. M. W. Turner, illustrators like John Flaxman, and aesthetic theorists like John Ruskin.[2]

Melville's statement of how Hawthorne might proceed with the "Agatha" story – "You have a skeleton of actual reality to build about with fulness & veins & beauty" – describes his own practice of weaving narrative around the "skeleton" of his sources. As other statements of the "Agatha" correspondence reveal, he had many ideas about how to build onto the bones of "actual reality."

Symbols

In describing to Hawthorne how he might develop the lawyer's story, Melville turned immediately to symbols. His mind worked instinctively in metaphors. "Supposing the story to open with the wreck," he begins, "then there must be a storm": a storm that creates symbolic significance at the same that it serves the logistical purpose of bringing the sailor Robertson to shore. (Melville persistently misnames him Robinson, perhaps with Defoe's Crusoe in mind.) And so that storm must begin with a "preceding *calm*" in which Agatha walks along the seaside cliffs, "filled with meditations." "The sea with an air of solemn deliberation, with an elaborate deliberation, ceremoniously rolls upon the beach. The air is suppressedly charged" with solemn meaning, like the sea. The next sentences emphasize Agatha's inclination to view events as carrying symbolic significance beyond themselves:

> Suddenly she catches the long shadow of the cliff cast upon the beach 100 feet beneath her; and now she notes a shadow moving along the shadow. It is cast by a sheep from the pasture. It has advanced to the very edge of the cliff, & is sending a mild innocent glance far out upon the water. There, in strange & beautiful contrast, we have the innocence of the land placidly eyeing the malignity of the sea.

Beginning with the factual description of Agatha walking along the cliffs, Melville then personifies the sea (rolling "with an air of solemn deliberation") and associates sea and sky with the impending disaster (air "suppressedly charged"). The sheep gazing out to sea becomes a metaphor for "the innocence of the land" in "beautiful contrast" with the "malignity of the sea"; similarly the sheep's innocence supplies a metaphor for Agatha's youth and injects a note of dramatic irony and foreshadowing into a pastoral scene.

Ever aware of symbols, Melville also creates a character capable of reflecting on them herself, so that the symbols carry as much of the story's impact as events and characters do. Later, for example, Melville describes the mailbox to which Agatha daily resorts to seek Robertson's letters. Each day the mailbox is empty. With what seems almost obsessive absorption in the life of the symbol itself, Melville dwells at length on the mailbox's fate: "As her hopes gradually decay in her, so does the post itself & the little box decay. The post rots in the ground at last. Owing to its being little used – hardly used at all – grass grows rankly about it. At last a little bird nests in it. At last the post falls." The mailbox as metaphor of Agatha's decaying hopes enlarges in meaning to encompass the breakdown of communication between her and Robertson, the untrustworthiness of letters themselves (doubly ironic since Melville is writing all this in a letter to Hawthorne), and by extension the instability of narrative. Yet the "little bird" nests in the box, an apt symbol of Agatha's resilience and resourcefulness.

It may seem a truism to comment on Melville's abiding interest in symbolism. Anyone who has read *Moby-Dick* or any number of his other works will be forcefully reminded on every page of symbols and the human power to wrest meaning from them. What seems remarkable in the "Agatha" correspondence is Melville's preoccupation with symbols as organizing and charging his story. The lawyer Clifford responded to the legal questions surrounding the inheritance, to the characters of Agatha and Robertson, and to the pathos of her suffering. Melville, while acknowledging these important elements of the narrative, finds its heart in powerful symbols that resonate with profound significance. Once he has pointed them out to a reader, they seem to take off, becoming active players in the story's drama.

Sympathy

At the same time that Melville launches immediately into the story's symbolic meanings, he stays firmly grounded in its social realities, that is, the immediate experiences of people whose anguish arouses his sympathy. Agatha, who lives in dignified destitution, represents a suffering Melville wrote about again and again. From his earliest novels, where he dwelt on the lives of rootless and downtrodden sailors (especially in *Omoo*, *Redburn*, and *White-Jacket*), to his indictments of poverty in "Bartleby, the Scrivener" and *Israel Potter*, from his early representations of racially dispossessed Polynesians in *Typee* and *Omoo* to the oppressed African Americans and Native Americans of *Moby-Dick*, "Benito Cereno," and *The Confidence-Man*, and in his frequent studies of working women and men, Melville maintains an abiding concern with human affliction. Agatha is to him not only a character, but, like Pip in *Moby-Dick* or Isabel in *Pierre*, a member of an exploited and neglected class.

Robertson too wins Melville's sympathy. Rather than judge him harshly as Clifford does, treating him as a sinner, Melville insists that Robertson's behavior has a social explanation as well as a moral framework: "The probable facility with which Robinson first leaves his wife & then takes another, may, possibly, be ascribed to the peculiarly latitudinarian notions, which most sailors have of all tender obligations of that sort. In his previous sailor life Robinson had found a wife (for a night) in every port." Melville describes such behavior with considerable tolerance in *Redburn*, where one sailor has a wife on either side of the ocean, and in *Billy Budd*, where he portrays the sailors as inexperienced in the complex moral systems of the land: "The sailor is frankness, the landsman is finesse" (p. 86). Robertson's "latitudinarian notions" grow out of particular circumstances and speak to his social class more than to any innate evil. Melville, in fact, seems to admire his creative relationship to conventional systems of marriage and the law. As a confidence man and trickster, Robertson embodies tendencies that Melville explored often in his writing.

"Sympathy" can refer to a writer's capacity to imagine the misery of others and view it with tolerance and understanding. As a term for certain kinds of writing, a nineteenth-century literature of "sympathy," it is often associated with the "sentimental" and thus, traditionally at least, with writing about domestic or romantic subjects. But it speaks to larger political and metaphysical concerns as well, as a term some writers used to describe literature that opens the heart as well as the mind. In letter to Hawthorne in June 1851, Melville exclaimed, "I stand for the heart. To the dogs with the head!" (*L* 192). In an era with little social reform legislation or institutional support for the poor, homeless, enslaved, or diseased, reformers depended on their readers' sympathies to produce social change. While seldom an activist, Melville spoke out openly against flogging on naval ships (*White-Jacket*), produced searing exposés of slavery (*Mardi*, "Benito Cereno"), and wrote vivid portrayals of rural and urban poverty (*Pierre*, "The Piazza," "Bartleby," *Israel Potter*). His heated response to the predicaments of his characters suggests a keen eye for social inequities and a heart moved to sympathize with others. That sympathy extended from describing the misery of sufferers to condemning the society that produced it.[3]

Memorials

Critics and biographers have not arrived at any consensus about Melville's religious and philosophical views. Though raised by Christian parents, he observed and wrote about a range of religions, from Polynesian animism and polytheism to the broad array of Islamic, Jewish,

Persian, and Hindu beliefs he explored in *Mardi*, *Moby-Dick*, *The Confidence-Man*, and *Clarel*, among other works. As consumed with philosophy as with religion, he nevertheless exhibited considerable skepticism about any binding system of thought. Yet, as the "Agatha" correspondence suggests, he also respected a certain majestic power that he associated with the sublime – even the sacred. Sometimes this reverence emerged, as in *Moby-Dick* or *Clarel*, in the numerous ways he responded to the Bible. At other times, it evinced itself in a habit of deference to the deeply profound, moving, or significant: something his characters encounter powerfully in the presence of tombs and other reminders of death.

Melville's elegiac impulse appears in the "Agatha" correspondence when he describes Robertson's ship. After narrating the shipwreck, Melville returns to and lingers over the vessel itself, which develops into an almost sacred object: "Now this wrecked ship has driven over the shoals, & driven upon the beach where she goes to pieces, all but her stem-part. This in course of time becomes embedded in the sand – after the lapse of some years showing nothing but the sturdy stem (or, prow-bone) projecting some two feet at low water. All the rest is filled & packed down with the sand. – So that after her husband has disappeared the sad Agatha every day sees this melancholy monument, with all its remindings." Like the decayed mailbox, the ship becomes a "melancholy monument," something that reminds her not only of Robertson's fate but also of the actions of fate itself. As with the statue of Ozymandias in Shelley's poem, or Melville's beached whale skeleton wreathed in vines in *Moby-Dick* (chapter 102), the buried "prow-bone" of the ship speaks to divine will and agency, inscrutable as they are. It creates a "monument" to the past and to whatever may console humanity in the face of death.

As intellectually free-ranging, ironic, skeptical, and independent as Melville's thought tends to be, his characters also stop themselves at such monuments throughout his work: at the grave of a dead king in *Typee*, in the cellar sanctified by death in *Redburn*, at the Seaman's Bethel in *Moby-Dick*, in the Tombs prison in "Bartleby," in the forgotten fields of *Battle-Pieces*, at the Mar Saba palm in *Clarel*, at the mast from which Billy is hanged in *Billy Budd*. These sites of intense meaning call up an awed silence in Melville's characters, hushing them in the presence of death, suffering, and the terrifying truths of existence.

The Suggestive

Melville seems constantly aware throughout his career of the fertile relationship between writer and reader. In passing along Clifford's diary and his own extended remarks, Melville also entrusted to Hawthorne the task of reading and interpreting the papers thoughtfully. "You will find out the *suggestiveness* for yourself," he advises him (emphasis added), offering Hawthorne the freedom to think independently: "you must of course be your own judge – I but submit matter to you – I dont [*sic*] decide." Although he makes many remarks, calling them a species of "strange impertinent officiousness," Melville respects the reader's, Hawthorne's, relationship to the story, his "great power" of imaginative thinking.

Melville also understands the relationship between writer and reader as an ongoing dialogue, a collaboration. The fact that the "Agatha" story appears in letters implies a hope that it will perpetuate a conversation between the two authors, and many of Melville's books proceed in this communicative vein. Ishmael's chatty narration implies a willing interlocutor. When he asks readers to "Call me Ishmael," he expects them to do just that. Most of Melville's nautical narrators assume the congenial tone of a shipmate lounging in the rigging and trading yarns. Notice, for example, his direct invocation of the reader in the opening sentences of *Typee*: "Six months at sea! Yes, reader, as I live, six months out of sight of land" (p. 3). Even as reserved a character as the narrator of "Bartleby," a stiff, pompous, and professional sort, begins by saying confidentially, "I am a rather elderly man" (*PT* 13).

Many of Melville's works move through dialogue as well. *The Confidence-Man* and *Clarel* develop more out of conversations between characters of widely varying identities than out of action or physical conflicts between them. Just as with the characters, so with writer and reader: Melville's narrators create space in the story for the reader to intervene and take up the conversational thread.

Melville's narrative and poetic works are "suggestive," then, in several senses. In one way, they often suggest meanings through elliptical, ironic, symbolic, or other indirect means, trusting in the reader's ability to make sense of their subtleties. They also work suggestively as a way of arriving at a truth that flees from a direct approach. Joining together with other voices (those of the characters) and other texts (the many sources and literary inspirations he draws from), writer and reader embark on a journey of discovery. "Suggestiveness" seems ultimately a practical strategy for traveling in the "latitudinarian" spaces of the literary imagination. One cannot reach the horizons of thought by any direct route.

This study of the "Agatha" correspondence offers a way to begin mapping Melville's literary genome, isolating certain characteristic patterns and preferences. Without offering a comprehensive survey of his writing habits, it identifies a few literary traits. There are many others. Critics have noticed Melville's humor, his love of wordplay and jokes, his engaging rhetoric and tone. Others have seen his irreverence, his subversion of readers' expectations, his irony, bawdiness, and blasphemy. For some he speaks in the voices of his times, absorbing a "correspondent coloring" ("Mosses," *PT* 246) from maritime, urban, and other popular vernaculars. For others he writes out of a classic literary tradition, in biblical, Shakespearean, Miltonic, and Emersonian registers. Melville has appeared as a genius of an extraordinarily plastic kind, weaving different literary strands into gloriously hybrid textual tapestries; or as an inspired amateur, self-taught, fumbling his way into eloquence. The "Agatha" correspondence may not reveal the full dimensions of a career in which Melville experimented with and often threw out a bewildering variety of literary forms and genres. But it may give us an authorial fingerprint, which in its distinctive design draws attention to the larger body of work.

We turn now from forensic analysis of this remarkable literary fragment to readings of his published novels, stories, and poems.

PART II

Melville's Early Yarns

CHAPTER 3

"Making Literary Use of the Story": *Typee* and *Omoo*

Herman Melville's contemporaries relished the vivid nautical ambiance, sensational adventures, and lively, graceful prose style of his first books. For many nineteenth-century readers, nothing Melville wrote was nearly as good as *Typee*. After his death, by contrast, scholars and biographers began to read his early volumes as a literary apprenticeship leading up to *Moby-Dick* and as fodder for biographies that emphasized the growth of "an artist in the rigging" (*R* 121). Later critics focused more particularly on these books apart from their relation to *Moby-Dick*, tracing Melville's creative explorations of his own life.[1] As interest in Melville's social, political, and racial themes expanded, *Typee*, *Omoo*, and *Mardi* came under scrutiny as works that alternately romanticize and satirize "civilized" humans and their "exotic" counterparts. Viewed as exhibiting either the colonizing perspective of invading Europeans or the postcolonial experience of the ravaged islander, these books have been studied in terms of Melville's treatment of the racial other as well as white European settlers and travelers.[2] *Redburn* and *White-Jacket*, less concerned with travel than with shipboard and urban life, have aroused interest in issues of labor, race, and class.[3] As literary texts, these five works have appeared significant in terms of their relationship to other literary sources;[4] their social, sexual, and cultural themes;[5] and the ways in which they develop a sensitive, observant narrator and expose his characteristic ways of reading an alien experience.

For Melville, as a young author at first only dimly aware of the career that lay ahead, his early writing signified a vigorous entry into New York's competitive literary market. Because of the lack of international copyright laws, that competition operated on different fronts: one in England, where American authors printed their books in order to avoid having them pirated and sold in cheap editions elsewhere; and one within the US, where publishers aggressively marketed new books to a nation that hungered for literature and the cultural authority that went with it. Fledgling American authors thus faced a publishing environment that presented both extraordinary opportunities and terrifying pressures. Melville, noting the successes of James Fenimore Cooper, Richard Henry Dana, and Washington Irving in selling narratives of maritime life and travel, took a daring plunge and was astonished to find that the gamble paid off. The celebrity of *Typee* and *Omoo* led him to attempt the even more ambitious *Mardi*, an innovative hybrid of adventure, travel, and philosophical romance that shows the influence of his reading great English and European authors. When *Mardi* failed to earn positive reviews, Melville returned to more sober attempts at autobiographical fiction, but he never abandoned his romantic ambitions, and *Redburn* and *White-Jacket*, though far more restrained, show his eager response to philosophy and literature, even as they maintain a certain grave social realism.

Melville enjoyed the remarkable experience of beginning his career as a popular author, admired by critics on both sides of the Atlantic as a new phenomenon. He was also hailed largely as a sailor-author, identified with nautical lingo and experiences, and his early books evince his anxiety over demands for maritime adventures when he was beginning to model himself on the poets, dramatists, philosophers, and epic visionaries of the past. This mixture of bold self-assertion and anxious self-scrutiny lends his early texts a problematic but also fascinating complexity. The protagonist's or narrator's ambivalence, interpreted variously as cultural defensiveness, psychological insecurity, or literary inexperience, has come to be seen as one of Melville's most enduring discoveries, the source of biting irony, sly humor, and lyrical expressiveness in his prose.

"So Interesting a Story of Reality": *Typee*

Melville's inventiveness manifests itself throughout *Typee* in the way he assembles existing genres – travel account, captivity narrative, anthropological study, escapist fantasy, maritime yarn – into a thrilling adventure. In the "Agatha" correspondence, he spoke to Hawthorne of John H. Clifford's expectation that Melville would make "literary use" of any intriguing story that came his way. *Typee* offers the first example of how Melville developed a multi-layered text from seemingly spontaneous, unstudied sailors' yarns. At the same time, he strove to make the book "so interesting a story of reality," as he said of the "Agatha" tale.

Typee is a supposedly autobiographical account of how Melville jumped ship with Toby Greene in the Marquesas, fled inland, suffered a debilitating leg injury, and dwelt among Taipis (he adopted Captain David Porter's spelling of their name), who had the reputation of being ferocious cannibals. Toby leaves for the coast to get medical help but never returns. While awaiting rescue, Melville's narrator, whom the islanders call Tommo, lives among seemingly peaceful, happy people amid groves of breadfruit and coconut. He enjoys pleasant relations with Mehevi the king, Kory-Kory his "valet," Marnoo the traveling orator, and Fayaway, his beautiful companion, and he observes life in a community that seems to resemble a utopian ideal. The only problem is that the islanders may wish to eat him, and they certainly hope to tattoo him, both of which possibilities fill him with horror. Eventually he makes his way to the shore in company with the Typees, who are hoping to barter with a visiting ship's crew, and he escapes by leaping into a departing whaleboat, leaving Fayaway in tears, and viciously striking one of the chieftains, Mow-Mow, with a boathook. The book as we have it today ends with appendices in Melville's voice: one (added to the American revised edition, after the book appeared in England) explaining Toby's whereabouts during Tommo's captivity; the other (dropped in the American revised edition) defending the actions of the British during their brief takeover of the Sandwich Islands, or Hawai'i.

When Melville began writing *Typee* (which, whatever the facts of his sojourn in the Marquesas, is highly fictionalized), he struggled with his publishers' demands for a realistic travel narrative. His London publisher, John Murray, saw Melville's book, which he soberly titled *Narrative of a Four Months' Residence Among the Natives of a Valley of the Marquesas: or, A Peep at Polynesian Life*, as ideal for his Home and Colonial Library, a series on travel and exploration. He by no means desired a work of fiction, and in correspondence with Murray, Melville strove to satisfy the publisher's requirements for accuracy, realism, and facts. Yet he also understood the exotic appeal of his subject and, fired with youthful enthusiasm, took pleasure in stretching his facts to stimulate a reader's fancy. Melville's first work, not quite a novel and not quite a travel narrative either, was also a sailors' yarn, a term that, with its associated images of spinning and twisting the fibers of action, circumstance, and discourse, became a potent image of his writing throughout his career.

In his early work, Melville used the yarn to suggest a spontaneous and naive form of storytelling that, as he said eloquently later in *Billy Budd*, partook of divine inspiration: "when not actually engaged on the yards yet higher aloft, the topmen, who as such had been picked out for youth and activity, constituted an aerial club lounging at ease against the smaller stun'sails rolled up into cushions, spinning yarns like the lazy gods" (p. 68). Melville announces just such godlike freedom and seeming ease in the preface of *Typee*:

> Sailors are the only class of men who now-a-days see anything like stirring adventure; and many things which to fire-side people appear strange and romantic, to them seem as common-place as a jacket out at elbows. Yet, notwithstanding the familiarity of sailors with all sorts of curious adventure, the incidents recorded in the following pages have often served, when "spun as a yarn," not only to relieve the weariness of many a night-watch at sea, but to excite the warmest sympathies of the author's shipmates. (p. xiii)

While satisfying the public's hunger for factual narrative, Melville also indulged his pleasure in telling a seemingly artless form of fiction.

But Melville had to learn how to *write* yarns, and his first works show the joys and strains of acquiring that knowledge, as he struggled with the initially unwieldy medium of written words. In *Typee* and its sequel *Omoo*, that strain evinces itself in the places where the yarn wears thin and frays, where the narrator seems not altogether comfortable in his story or encounters a cultural experience for which his early training has little prepared him – tattooing, for example, or suggestions of cannibalism. In *The Adventures of Huckleberry Finn*, Mark Twain was later to admit, through Huck's voice, to telling quite a few of what he called "stretchers." Although Melville's narrators do not seem as comfortable stretching the truth, in practice their elastic yarns accommodate various, sometimes conflicting, literary aims.

Melville gives a sense of the artful possibilities of the stretched yarn in his first chapter of *Typee*, when he describes the crew of the whaling vessel as desperate for the comforts and delights of the shore after "six months at sea!" In what seems his most frolicsome vein, the narrator nevertheless hints at the dangers and violence to come:

> There is but one solitary tenant in the chicken-coop, once a gay and dapper young cock, bearing him so bravely among the coy hens. But look at him now; there he stands, moping all the day long on that ever-lasting one leg of his. He turns with disgust from the mouldy corn before him, and the brackish water in his little trough. He mourns no doubt his lost companions, literally snatched from him one by one, and never seen again. But his days of mourning will be few; for Mungo, our black cook, told me yesterday that the word had at last gone forth, and poor Pedro's fate was sealed. His attenuated body will be laid out upon the captain's table next Sunday, and long before night will be buried with all the usual ceremonies beneath that worthy individual's vest. Who would believe that there could be any one so cruel as to long for the decapitation of the luckless Pedro; yet the sailors pray every minute, selfish fellows, that the miserable fowl may be brought to his end. They say the captain will never point the ship for the land so long as he has in anticipation a mess of fresh meat. This unhappy bird can alone furnish it; and when he is once devoured, the captain will come to his senses. I wish thee no harm, Peter; but as thou art doomed, sooner or later, to meet the fate of all thy race; and if putting a period to thy existence is to be the signal for our deliverance, why – truth to speak – I wish thy throat cut this very moment; for, oh! how I wish to see the living earth again! (p. 4)

In this early moment of *Typee*, the narrator sketches a comical picture of the sailors' frustrations being taken out on a hapless fowl, but he also gives a portrait of social conflict, suggesting the crew's subjection to a gluttonous tyrant at whose pleasure they await their liberation. Like Pedro, the sailors are fed on moldy fare and mourn their captivity. Cut off from home and the companionship of "coy" damsels, the sailors are left deprived, like the once brave cock standing on one "everlasting" leg. Poised between the powerful captain and the

African cook Mungo, the sailors enjoy the privileges of neither class nor race. In the end, violence will be done to the "unhappy" cock, as symbolically it has been done to the sailors, and some one of them will be sacrificed to the captain's appetite for "fresh meat." Melville even implies a spectacle of Christian martyrdom in the image of the bird being killed on Sunday and buried with "all the usual ceremonies" in a dignified rite.[6] While appearing as the amusing subject of the narrator's yarn, Pedro shifts to representing the sailors and their distress in various subtle registers of class, gender, and religion, all within a few sentences.

Pedro also foreshadows the fate of Tommo, who likewise becomes a captive and "mourns no doubt his lost companions, literally snatched from him one by one." As a hostage among the Typees, Tommo will get to sport like "a gay and dapper young cock" among the hens, but with the mysterious injury to his leg, he is also incapacitated and forlorn, as Pedro was, and he anticipates being eaten by his hosts. Faced with messages filtered through conflicting racial, linguistic, and cultural screens, Tommo finds himself in as confusing a world as Pedro's, and he longs, in a sense, for the violent finale that will set him free. At this early stage of the yarn, Tommo indicates the sinister pressures on his seemingly genial story.

Melville's yarn-spinning in *Typee* reveals a complicated set of objectives and clearly involves more than the seemingly effortless production of amusing stories. We might identify five narrative strands in his yarn: (1) a romantic tale of desire titillated and at least partly satisfied in a tropical paradise; (2) an entertaining and edifying account of travel to a distant Polynesian island; (3) a passionate and satiric diatribe against European military and missionary incursions into the Pacific; (4) a horrific encounter with human savagery as envisioned in stories of cannibalism and war; and (5) a discovery of art in the graceful expressions of a Polynesian aesthetic. These different strands, sometimes at odds with each other, create considerable tension in Melville's yarn.

The romantic and escapist narrative of flight to Polynesian paradise was probably the least difficult of these different stories to write. However much Melville based the captivity plot on actual experience, he knew enough about the islands to write convincingly of their beauties and sensual delights. Conjuring up the allure of the exotic, Melville's narrator quickly captures the popular appeal of his material:

"The Marquesas! What strange visions of outlandish things does the very name spirit up! Lovely houris – cannibal banquets – groves of cocoa-nut – coral reefs – tatooed [*sic*] chiefs – and bamboo temples; sunny valleys planted with bread-fruit trees – carved canoes dancing on the flashing blue waters – savage woodlands guarded by horrible idols – *heathenish rites and human sacrifices*" (p. 5). The first ten chapters contain the book's most adventurous scenes, as the narrator and Toby hack their way through dense cane brakes, ascend perilous cliffs, launch themselves into cataracts and ravines, and behave like contemporary action heroes. Arriving exhausted in the valley, they are rescued by the Typees, who feed them delicious food and supply them with delightful companions. Once Tommo's initial fears of danger have been allayed, he gives himself over to the pleasures of life in the Happy Valley.

Surprisingly, though, the tale of sensational adventure and erotic desire occupies relatively little of the rest of the novel. Fayaway surfaces only occasionally throughout the story, though memorably enough for Melville's first readers, who saw her as a seductive island paramour. She appears most strikingly as a living mast for Tommo's lake canoe, in a sensuous and at the same time absurd display of her naked body:

> With a wild exclamation of delight, she disengaged from her person the ample robe of tappa which was knotted over her shoulder (for the purpose of shielding her from the sun), and spreading it out like a sail, stood erect with upraised arms in the head of the canoe. We American sailors pride ourselves upon our straight clean spars, but a prettier little mast than Fayaway made was never shipped a-board of any craft. (p. 134)

Except for scattered references to her beauty and to various peculiarities such as her eating fish raw or having minute facial tattoos, Fayaway does not appear again until the end of the story when Tommo, making his abrupt and violent departure, tosses her a roll of calico by way of guilty farewell. Yet although Melville undercuts the island romance by the way Tommo neglects Fayaway, he nevertheless makes her emblematic of the allure of the Pacific islands. As an image of female beauty forsaken and betrayed, she will return in Melville's fiction as Yillah in *Mardi*, Lucy in *Pierre*, Agatha in the correspondence with Hawthorne, Hunilla in "The Encantadas," and Ruth in *Clarel*.

The romance of the islands does not include only female beauty. Tommo is equally captivated by the island's men, especially the noble chief Mehevi and the "taboo" (i.e. protected by ritual edict) orator, Marnoo. These evoke a more complicated range of responses than Fayaway does. In Tommo's first meeting with Marnoo, for example, Melville emphasizes Tommo's intense interest in the beautiful youth. This speaks to more than the question of homoerotic attraction, although Tommo registers plenty of that: "His unclad limbs were beautifully formed; whilst the elegant outline of his figure, together with his beardless cheeks, might have entitled him to the distinction of standing for the statue of the Polynesian Apollo; and indeed the oval of his countenance and the regularity of every feature reminded me of an antique bust" (p. 135). But Marnoo's beauty is also part of his social prestige and makes him a rival to, rather than an object of, Tommo's own power to draw attention to himself. Melville suggests that male beauty, and its promise of romance, freedom, and delight, comes with certain social tensions not visible in his relations with Fayaway.

A second strand of Melville's yarn, the realistic travel narrative that Murray and many of Melville's readers favored, presents a different set of challenges from those of the exotic romance. Melville would have known that his readers sought "unvarnished truth" (p. xiv), moral improvement, and uplift. Given the sensational nature of his plot, he knew that he would need to bolster its inventions with sober truth, documentary evidence, and moral authority. At about the point when Toby departs, then, and Tommo emerges from his lethargy and begins to enjoy himself, Melville shifted his practice from spinning to splicing his strands of rope. The extended midsection of the book relies less on an adventure plot – hair's-breadth escapes, sensual delights, and erotic dalliance – and more on observation, reflection, and cultural commentary twisted into the narrative. To build this section and display his credentials as an authority in what later came to be called cultural anthropology, Melville relied on outside written sources, especially accounts by David Porter, Charles Stewart, and Georg H. von Langsdorff. Although in the first British edition of *Typee* Tommo claims disingenuously that Porter's book is a "work, however, which I have never happened to meet" (p. 6), it is clear that Melville did meet Porter in print, and a number of other travelers and authorities besides.[7] These borrowings not only enlarged his story but also led him to obscure the original events so that, in the most obvious example, Tommo claims to have spent four months amongst the Typees rather than the four weeks Melville actually spent on the island. This shading of the truth has bothered Melville scholars strenuously for some time.

Tommo's blending of other texts into his own, while explicable as the contrivance of a novice author to give his work greater legitimacy, raises serious questions about Melville's intentions in *Typee*. The book does not answer them with any certainty. In the book's borrowings from Porter, as scholars have shown, Melville seems to trust someone whose actions he deplored.[8] Porter invaded the Taipi Valley and left it in ruins. He helped to inflate the Taipis' reputation for savage ferocity. Yet Melville recycles a number of Porter's attitudes while at the same time indicating Tommo's awareness of their hypocrisy and falsehood. It would be a mistake, then, to treat the factual material in *Typee* – the often amusing but generally pedantic disquisitions on island religious practices, festivals, dogs and mosquitoes, tappa-making, marriage customs, and so on – as merely filler. In these passages, Melville is actively contending with his sources in ways that are generally invisible to twenty-first-century readers but that indicate both acceptance and rejection of print authorities. Melville's use of other authors in his own work suggests a significant tension in the yarn.

More tension stresses a third strand of the narrative, its engagement with the political and religious controversies raging in Melville's culture in the 1840s. Melville arrived in the Marquesas at a critical moment, when France had just declared its sovereignty over the islands and when European and American missionaries were establishing their own form of sovereignty through attempts to convert to Christendom people they considered savage heathens. Since both political and religious incursions into the Pacific generally received glowing praise in the mainstream publications of Melville's day, Tommo's criticisms of "civilization" and its "depredations" were seen by some reviewers as heretical attacks on a national orthodoxy. Tommo articulates these views with little verbal restraint: "Thrice happy are they who, inhabiting some yet undiscovered island in the midst of the ocean, have never been brought into contaminating contact with the white man" (p. 15). These attitudes burst forth from the book's more romantic interludes and sober factual accounts with a rhetorical urgency that seems to signal Tommo's – if not Melville's – convictions.

In fact, some of these attitudes owed as much to print sources as the book's other literary strains. If we see them as representative of Melville's views, we commit the same error as those who read *Typee* as autobiographical truth. Such passages suggest rather the complexity of Melville's topic and the ideological conflicts it betrays. Nowhere is that conflict more visible than in the fourth narrative strand, namely the Gothic horror story of savage violence erupting in cannibalism. These passages call up some of Melville's most charged language:

> I observed a curiously carved vessel of wood, of considerable size, with a cover placed over it, of the same material, and which resembled in shape a small canoe. . . . prompted by a curiosity I could not repress, in passing it I raised one end of the cover; at the same moment the chiefs, perceiving my design, loudly ejaculated, "Taboo! taboo!" But the slight glimpse sufficed; my eyes fell upon the disordered members of a human skeleton, the bones still fresh with moisture, and with particles of flesh clinging to them here and there! (p. 238)

Tommo's horror at the spectacle of human meat is rendered forcefully and provides a critical turning point in the story, as he imagines that he has seen evidence to support his fears of the villagers' cannibalism.

Whether Melville is describing something he saw, read, or imagined, his "invention" of Taipi cannibalism has a powerful effect on the narrative, once again stressing the elastic fibers of the yarn. The specter of cannibalism locates violence firmly among the Polynesians at a point in the narrative when Tommo's attacks on European savagery would prove inconvenient. He wants to go home again, and he needs Marquesans to be the savages now. Ironically, however, Melville makes Tommo the savage in the final passages when, fleeing from Mow-Mow, an armed chief, he strikes him in what he claims is self-defense:

> Even at that moment I felt horror at the act I was about to commit; but it was no time for pity or compunction, and with a true aim, and exerting all my strength, I dashed the boat-hook at him. It struck him just below the throat, and forced him downwards. I had no time to repeat my blow, but I saw him rise to the surface in the wake of the boat, and never shall I forget the ferocious expression of his countenance. (p. 252)

The fact that the blow may prove fatal – Melville never explains – implicates Tommo in violence that he has elsewhere called savage, and threatens to upset the balance between barbarism and civilization that Tommo has maintained throughout the book. The further insult of heaving a musket at Kory-Kory and a roll of cloth at Fayaway, thus undermining any pretense of sentiment or rationality, signals the final fraying of Tommo's several yarns. The book ends with the narrator crumpling in his rescuer's arms, not with the jaunty confidence of the master storyteller but with the fear and self-loathing of a fugitive.

One last strand may help to finish off these frayed ends and suggest a more coherent, if not fully integrated and unified, narrative aim. Tommo's exposure to Marquesan arts, such as carving, fanciful decorations, textile manufacture, and especially tattooing, provides him with an aesthetic framework that allows him to include a wide range of competing concerns within his narrative. Marnoo's tattooing shows him how. The design on Marnoo's body is remarkably complex and multiform:

> Traced along the course of the spine was accurately delineated the slender, tapering, and diamond-checkered shaft of the beautiful "artu" tree. Branching from the stem on either side, and disposed alternately, were the graceful branches drooping with leaves all correctly drawn, and elaborately finished. Indeed, this piece of tattooing was the best specimen of the Fine Arts I had yet seen in Typee. . . . Upon his breast, arms, and legs, were exhibited an infinite variety of figures; every one of which, however, appeared to have reference to the general effect sought to be produced. (p. 136)

With its graceful organic lines and shapes, Marnoo's tattooing adapts itself fluidly to his body and its movements. The many different motifs, and the many occasions on which they have been inscribed on his skin, do not seem to interrupt or break up the overall pattern.

Tommo, of course, resists the unifying aesthetic of tattooing, seeing it as a violation of his identity. Although he calls Karky, the tattooist, an artist, he expresses little interest in becoming a "human canvas" (p. 218) for his artistic productions. Melville, however, seems more open than Tommo to the possibilities of tattoo art, particularly its tolerance of multiplicity and openness. What Tommo considers ugly, barbaric, and horrifying, Melville suggests is at the same time mysterious, refined, and sophisticated. Similarly in the open design of his book, with its embrace of different and competing narrative strands, Melville seems to invite an art that owes a great deal to Polynesian tattooing.[9]

"Items . . . [that] Seem Legitimately to Belong to the Story": *Omoo*

If we think of the tattooing in *Typee* as an aesthetic model for Melville's narrative, then it seems, like the making of yarns, an apt image of storytelling that blends different motifs into an elastic design. Both tattooing and yarns are arts that arise among working communities, rather than in an elite or literate culture. As a novice writer, Melville seems to have been drawn to this kind of spontaneous art inspired by communities, whether of sailors or islanders, and he seems to have spliced in other literary sources and influences as Karky might have added a few leaves or vines to Marnoo's spine, as decorative elements in an organic pattern. Melville's openness to Polynesian arts may have lent itself productively to the making of *Typee* – a book that many of his readers found irresistible.

When Melville came to write his second novel, *Omoo*, published in 1847, he was a literary success, not a beginner, and a celebrity, rather than an outsider. Responding to the pleasure of readers who clearly appreciated his storytelling gifts, Melville apparently felt little hesitation in keeping the yarn going; *Omoo* begins exactly where *Typee* leaves off, with a narrator now called Typee. According to Melville's introduction, the title *Omoo* "signifies a rover" (p. xiv), and he intended the book to show the beachcomber life of renegade whites in the Pacific, as well as giving, more controversially, a *"familiar* account of the present condition of the converted Polynesians, as affected by their promiscuous intercourse with foreigners, and the teachings of the missionaries, combined" (p. xiii).

The plot is as seemingly spontaneous as that of *Typee*. Signing on to a whaling vessel, the *Julia*, Typee finds himself among a derelict crew led by a sick captain and disorderly first mate. When Jermin, the mate, and Captain Guy go ashore in Tahiti for medical help, a disaffected Maori sailor, Bembo, nearly drives the ship upon rocks, intending to murder the crew. In the chaos that ensues, the men mutiny. Typee and the ship's doctor, Long Ghost, go along with the plot, ostensibly to contain the men's more radical and violent impulses; all end up in an onshore prison called the Calabooza Beretanee under the indulgent supervision of Captain Bob, who allows Typee and Long Ghost to slip away and roam the islands on a kind of extended holiday. The two men enjoy their roving, which includes an interlude of working for potato farmers, Zeke and Shorty, and visiting villages scattered among the islands. At the end, Typee reaches the limit of his patience with the rakish Long Ghost, and signs on another whaling vessel, bidding his companion a friendly but relieved farewell.

According to the reviews, Melville once again succeeded in entertaining his readers with a pleasurable mixture of amusement, edification, satire on the missionaries and political powers at work in Tahiti, and occasional romantic glimpses of its beauties. The careful balance he maintains in *Typee* between romance and satire, however, between civilized amusement and Gothic horror, seems to have disappeared from *Omoo*, to be replaced with a more unsettling stew of ingredients. Although *Omoo* is less well known now than *Typee*, it merits careful attention for the alternative image it presents of yarn-spinning, invention, and making "literary use" of a story. Whereas *Typee* represents as a redemptive myth the creation of narrative out of multiform experiences and texts, *Omoo* exposes the damaging consequences of the literary appropriation of other people's property, livelihoods, and stories. Whereas *Typee* submerges the protagonist in a paradisiacal flow of delight, the main trope of *Omoo* is depredation and theft, with the protagonist as one of the chief offenders. Here Melville's narrator does not so much spin yarns as steal narrative "whole cloth" from the sailors, the Tahitians, the white Europeans, and previous chroniclers of the Pacific islands.

In his thefts, Melville reveals, indeed invents, a literary persona as creative and beguiling as the more passive figure of Tommo. The narrator becomes a trickster who dramatizes a series of lucky escapes and narrow victories played out against the somber backdrop of Europe's ravishment of Tahiti's island paradise. If a less cheerful investigation of cultural encounter than *Typee*, *Omoo* provides a more complex picture of the making and taking of stories. When Melville told Hawthorne in the "Agatha" correspondence that he had collected certain "tributary items" to add to Clifford's narrative, he did not appear to notice the implications of his casual plunder of other people's

experiences. Instead he told Hawthorne that these items "seem legitimately to belong to the story," a proprietary attitude that he explores
and seems to find reprehensible in characters like Long Ghost.

As an example of the kind of yarn being spun in *Omoo*, we might
look more closely at Long Ghost, the book's primary trickster, and at
Melville's descriptions of Typee's and Long Ghost's visit to Eimeo (the
older name of Moorea), where they sign on as farm laborers but eventually charm their employers, Zeke and Shorty, into treating them
more as honored guests instead. Long Ghost, a debonair confidence
man who "did not eschew his own medicines" and kept "his invalids
in good-humor, spinning his yarns to them, by the hour, whenever he
went to see them" (p. 36), becomes particularly lively and entertaining. He pretends at first to be too sick to work and regales his employers with more yarns to prevent them from resenting the ruse.
Then, after a remarkable recovery, he joins a hunting expedition and
in the feast that follows beguiles the unsophisticated party with his
geniality: "There was no end to my long comrade's spirits. After telling
his stories, and singing his songs, he sprang to his feet, clasped a young
damsel of the grove round the waist, and waltzed over the grass with
her. But there's no telling all the pranks he played that night" (p. 223).
The doctor's frolics win grudging respect from Typee, who admires
his ingenuity in all kinds of endeavors. But he does not know quite
what to make of Long Ghost's antics, which often savor to him of
chicanery.

Melville's narrator recognizes a certain kind of artistry in his friend's
creative efforts, but it is a far cry from the natural aesthetic of Typeean
tattooing, and more like the entrepreneurial and mechanical genius of
an American inventor such as Benjamin Franklin. "In gastronomic
affairs," for example, "my friend was something of an artist; and by
way of improving his knowledge, did nothing the rest of the day but
practice in what might be called Experimental Cookery: broiling and
grilling, and deviling slices of meat, and subjecting them to all sorts of
igneous operations" (p. 225). Long Ghost's "art" consists in creatively
operating on his raw materials, experimenting with and fashioning all
kinds of new dishes for his own ravenous sampling. But, in the end,
Typee begrudges the doctor his artistry, which he considers little more
than trickery and lying. As the potato farmers begin to notice that Long
Ghost is improving in health, Typee reflects that the trickery has
gone far enough: "To tell the truth, I was not a little pleased to see the

doctor's reputation as an invalid fading away so fast; especially, as on the strength of his being one, he had promised to have such easy times of it, and very likely, too, at my expense" (p. 225).

The distaste generated by Long Ghost's antics introduces a serious strain into a narrative that might otherwise appear as picaresque high jinks and roguery. Long Ghost demonstrates the dark side of spinning wild and improbable yarns. Stealing kisses from island maidens and food from his generous hosts, Long Ghost exhibits a con-artistry quite different from what the geniuses of Polynesian tattooing, woodcarving, and weaving of cloth produce. As opposed to these organic and unifying arts, his storytelling is self-interested, disruptive, and sneaky. Typee revolts from it eventually and leaves the doctor behind. Nevertheless he raises the question of whether he, the book's narrator, is also, like the doctor, pulling the reader's leg and picking the reader's pockets. *Typee* casts a dreamy Polynesian spell on the reader; *Omoo* beguiles the reader in other less charming ways, making "literary use" of an old story of robbery and deceit. This depredation operates on a political stage, with the Western powers of nation-building and religious conversion cowing the Tahitian islanders into submission. But it also takes place within a literary frame, with the narrator suggesting that the reader has been robbed of one kind of pleasure by being given something else more ephemeral and unsatisfying: a kind of Experimental Cookery instead of real food.

The spinner of yarns in *Typee* and *Omoo* exhibits, on balance, considerable dexterity in "making literary use" of the materials of his narrative. When he turned to his next novel, *Mardi*, Melville sought a nobler role for himself, as someone who could plumb the depths of literary invention itself.

CHAPTER 4

"A Regular Story Founded on Striking Incidents": *Mardi, Redburn,* and *White-Jacket*

After the successes of *Typee* and *Omoo*, Melville apparently felt emboldened to venture in new directions in his writing. His literary knowledge deepened and matured in the late 1840s, as he read European authors voraciously – Rabelais, Montaigne, Shakespeare, Sir Thomas Browne, Spenser, Dante, Milton, Camoëns – as well as maritime chroniclers and popular American writers like James Fenimore Cooper, Richard Henry Dana, and J. Ross Browne. He maintained a lifelong habit of studying the Bible closely, as well as poring over encyclopedias and compendia of discoveries in science, travel, and natural history. He read critically, too, marking passages with marginal notes that show an eager mind and a desire to learn from as well as argue with cultural authorities from the past. No longer satisfied with writing autobiographical narratives loosely structured around sailor yarns and interwoven with travel narratives by other writers, Melville aspired to heights inhabited by his literary heroes. His next three novels, written at a feverish pace over a brief period, would in different ways show the imprint of what he had learned.

In the "Agatha" correspondence, Melville described his fascination with the story supplied by lawyer John H. Clifford, speaking of its hold on his imagination as he searched for the best way to write it: "I confess, however, that since then [hearing the story] I have a little turned the subject over in my mind with a view to a regular story to be founded on these striking incidents." Although he claims to give the story to Hawthorne to write, he cannot let go of it himself and devotes numerous pages to the "striking incidents" themselves and to the problem of creating a "regular story" from them. We might think of his earlier novels as likewise experimenting with the problem of making a logical structure for – a "regular story" of – the "striking incidents" both in Melville's nautical experience and in his imaginative and intellectual life, which was expanding to absorb more and more of his creative energies. In *Mardi*, *Redburn*, and *White-Jacket*, in different ways, a narrator struggles to give shape to the expanding size and significance of his subject, to balance the power of what is "striking" him against the demands for a "regular" or manageable text. Whereas, in *Typee* and *Omoo*, Melville adopted plot structures that allowed him to be highly *irregular*, to spin yarns and events without a particularly confining narrative structure, in his next books he attempted a structure that would allow him to contain, not always successfully, the vast expanses of his thought and imagination within a regular story.

"Mark it Deeper": *Mardi*

Like *Typee* and *Omoo*, *Mardi*, published in 1849, begins on a whaling ship cruising the Pacific, with a disaffected sailor longing to escape. In this case the at first unnamed narrator encounters little resistance from his quite reasonable captain, and he and his "chummy" Jarl steal a whaleboat and set out for unnamed islands to the west. They happen upon what appears to be a deserted ship but which has in fact been commandeered by a Polynesian named Samoa and his wife Annatoo, after being attacked by pirates. When the ship sinks in a storm which Annatoo does not survive, Samoa, Jarl, and the narrator escape in a boat and drift for some time before falling in with a mysterious craft. It bears a beautiful woman named Yillah hidden in a tent, and the narrator divines that she is the captive of a wicked-seeming priest, Aleema, and his sons. Murdering Aleema to protect Yillah, the narrator eventually lands with her on an island ruled by the great king Media. The inhabitants take the narrator for a demigod and call him Taji. He graciously accepts his divine status and settles in for an extended idyll with his lovely bride, until Aleema's sons steal her away. Enraged and grieved, Taji wins Media's aid in seeking Yillah throughout his archipelago, Mardi, accompanied by a retinue that includes Babbalanja the talkative philosopher, Mohi the aged historian, and Yoomy the enthusiastic poet. The group travels among a wide range of island kingdoms that, it becomes clear, represent satirical, *Gulliver*-like versions of European countries and slaveholding America, but Yillah is nowhere to be found. Instead a mysterious dark queen, named Hautia, appears to be pursuing Taji, her handmaidens casting at him flowers that have significant meanings. In the end, Taji's companions drop away, leaving him to pursue Yillah's abductors in wrathful vengeance, "over an endless sea" (p. 654).

Clearly in *Mardi* Melville was trying to break from the pattern of autobiographical nautical adventure established in his first two books by entering the world of literary romance, i.e. fictional work that operates at the boundaries of reality and imagination, such as Hawthorne was producing in his short tales. Inspired by his extensive reading of European writers to enter the authorial lists himself, Melville was attempting to make his mark on the world of literature.

But that enterprise, with its associated risks of leaving an indelible and damaging mark on his subject, raised considerable difficulties for him as a writer.

The word "mark" appears in the August "Agatha" letter with various significations. At first, Melville uses it in relation to Agatha's reflections, her remarks, on the landscape: "She marks how the continual assaults of the sea have undermined it [the shore]." Melville then advises Hawthorne to "mark" his words, as well as Robertson's actions: "Mark his trepidation & suspicion when any one called upon him. – But why prate so – you will mark it all & mark it deeper than I would, perhaps." In his diary of the events, Clifford notes the letter "directed to James Robertson the deceased, post marked Falmouth Mass[tts]." The verb thus migrates from meaning "note" or "notice," to "attend well to" to, finally, "inscribe or print with a distinguishing symbol." It also borrows from connotations of marking off or delineating, damaging or scarring, making visible, and assigning boundaries or other assertions of ownership. As Melville moved in his early books from spinning yarns to crafting more literate forms of storytelling, ones that reflected his vast and self-designed course of reading, images of marking crept into his prose with greater frequency and variety. These images suggest a certain tension over the relationship between oral and written forms of storytelling, between narratives spun in air and those recorded in print.

In particular, Melville's early novels present an intriguing pattern of marked men, characters whose markings reflect the influence of arts like tattooing but also draw attention to punitive marks or scars, as well as the marks of a writer upon a page.[1] Hence, as we have seen, *Typee* offers portraits of natives marked in artistic ways: Mehevi with his broad and warlike facial stripes, Marnoo with organic vines growing up his legs, old sages with blurred outlines and bleeding colors. *Omoo* presents, among the many tattooed islanders, Melville's first marked white man, Lem Hardy, with a dramatic facial tattoo of a "blue shark, nothing but fins from head to tail." Hardy's marks elicit horror: "What an impress! Far worse than Cain's – *his* was perhaps a wrinkle, or a freckle, which some of our modern cosmetics might have effaced; but the blue shark was a mark indelible" (p. 27). In comparing Hardy to Cain, Melville suggests the punitive power of the mark to alienate the marked man from his fellows.

Mardi, however, introduces a wider and more complex range of human markings and suggests the ways that men may be variously and creatively marked. Some of these associations are delightfully casual. For example, the only other white sailor identified by name besides Jarl, the narrator's chum, is a harpooner called "Mark," who tends to sleep on watch, thus missing the mark when Jarl and Taji slip away under cover of night. Another character, the islander Samoa, is both a "man of mark" and a man of "marks" (p. 98) or tattooings, "embracing but a vertical half of his person, from crown to sole" (pp. 98–9).

The most dramatic marked man is Taji himself, who acquires a Cain-like brand, somewhat mysteriously, as the narrative proceeds. While he enjoys his status throughout the novel as roaming demigod, Taji also feels guilt over the murder of Aleema the priest, which seems to have left its traces on his brow. At a critical moment, when Taji confesses his crime to his companions, Yoomy the poet reacts emotionally to Taji's brand: " 'Ah, Taji! I had shrank from you,' cried Yoomy, 'but for the mark upon your brow. That undoes the tenor of your words' " (p. 423). Yoomy seems to see Taji's mark not as a punitive sign, like the marks on Cain's or Lem Hardy's visages, but as a protective imprint, like the marks of taboo that allow Marnoo to travel freely in *Typee*. Nevertheless, Taji's mark is morally ambiguous, and at the end of the novel, when he vengefully continues to pursue his quarry, Melville, like Mary Shelley in *Frankenstein*, obscures the question of whether the protagonist is a reckless demon or a noble, Byronic hero.

The presence of significant marks in *Mardi* seems to speak to Melville's preoccupation with the status of writing itself, and Taji's moral ambiguity seems of a piece with Melville's concern about his relationship to the texts he plundered to construct his narrative. While Melville did not commit murder to write *Mardi*, he in a sense killed off the carefree, genial personas of Tommo and Typee to create Taji, whose story is both more reckless and far-ranging than those of *Typee* and *Omoo* and also more literary, borrowing heavily from the world of books and newspapers, literary imagination and print culture. In his previous works, Melville spun yarns and wove other people's books into his text. In *Mardi*, he sets out to "mark it deeper," to inscribe his authorial presence on the Pacific as if it were a stretch of canvas, or skin, awaiting his literary markings. Scholars have noted Melville's fascination with the "blank page" of his imaginings and have identified a complex of fears and guilt about writing over this blank page in a gesture that partakes of imperial conquest, proprietary appropriation, ideological mastery, even sexual violence.[2] Such readings may neglect to address the liberating joy Melville clearly expressed in expanding his literary vision in *Mardi* to take in new ideas, authors, and language. But they certainly identify his ambivalence over his vision of unfettered authorship at large in the Polynesian archipelago.

The greater part of the book consists of lengthy conversations among authors. Babbalanja, Mohi, and Yoomy, while spinning their philosophy, history, and poetry within a decidedly oral culture, nevertheless represent South Seas versions of the literary arts in Europe. Media and Taji, while not literary artists themselves, are deeply educated and engaged in intellectual debates over politics, religion, culture, and society. Just as significant as what the characters say or do is the presence in the text of authors, who import a rich array of allusions to philosophical, literary, sacred, scientific, and popular texts (including popular books on the language of flowers that Melville read with his wife Elizabeth). As he told his publisher John Murray, he intended the book not as a work of travel or nautical adventure but as a romance. In fact, he had in mind *philosophical* romance, a book less concerned with plot than ideas, and one that would investigate the meaning of human existence through fanciful evocations of an imaginary but parallel universe. That story would also be told in a language as rich and poetic as its subject, leaving the realistic lingo of the sailors far behind. With its evocations of dreams and madness, revery and intoxication, the novel launches itself into a superliterary universe that Melville's early readers had no reason to suspect him of inhabiting. At the same time, its trenchant critiques of European despotism and American slavery, religious orthodoxy and colonialist expansion, make it one of Melville's most politically sophisticated and far-ranging satires.

The broad reach of Melville's aims in *Mardi* reveals itself in many ways, as he explores most human systems of knowledge and belief. The book also records another set of markings, those of time and nature, and in those mystical signs Melville seems to find something concrete and irreducible to balance with the vast immensities of *Mardi's* cosmic space. In chapter 132 the adventurers visit the Isle of the Fossils, where they find rocks that seem to contain eons of history, unmistakable signs of past events: "Like antique tablets, the smoother parts were molded in strange devices: – Luxor marks, Tadmor ciphers, Palenque inscriptions. In long lines, as on Denderah's architraves, were bas-reliefs of beetles, turtles, ant-eaters, armadillos, guanos, serpents, tongueless crocodiles: – a long procession, frosted and crystalized in stone, and silvered by the moon." As Babbalanja explains, " 'These are the leaves of the book of Oro [God]. Here we read how worlds are made; here read the rise and fall of Nature's kingdoms'" (p. 415). Although Melville goes on in the rest of the chapter to mock natural history and theories of evolution, this reverent treatment of nature's inscriptions suggests the ways in which he sought to "mark it deeper" in *Mardi* by anchoring the airy spun fibers of his narrative to a bedrock of ancient prehistory. "Frosted" and "crystalized," these markings become luminous artifacts, beautiful in themselves, apart from the stories they tell.

Melville hoped to make his mark as an author in *Mardi*, to distinguish himself from the common herd of literary hacks and raise himself to the plane of the artists he admired. If he did not entirely succeed, he nevertheless established his daring and adventurous spirit. "I have created the creative!" his author-character Lombardo cries (p. 595). Even when *Mardi* failed in the literary marketplace, Melville surged ahead with a new sense of reckless authorial power. The sobering reviews of *Mardi*, however, pressed him to rein in his exuberance and discipline his narrative. The results in *Redburn* and *White-Jacket* suggest that this discipline, this creation of a more "regular story," may have toned his writing and prepared him for the ambitious ventures that lay ahead.

"A Skeleton of Actual Reality": *Redburn* and *White-Jacket*

A traditional reading of Melville's course after *Mardi* is that, chastened by the lukewarm reception of his rhapsodic book, he returned to the nautical scenes of his first successes. Yet, constrained by the narrow expectations of his readers and conditions of his popularity, he wrote out his frustration by creating protagonists who live not in island paradises but in shipboard infernos. Famously declaring to his father-in-law Lemuel Shaw that *Redburn* and *White-Jacket* were "two *jobs*, which I have done for money – being forced to it, as other men are to sawing wood," Melville lamented that "I have felt obliged to refrain from writing the kind of book I would wish to" (*L* 138). In spite of the considerable admiration that both books have aroused, scholars and readers tend to view them as secondary works, rehearsals for the far more magnificent achievement of *Moby-Dick*.

Yet Melville went on to tell Shaw that even though he would prefer "to write those sort of books which are said to 'fail,'" nevertheless "in writing these two books, I have not repressed myself much – so far as *they* are concerned; but have spoken pretty much as I feel" (*L* 138–9). He seems to have been drawn, as he was later to articulate the matter to Hawthorne in the August "Agatha" letter, to stories of "real" life: "You have a skeleton of actual reality to build about with fullness & veins & beauty." "Actual reality," in *Redburn*, *White-Jacket*, and the "Agatha" correspondence, meant to Melville not only the lived experiences of real people but also a kind of suffering that produces agonized reflection, endurance, and eventually wisdom, such as he was later to attribute to Solomon in *Moby-Dick*. This kind of experience calls for a writer who is not so much a spinner of yarns or an imaginary voyager as an Ancient Mariner, driven to tell his tale by some compulsion. Yet both *Redburn* and *White-Jacket* also considerably expanded Melville's literary skills by tempering his prose, imposing a certain rigor, as he focused his sights more narrowly on his characters and their maritime worlds.[3]

Melville based *Redburn* on his own first voyage, at the age of nineteen, on a merchant ship traveling to Liverpool. The protagonist, Wellingborough Redburn, is the son of a gentleman who, like Melville's father Allan, having fallen upon hard times has died, leaving his family to suffer in poverty and distress. The young man decides to make his fortune by going to sea. The early chapters give a comical picture of the youth's naiveté, as he imagines dining companionably with the captain and enjoying the genteel pleasures of oceangoing life. Instead he finds himself performing menial labors on deck and horrifying ascents into the rigging during an apprenticeship that exposes him to the harsh hazing of the crew. When he arrives in Liverpool, hoping to use his father's guidebook to seek out the sites of history and culture, he discovers that the book and the gentlemanly world his father inhabited are hopelessly out of date. Instead he, a poor sailor lad, lives in the sailor haunts and Booble Alleys of the port, where he witnesses, in a memorable episode, a starving woman and her children dying in a cellar. His one friend in Liverpool, Harry Bolton, spirits him away to an opulent gambling den and brothel in London, where he spends a night in opiated splendor, but the next day brings them back to their dreary reality. Harry, desperate and in debt, signs on for the return voyage, where Redburn hopes to help him make a new start. Instead, Harry shows his unfitness for sailor labor and endures a miserable voyage, subject to the teasing and ridicule – and probably sexual assaults – of the sailors. On their arrival in America, Redburn returns to his family, leaving Harry to make his uncertain way in the rapacious city of Manhattan. While seeming a simple sailor's story, the book also suggests the mature writer who will emerge from this early experience of the "striking" cruelties of existence.

Beginning in the first chapter of *Redburn*, Melville gives some sense of what that mature writer born out of suffering "actual reality" looks like. The narrator has been describing his "long reveries about distant voyages and travels, and … how fine it would be, to be able to talk about remote and barbarous countries" (p. 5). Redburn's fantasies suggest the powerful allure of travel, but characteristically Melville extends this description of adolescent reverie into a more complex meditation on literary imagination and on textuality itself when Redburn encounters an actual traveler:

For I very well remembered staring at a man myself, who was pointed out to me by my aunt one Sunday in church, as the person who had been in Stony Arabia, and passed through strange adventures there, all of which with my own eyes I had read in the book which he wrote, an arid-looking book in a pale yellow cover.

"See what big eyes he has," whispered my aunt, "they got so big, because when he was almost dead with famishing in the desert, he all at once caught sight of a date tree, with the ripe fruit hanging on it."

Upon this, I stared at him till I thought his eyes were really of an uncommon size, and stuck out from his head like those of a lobster. I am sure my own eyes must have magnified as I stared. When church was out, I wanted my aunt to take me along and follow the traveler home. But she said the constables would take us up, if we did; and so I never saw this wonderful Arabian traveler again. But he long haunted me; and several times I dreamt of him, and thought his great eyes were grown still larger and rounder; and once I had a vision of the date tree. (pp. 5–6)

In this description, Redburn eyes the stranger whose narrative he has read, in his mind merging the famous voyager with his "arid-looking book in a pale yellow cover." The traveler who went to "Stony Arabia" writes a chronicle whose cover resembles the pale yellow desert where he nearly died of hunger. The aunt's excited whisper conveys the power of the man's story to arouse readers; for that very pale yellow book has broadcast his adventures far and wide. But the man has paid dearly for his book. He bears the signs of an unspeakable experience in eyes that grew large because of the ripe fruit he desired and, perhaps, could not touch. He is a marked man, like Taji in *Mardi*, and the boy Redburn, watching him, becomes marked too; his eyes widen so much that they, like the traveler's, seem "stuck out … like those of a lobster." As comical as this moment appears, it is also grotesque, suggesting that the boy's wonder partakes of the forbidden. Just as the traveler risks some mysterious kind of mark if he partakes of the ripe fruit, the boy Redburn risks losing himself if he stares too long. In fact, his aunt warns him that pursuing the traveler is a crime: "the constables would take us up." And so Redburn must content himself with remembering and imagining the mystic traveler. But later he will write a book of his own, perhaps creating a textual version of his own marked body.

This brief tale suggests what it is like to gaze on the wondrous and strange and to imagine the unthinkable, even for a young boy. And Redburn remains very young throughout the novel, even as he somewhat matures. The story of his voyage to Liverpool and back offers a comical reduction of Tommo's and Typee's wanderings in the Pacific far away and Taji's journey to the edge of the cosmos. Yet at the same time, Redburn's immersion in the world of sailors and criminals, confidence men, prostitutes, and the suffering poor tests his ethical foundations as rigorously as Taji's voyage challenges his. In his first coming-of-age story, a book that Melville disclaimed as a mere "job," he nevertheless provides a vivid portrait of a young writer facing the world and registering its impact on a sensitive and impressionable imagination. Making a "regular story" from these "striking incidents" requires a discipline that Redburn struggles throughout the narrative to learn.

White-Jacket, written quickly after the completion of *Redburn* and published in 1850, presents a much more seasoned narrator who has signed on to a naval ship, the *Neversink*, and tells the story of the white jacket he constructs from an old duck-cloth shirt and of the character he becomes by assuming the nickname "White-Jacket." Taking his place among a diverse and rigidly organized crew, White-Jacket observes the horrors of military life, especially the mind-numbing discipline enforced by frequent public floggings. White-Jacket offers a detailed account of life on board: the never-ending routine of work, food, sleep, a daily measure of grog, and the occasional outbreak of more violent spirits among the restive crew. The narrator takes solace in the companionship of like-minded men, especially Jack Chase, an Englishman, gentleman, and hero of the Napoleonic War. Other shipmates, like Lemsford the surreptitious poet, Mad Jack the rebellious mate, and Ushant the majestic captain of the forecastle, relieve the monotony of military life and provide congenial company for someone of White-Jacket's literary sensibilities. While satirizing the venality and incompetence of officers like Captain Claret and Cadwallader Cuticle, the ship's surgeon, Melville also devotes serious, passionate, and extended passages to the violence encoded in the Articles of War and an oppressive social hierarchy that makes slaves and juveniles of the men. Calling naval ships the "Gomorrahs of the deep" (p. 376), he also hints at a world of rampant sexual predation where a man might need a very sturdy jacket to protect his vulnerable body.

White-Jacket has been admired for its meticulous detail, its passionate attack on the practice of flogging, and its probing meditation on issues of labor, class, and injustice done to men who resemble slaves more than genial sailors. It has also been viewed as a kind of twin sibling to *Redburn*, much as *Omoo* is often paired with *Typee*, but in fact *White-Jacket* stands apart from the works that precede it in being uncommonly focused and serious in its political and social aims.

It has also been understood as a complicated metaphor for the writing process itself, which, as White-Jacket develops as a character, becomes entwined with the writing of a text on or through the white canvas of his identity.[4] Rather than spinning a yarn, White-Jacket seems enmeshed in the threads and fibers of his garment, so that eventually it becomes a straitjacket from which he must laboriously free himself, cutting and ripping it open when it threatens to confine and drown him at the end: "I essayed to swim toward the ship; but instantly I was conscious of a feeling like being pinioned in a feather-bed, and, moving my hands, felt my jacket puffed out above my tight girdle with water. I strove to tear it off; but it was looped together here and there, and the strings were not then to be sundered by hand. I whipped out my knife, that was tucked at my belt, and ripped my jacket straight up and down, as if I were ripping open myself. With a violent struggle I then burst out of it, and was free. Heavily soaked, it slowly sank before my eyes" (p. 394). Many critics have viewed this image of the confining jacket as Melville's way of signifying the demands of his craft, as he struggled to free himself from realistic nautical narrative to create new forms.

But the discipline of *White-Jacket*, while oppressive to the main character and painful to the writer, may nevertheless have proved salutary, at least in the way it allowed Melville to map and contain a vast subject. As ambitious in its way as *Mardi*, *White-Jacket* seeks to explore a world made large not only in geographical but also in social and epistemological terms. Rather than traveling over the cosmic expanse of an imaginary archipelago, White-Jacket explores the hidden recesses of a ship that seems to contain multitudes, whole realms of knowledge and of social experience as manifested in the secret lives of the officers and crew in the complex hierarchy of the ship. Whereas Redburn stumbles accidentally upon the hidden world of the under-classes, White-Jacket systematically seeks it out, rendering his discoveries in sometimes Gothic but also sympathetic terms. Imagining the ship as the physical embodiment of a teeming social structure, he creates a Dantean vision of its moral and spiritual depths as well.

In many ways, then, *White-Jacket* anticipates the encyclopedic expanse of *Moby-Dick*, with its epic proportions and at the same time minute attention to detail. Melville made no lofty claims for *White-Jacket*, announcing in a brief, factual prefatory note that "My man-of-war experiences and observations are incorporated in the present volume." As with his other novels, however, Melville was experimenting with making a "regular story" from the "striking incidents" of his subject. *White-Jacket* succeeds by making "regular" – i.e. ordinary but also disciplined, organized, and regulated – that which is "striking." Thus, the experience that Melville found painful in the extreme, and that included the literal striking of sailors' naked backs, takes form in a narrative that shapes it rigorously, while at the same time exposing its immense psychological, philosophical, and social implications. Such discipline served him well when he turned to the equally "striking" incidents of *Moby-Dick*.

PART III

Writing New Gospel in *Moby-Dick* and *Pierre*

CHAPTER 5

"So Much of Pathos, &
So Much of Depth":
Moby-Dick

The story of Agatha, a woman betrayed, isolated, and forlorn, may have attracted Melville in 1852 in part because he had spent over three years immersed in narratives of human suffering and heroism: *Moby-Dick* (1851) and *Pierre* (1852). Nothing in his earlier work achieved the grand dimensions of these novels. His first five sea stories had experimented with a wide range of styles and emotional registers, from the comic to the mystical, the satiric to the metaphysical, the realistic to the romantic. They reflect the various impacts of his early maritime experience, his wide reading, the fluctuating reception of his books, and the pressures of economic necessity that forced his growth as a writer. Told often as yarns, they develop complex designs, playing suggestively with ideas of weaving disparate strands together and sometimes tying the teller in knotted webs of narrative fabric, from which he must, like White-Jacket, eventually cut himself loose. Even if Melville had never written more than these five novels, he would have demonstrated the richness and versatility of his gifts as a storyteller.

With the conclusion of *White-Jacket*, in an image of the world as a frigate manned by oppressed souls, Melville articulated a vision of suffering humanity that was to expand his range and carry him into his next novels and many of his short stories as well: "we the people suffer many abuses. . . . Yet the worst of our evils we blindly inflict upon ourselves; our officers can not remove them, even if they would. From the last ills no being can save another; therein each man must be his own saviour" (p. 399). With this declaration, Melville voiced a concern, seldom so forcefully expressed before, with the sorrows of "we the people" the world over. His next novels would look more deeply for their meanings into the hearts of men and women and would broaden their thematic scope and literary invention accordingly.

Scholars and biographers have accounted in different ways for this widening of Melville's concerns. The era of Andrew Jackson and the myth of proud, young American democracy collided with the realities of internal dissension over slavery and abolition, manifest destiny and Western expansionism, religion and reform, regional and national interests. Melville's trip to London and the European continent in 1849 exposed him to a wealth of authors, ideas, and philosophical influences that deepened his perspective immeasurably. His subsequent move from New York to the Berkshires in 1850, a risky financial and professional gamble, raised his literary sights. Some have seen *Moby-Dick* as part of the slow, long growth that Melville described, in a letter to Hawthorne, as an "unfolding." Others have seen it as a radical break from his earlier work, nourished by the expanded sense of literary genius recorded in his essay, "Hawthorne and His Mosses" and by his stimulating friendship with Hawthorne. It would be hard to identify the exact confluence of events and influences that engendered *Moby-Dick*.

But we might take as a starting point Melville's advice to the reader in the second sentence of *Moby-Dick*'s "Extracts," the long opening section of "random allusions to whales he could anyways find in any book whatsoever, sacred or profane." Mocking the Sub-Sub Librarian who has assembled these motley references to whales, Melville warns, "Therefore you must not, in every case at least, take the higgledy-piggledy whale statements, however authentic, in these extracts, for veritable gospel cetology" (p. xvii). In implicitly identifying *Moby-Dick* as a "gospel cetology," Melville makes the boldest of claims for the novel as a new bible, a book of truth. Throughout his early novels, Melville oscillates between criticism of and reverence for holy scripture. But in *Moby-Dick* and *Pierre* he asserts a new conviction of his capacity to write a gospel of his own. Pierre says it most openly and controversially when describing to his sister Isabel his conception of the author's task: "I will write such things – I will gospelize the world anew, and show them deeper secrets than the Apocalypse! – I will write it, I will write it!" (p. 273). Pierre has in mind something that will revise all prior philosophies and theologies, and Melville is most likely satirizing such vaunting ambition in a writer. But perhaps he can do so because he had such ambitions himself in *Moby-Dick*.

The problem of Melville's relationship to theology is old and vexed. It is important to remember that he maintained a perennially open and restless mind. But as he indicated to Hawthorne in the "Agatha" correspondence, he saw the meaning of human existence not just as a question of doctrine but as a matter of "so much of pathos, & so much of depth." In *Moby-Dick* and *Pierre* he tried to find new literary form for the pathos and depth of his subjects, and in doing so experimented with nearly every available literary genre. Ishmael suggests as much in the first chapter of *Moby-Dick* when he says, "I cannot tell why it was exactly that those stage managers, the Fates, put me down for this shabby part of a whaling voyage, when others were set down for magnificent parts in high tragedies, and short and easy parts in genteel comedies, and jolly parts in farces" (p. 7). *Moby-Dick* embraces high tragedy, comedy, farce, and heroic epic – while at the same time and continually calling out for a new "veritable gospel." Through the multiplicity of their aims and forms, Melville's next novels break through generic boundaries to represent truths that Melville considered deep and shattering. In a sense, then, he was inventing a bible of his own.

"The Malignity of the Sea": Ahab and Tragic Rebellion

The form Melville selected for his new gospel was a narrative of whaling, the one nautical experience he had not yet explored in full. At first sight, little in the plot would indicate its grand tragic potential. A sailor named Ishmael signs on to a mysterious craft, the *Pequod*, after his new friend, a tattooed Polynesian called Queequeg, promises to ship with him wherever he chooses. Although the captain, Ahab, lies ailing somewhere out of sight, and although a sinister character named Elijah tries to warn him away, Ishmael feels sure that the *Pequod* is the ship for him, and he and Queequeg go aboard. Once they sail, Ahab emerges from his cabin, telling a dark tale of the murderous whale Moby Dick, who has shorn away his leg. In a dramatic scene on the quarter-deck (chapter 36, "The Quarter-Deck"), Ahab thunders his desire for vengeance, telling the men they have shipped for one thing:

to hunt and kill the great white whale. Incited by hopes of earning a gold doubloon, the white American mates – Starbuck, Stubb, Flask – and multiracial harpooners – Queequeg, Tashtego, and Daggoo – stoically serve his will, as do the mostly compliant crew.

For the long middle and late sections of the book, the ship chases whales, while Ishmael muses on all things cetological. Analyzing the technology of whale hunting as well as the natural history of whales, he offers a global view of whaling as a nexus of matters scientific, legal, political, cultural, historical, and anything else he can think of. His disquisitions are punctuated by whale hunts and detailed descriptions of the "trying-out" or refining of whale oil, by "gams," or periodic social encounters between ships, and also by the characters', especially Ahab's, Shakespearean soliloquies.

In the second half of the book, Ahab emerges more fully as a character, shadowed by a mysterious apparition known as Fedallah, who delivers various prophecies concerning his, Ahab's, and the ship's eventual encounter with the white whale. Ahab also forms an affectionate bond with the young African American cabin boy, Pip, who has gone mad after falling overboard and drifting alone in the sea. Although moody Ahab seems to soften as the voyage progresses, showing affection for both Pip and Starbuck, his quieter moments give way in the end to burning vengeance: the *Pequod* finally engages with Moby Dick in a fierce struggle over three days. In a maneuver that Melville knew would strain his readers' credulity but which had actually occurred in the case of the *Essex* in 1820, Moby Dick strikes the ship and causes it to sink. All drown but Ishmael, who manages to float to safety on a lifebuoy made from a coffin Queequeg built for himself when he was ill.

As a brief summary of this well-known story suggests, the plot is relatively simple and straightforward. What makes it, then, so compelling? One answer is that the story concerns, as Melville stated of his proposed story in the "Agatha" correspondence, the "malignity of the sea." This idea suggests Ahab's defiance of the gods and the grandeur of his tragic quest for vengeance.

Consider the peculiarity of Melville's phrase. The "malignity of the sea" does not suggest that the sea is merely indifferent or unfathomable. It indicates that the sea, or the power it represents, is evil and means to do harm. In many ways this concept excuses and ennobles Ahab's irrational hatred of the whale. As Ishmael explains,

All that most maddens and torments; all that stirs up the lees of things; all truth with malice in it; all that cracks the sinews and cakes the brain; all the subtle demonisms of life and thought; all evil, to crazy Ahab, were visibly personified, and made practically assailable in Moby Dick. He piled upon the whale's white hump the sum of all the general rage and hate felt by his whole race from Adam down; and then, as if his chest had been a mortar, he burst his hot heart's shell upon it. (p. 184)

Ishmael's explanation seems quite logical (and psychological) in showing how Ahab's anger against his fate focuses and falls upon the agent of it, one white whale. But it requires that the reader consent to a terrible hypothesis: that the universe is evil, that it contains "truth with malice in it," that all humanity shares in the "general rage and hate felt by his whole race from Adam down." To understand and sympathize with Ahab's suffering, one must accept his view of a hostile universe, must in a sense be as "crazy" as he is.

If this "malignity" is indeed Melville's theme, it resides like Ahab's bomb at the center of the narrative, threatening to explode and take everything with it. But the book encloses its destructive power in a structure of tragic motifs that seem to hold this violence at arm's length and even make of it something noble and sublime. Ahab has often been associated with a tragic arc in *Moby-Dick*. With his "nervous lofty language" (p. 73), his Shakespearean speeches, his Lear-like attachment to the mad fool Pip, and his reckless attack on the "pasteboard masks" (p. 164) of existence, he resembles the heroes of classical Greek, Renaissance, Miltonic, and Romantic tragedies. Ishmael explicitly announces that "to meanest mariners, and renegades and castaways, I shall hereafter ascribe high qualities, though dark; weave around them tragic graces" (p. 117). Frequent references to fate evoke the classical Greek sisters and the overwhelming fate of Greek tragedy: the sailors "plunged like fate into the lone Atlantic" (p. 105); Ishmael imagines himself as "a shuttle mechanically weaving and weaving away at the Fates" (p. 214); and Ahab constructs a fatal harpoon of "pole, iron, and rope – like the Three Fates" (p. 490).

What are the effects of such obvious, some might say heavy-handed, borrowing from classical tragedy? One is like that which Harriet Beecher Stowe achieves by lending "tragic graces" to a slave, Uncle Tom. By ennobling a figure many might consider ordinary – a whaling captain is a sort of butcher, after all – Melville clothes Ahab in a certain classic dignity. Another is an opposite effect, such as that which Lawrence Levine suggests for American adaptations of Shakespeare's plays: by writing comic endings for tragedies, presenting tragedy alongside farcical entr'actes, and using the trappings of melodrama, American producers of popular theater created a hybrid, democratic art that punctured the pretensions of classical forms. Thus when tragic Ahab sobs like a "heart-stricken moose" (p. 163), or delivers one of his exalted rants, he behaves much as the popular actor Edwin Forrest did when he tore up the New York stage (and nearly tore up the city during the Astor Place riots of 1849, when mobs dramatically asserted their preference for his histrionic style over that of the more refined Charles Macready).[1] Writing tragedy in an American idiom, Melville announces himself as that Shakespeare born on the banks of the Ohio whom he lauded in "Hawthorne and His Mosses."

A third effect of Melville's evocation of the tragic is that it lends heroism not only to Ahab's sympathetic qualities, as with Uncle Tom, but also to his destructive wrath. Like Antigone, Ahab defies the gods, whom he sees as tricking humanity into faith. As he brilliantly argues,

> "All visible objects, man, are but as pasteboard masks. But in each event – in the living act, the undoubted deed – there, some unknown but still reasoning thing puts forth the mouldings of its features from behind the unreasoning mask. If man will strike, strike through the mask! How can the prisoner reach outside except by thrusting through the wall?" (p. 164)

Ahab suspects, as Pierre later will do as well, that the mask of existence conceals a vast emptiness within. He feels no obligation, then, toward a power that may be no more than a bully and brute: "Talk not to me of blasphemy, man; I'd strike the sun if it insulted me. For could the sun do that, then could I do the other; since there is ever a sort of fair play herein, jealously presiding over all creations" (p. 164). For Ahab, having recklessly cast aside faith, "Naught's an obstacle, naught's an angle to the iron way!" (p. 168). In his final moments, aware at last that he has been "befooled, befooled!" by the universe, Ahab nevertheless continues to trumpet his defiance: "Sink all coffins and hearses to one common pool! And, since neither can be mine, let me then tow to pieces, while still chasing thee, though tied to thee, thou damned whale! Thus, I give up the spear!" (p. 572).

Twentieth-century critics of the so-called Melville Revival (the first flowering of Melville criticism from the 1920s to about 1960) tended to admire Ahab's tragic quest and to see in it a version of America's defiant emergence from the chaos of the Second World War.[2] As Melville might slyly point out, however, such a view rests on a radical, self-destructive individualism that is as dangerous to the welfare of the American ship of state as the seeming conformity of the men. Depending on a view of a universe dominated by indifferent fates rather than a merciful Christian deity, this reading reposes as much faith in "malignity" as it does in love. Writing to Hawthorne, Melville declared that he had written a "wicked book, and [felt] spotless as the lamb" (*L* 212). By asserting the necessity of "malignity," he felt he had baptized his book in hell-fire.

"Learned in These Matters": Ishmael as Comic Skrimshander

As necessary to the book as its blasphemy is its comic affirmation of a very different kind of spirit, the embracing, communitarian tendency embodied in Ishmael. As often as scholars have recognized the tragic potential in Ahab, they have seen it in balance with Ishmael's comic vision, one that perceives not a meaningless void opening beyond the pasteboard mask but a vast world of meanings located in the living text of human experience. Ishmael bears the name of the biblical wanderer and outcast, son of Abraham and despised Hagar and progenitor of Arabs, but he is also a textual wanderer, traveling freely through the worlds of history, philosophy, science, law, natural history, culture, poetry, and politics. His elastic mind and flexible faith include all humanity in their purview. With his embrace of the "meanest" along with the highest, Ishmael places himself squarely in the comic and humanist tradition, the enlightened universe against which Ahab rails.

But who *is* Ishmael? The narrator of *Moby-Dick* has two significant aliases. One, the famous one, he adopts himself: "Call me Ishmael." This name seems to signify the wandering, isolated, and questing spirit mentioned above. The other comes from the landlord at the Spouter-Inn, who offers Ishmael a pine board for a bed: "'But wait a bit, Skrimshander; I've got a carpenter's plane there in the bar – wait, I say, and I'll make ye snug enough'" (p. 17). Earlier in the same chapter (chapter 3, "The Spouter-Inn"), Ishmael has observed "a number of young seamen gathered about a table, examining by a dim light divers specimens of skrimshander" (p. 14); and later, in chapter 57 ("Of Whales in Paint; in Teeth; in Wood; in Sheet-Iron; in Stone; in Mountains; in Stars"), Ishmael describes this particular form of maritime art more minutely:

> lively sketches of whales and whaling-scenes, graven by the fishermen themselves on Sperm Whale-teeth, or ladies' busks wrought out of the Right Whale-bone, and other like skrimshander articles, as the whale-men call the numerous little ingenious contrivances they elaborately carve out of the rough material, in their hours of ocean leisure. Some of them have little boxes of dentistical-looking implements, specially intended for the skrimshandering business. But, in general, they toil with their jack-knives alone; and, with that almost omnipotent tool of the sailor, they will turn you out anything you please, in the way of a mariner's fancy. (pp. 269–70)

Why does the landlord call Ishmael Skrimshander? Perhaps he sees in him someone with the "omnipotent tool of the sailor," someone who can "turn you out anything you please." And indeed, he is not far from right. A sailor can produce "lively sketches" to suit anyone's "fancy" as well as the artist or writer can.

As *Moby-Dick* progresses, it becomes clear that Melville sees Ishmael as something more than a mariner, someone whose authority rests not only on his maritime skills but also on his wide reading, restless intellect, and spiritual striving. But as in Melville's first five novels, being a sailor provides sufficient grounds, and indeed excellent training, for producing a story. Each of Melville's early narrators is, typically, a skrimshander who learns how to carve a scene or craft an object of utility or delight, as well as how to spin yarns, skip into the complicated rigging, tie knots, and ink tattoos on a comrade's arm. Even if he outgrows his nautical ways, resembling a writer or even a philosopher more than a sailor as the novel goes on, the narrator of any one of Melville's early books owes his very identity to his experience at sea. It makes sense that he would draw on the seaman's art to fashion his story.

Ishmael evinces this practical skill constantly throughout *Moby-Dick*. Beginning with a length of rope, he can construct as handy a metaphor as you might wish to see (chapter 60, "The Line"). He is, like Agatha, "learned" in all things maritime, but as much as learning he exhibits ingenuity, turning to clever use the episodes of the whaling voyage. Thus a recipe for chowder offers a vivid image of how a book is made (chapter 15, "Chowder"), a stand at the mast-head becomes an occasion for meditating on meditating (chapter 35, "The Mast-Head"), the weaving of a mat introduces ideas of fate and free will (chapter 47, "The Mat-Maker"), a fog-bound attack on a whale provides an opportunity for philosophically considering his death (chapter 49, "The Hyena"), and the chore of squeezing spermaceti produces a paean to human love and sexuality (chapter 94, "A Squeeze of the Hand").

As Melville advised Hawthorne in the "Agatha" correspondence, a writer must "mark it deeper," carving his insight into the plastic materials of his imaginings. Whereas the teller of a yarn broadcasts his words to the winds, like the poet Lemsford shooting his odes from the mouths of cannons in *White-Jacket*, the skrimshander etches his in a more durable medium. And whereas the tattoo artist applies his indelible dyes to living skin, the skrimshander cuts his into dead whale's tooth and bone. And so, as skrimshander, Ishmael is an artist of a somewhat necrophiliac kind. For just as "malignity" is necessary to Ahab's tragic action, so are whale teeth and bones, or the materials of death, oddly necessary to Ishmael's comic art. Ishmael's comedy is not simply a matter of being able to laugh, like the hyena in Melville's chapter 49, at the universe. It also consists in being able to construct meaning from the bare bones and shattered ruins of hope.

Such images of desolation appear in chapter 7, "The Chapel," when Ishmael asks why humans mourn their dead when religion tells them that they are far happier in the life after death: "how is it that we still refuse to be comforted for those who we nevertheless maintain are dwelling in unspeakable bliss; why all the living so strive to hush all the dead; wherefore but the rumor of a knocking in a tomb will terrify a whole city." Whereas Ahab might see this insight as proof of the emptiness of existence, Ishmael thinks more optimistically – "All these things are not without their meanings" – and concludes, "But Faith, like a jackal, feeds among the tombs, and even from these dead doubts she gathers her most vital hope" (p. 37).

Ishmael's pliable, skrimshandering imagination makes it possible to construct living narrative from dead matter. Just as the whale's skeleton in chapter 102, "A Bower of the Arsacides" provides the framework for the vines that give it life, so does Ishmael's comic vision find substance for fiction in the hard facts of the whale's corpse. Much of his narration takes place on, around, and inside that dead body as it examines every orifice, every detail of its history and every meaning held therein. As he dwells on the whale's tail (chapter 86, "The Tail"), for example, he makes it clear that he can appreciate its beauty only because the whale is dead: "the entire member seems a dense webbed bed of welded sinews; but cut into it, and you find that three distinct strata compose it: – upper, middle, and lower" (p. 375). Yet from this anatomy lesson proceeds a breathtaking display of poetic fancy. The tail's "Titanism of power" calls forth an ecstatic stream of reflections on the relationship between strength and beauty:

> Take away the tied tendons that all over seem bursting from the marble in the carved Hercules, and its charm would be gone. As devout Eckerman lifted the linen sheet from the naked corpse of Goethe, he was overwhelmed with the massive chest of the man, that seemed as a Roman triumphal arch. When Angelo paints even God the Father in human form, mark what robustness is there. And whatever they may reveal of the divine love of the Son, the soft, curled, hermaphroditical Italian pictures, in which his idea has been most successfully embodied; these pictures, so destitute as they are of all brawniness, hint nothing of any power, but the mere negative, feminine one of submission and endurance, which on all hands it is conceded, form the peculiar practical virtues of his teachings. (p. 376)

Within a few lines, Ishmael comments on the strength, structure, and beauty of the whale's tail; associates the whale with classical Greek gods and Roman arches, a Romantic poet and philosopher (Goethe), and the Renaissance painter Michelangelo; delivers an androcentric theory of gender and power in art and religion; and incidentally casts a sly aspersion on the merely "practical virtues" of Christ's teachings of submission and endurance.

Thence follows an exhaustive treatment of the different kinds of motion the tail can perform, again eloquently rendered and richly ornamented with allusions to Roman history, Miltonic and Dantean images of hell, and Persian mythology. The chapter concludes with a characteristically virtuosic reflection on Ishmael's own practice as thinker and artist:

> The more I consider this mighty tail, the more do I deplore my inability to express it. At times there are gestures in it, which, though they would well grace the hand of man, remain wholly inexplicable. In an extensive herd, so remarkable, occasionally, are these mystic gestures, that I have heard hunters who have declared them akin to Free-Mason signs and symbols; that the whale, indeed, by these methods intelligently conversed with the world. Nor are there wanting other motions of the whale in his general body, full of strangeness, and unaccountable to his most experienced assailant. Dissect him how I may, then, I but go skin deep. I know him not, and never will. But if I know not even the tail of the whale, how understand his head? much more, how comprehend his face, when face he has none. Thou shalt see my back parts, my tail, he seems to say, but my face shall not be seen. But I cannot completely make out his back parts; and hint what he will about his face, I say again he has no face. (pp. 378–9)

Again, within a few lines, Ishmael ranges from an extraordinary insight about whale "gestures" and their subtle communications to an implication about his own use as writer of "Free-Mason signs and symbols"; he reminds the reader of the complex relationship between surface and depth ("I but go skin deep") and his ironic perception that to go skin deep is to mark it deeper; he refers knowledgeably to the Bible, Jeremiah 18.17 ("I will scatter them as with an east wind before the enemy; I will shew them the back, and not the face, in the day of their calamity"), with both an apt allusion and a prophecy of what Moby Dick will do to the ship; and he suggests a bawdy reading of his efforts at making out the whale's "back parts." The whale's dead body, then, has proven fertile ground for Ishmael's lively imagination and learning. Passages like this one give ample evidence that Melville saw writing, as he told Hawthorne in the "Agatha" correspondence, as giving a reader what he needs to "find out the suggestiveness for [him]self."

As admirable, even redemptive, as Ishmael's comic skrimshandering may be, it ultimately carries nearly as much potential for destruction as Ahab's tragic gestures. In chapter 96, "The Try-Works," as in "The

Mast-Head," Ishmael learns the dangers of free thought and imagination when, wearied by looking in the infernal fires of the try-pots, he falls asleep at the helm and lets the ship drift off its course. The shock of awakening to this realization leads him to distrust his earlier perceptions of truth: "Look not too long in the face of the fire, O man! Never dream with thy hand on the helm! Turn not thy back to the compass; accept the first hint of the hitching tiller; believe not the artificial fire, when its redness makes all things look ghastly" (p. 424). In his rejection of the false lights of "artificial" fires, Ishmael recommends turning away from the world of art and artifice to that of nature and the "true lamp" of divine revelation. Melville here seems to indicate that the cunning artifice of the skrimshander can take humanity only so far in its quest for truth.

The dark side of Ishmael's comic skrimshandering displays itself, with "so much of pathos, & so much of depth," even more fully in chapter 42, "The Whiteness of the Whale." This meditation on the meaning of the whale's color, and on whiteness, light, and color as cultural and philosophical constructs, shows Ishmael's characteristic inventiveness, those traits of mental dexterity and restlessness that appear in characters as different as Long Ghost, White-Jacket, and Agatha's peripatetic husband Robertson. Viewed as a certain kind of sailor art, the chapter is highly decorative and ornate. Ishmael begins with a proposition: "What the white whale was to Ahab, has been hinted; what, at times, he was to me, as yet remains unsaid" (p. 188). Taking this simple, utterly bare statement as his canvas, he proceeds to fill in that canvas with a bewildering array of examples of whiteness, an array that "paints like the harlot" (p. 195) onto the screen of his imagination. As examples of the horror of whiteness proliferate – the white shark or bear or albatross, the white squall, the bleached ruins of Lima, the Antarctic waste – Ishmael appears to lose his way, his composure, as he does in "The Try-Works": "But thou sayest, methinks, this white-lead chapter about whiteness is but a white flag hung out from a craven soul; thou surrenderest to a hypo, craven Ishmael" (p. 194). Ishmael's surrender to his fears, though, precisely defines his comic response. Whereas Ahab sees a pasteboard mask as something to strike through in a tragic quest for meaning, Ishmael sees the "dumb blankness" itself as "full of meaning": even if its meaning is "the thought of annihilation," the reminder of the "charnel-house within" all the beguiling appearances of life. Rather than being paralyzed by fear and despair, Ishmael chooses and submits to this bleak knowledge: "like willful travelers in Lapland, who refuse to wear colored and coloring glasses upon their eyes, so the wretched infidel gazes himself blind at the monumental white shroud that wraps all the prospect around him." His choice is the comic choice, as he accepts his lot, refuses to fight the gods, as Ahab does, and adopts a rueful shrug: "Wonder ye then at the fiery hunt?" (p. 195). But his comic acceptance is in many ways as dark as, if not darker than, Ahab's tragic defiance.

"Those Very Perils": Epic Heroism in the Men

If we view *Moby-Dick* as drama and Ahab and Ishmael as the twin faces, or pasteboard masks, of tragedy and comedy, then the novel contains a certain symmetry and balance. Mid-twentieth-century adherents of New Criticism admired such principles of Apollonian order. But Melville introduces a third generic form to the literary chowder of *Moby-Dick* – the epic – and a third set of interests, those of the sailors, men who have none of the consolations of high art. In their primarily illiterate universe, Ahab's speeches and Ishmael's reveries have little meaning.

Instead the men live in the world of physical heroism, mindless violence, and democratic comradeship of the great national epics: the *Iliad* and *Odyssey*, the *Aeneid*, *Beowulf*, the *Lusiad* of Luis de Camoëns, even *Don Quixote*. These men might eventually resemble Agatha's father, the "old widower – a man of the sea, but early driven away from it by repeated disasters. Hence, is he subdued & quiet & wise in his life. And now he tends a light house, to warn people from those very perils, from which he himself has suffered." Like Captain George Pollard of the *Essex* (whom Melville would meet on his visit to Nantucket in 1852) and his first mate Owen Chase, whose narrative Melville had read at sea, the sailors have lived through unspeakable terrors with the physical courage and fortitude that Ishmael reveres in Starbuck: "Looking into his eyes, you seemed to see there the yet lingering images of those thousand-fold perils he had calmly confronted through life" (p. 115). Like the sturdy insensibility of the other mates, Stubb and Flask, Starbuck's courage is "a thing simply useful to him" (p. 116) in his chosen livelihood, but Ishmael sees in it the token of "that democratic dignity which, on all hands, radiates without end from God; Himself!" (p. 117). His concept of the men's dignity and democratic equality opposes the aristocratic world of elite theatrical forms like tragedy and comedy or the more intellectual realm of Ishmael's philosophy.

If the confrontation between man and whale provides tragic conflict for Ahab and comic opportunity for Ishmael, for the men it is a scene of pure terror and yet the stuff of their daily work and the medium in which they express their strength and virtue. The genre that takes up their struggle most properly is the epic. The plot of epic does not so much concern a battle between men and fate as in tragedy, or between men and their own natures as in comedy, as it is a conflict between men of one tribe or nation and those of another. Although the sailors of the *Pequod* come from all parts of the globe – Queequeg specifically from Polynesia, Daggoo from Africa, not to mention the Maltese, Tahitian, Chinese, Lascar, and other sailors – Ishmael groups them together and identifies them with America. They compete with ships of other whaling nations – the British, French, German, and Dutch that they meet in their periodic gams. And although this competition is primarily friendly, national honor is at stake, as when Stubb cheats the French of a particularly valuable cache of ambergris and exults in his victory: "these Crappoes of Frenchmen are but poor devils in the fishery" (p. 403). Ishmael himself, as one of the sailors, takes pride in the Nantucketers, "Red Men," like Tashtego, and other American heroes of whaling who have extended America's reach and influence over the globe and carried its civilization to the farthest corners of the world ("The Advocate").

The greatest of Melville's epic heroes is Queequeg. Like Homer's warriors or Beowulf and his men, he faces danger calmly and fearlessly. He exhibits precise and artful skill in his use of weapons. He decorates his body with pride. He speaks to the purpose, without the baroque elaborations that Ahab and Ishmael love. And he embodies an ethic of universal brotherhood that Ishmael mockingly identifies as more Christian than most Christians: as he explains to Captain Bildad, Queequeg is a member of "the same ancient Catholic Church to which you and I, and Captain Peleg there, and Queequeg here, and all of us, and every mother's son and soul of us belong; the great and everlasting First Congregation of this whole worshipping world" (p. 88).

Queequeg's dominance over the first twenty or so land-based chapters of *Moby-Dick* signals that the epic mode in the novel is no less important than Ahab's grand tragedy or the saving comedy of Ishmael. And indeed Melville's reading of Homeric epic in those chapters is as audacious as the way he reimagines classical tragedy and comedy elsewhere. The relationship between Ishmael and Queequeg, bosom friends who declare themselves "married," has been viewed recently through critical readings of Melville's early novels of the Pacific, in particular a psychosexual rendering of different kinds of homoerotic bonding. Queequeg at first appears to be another of the tattooed islanders picked up but then discarded on white men's travels.

Viewed through the frame of Homeric epic, though, Queequeg becomes a more significant figure. Melville could almost be imagining the life of Homer's Achilles and Patroclus in their tent when he represents Ishmael and Queequeg sleeping together, dressing and undressing, eating breakfast and sallying forth, sharing their money, worshiping the same gods, and pledging eternal amity, "yea, till poor Queequeg took his last long dive" (p. 61). Like Achilles, Queequeg is a prince and a superb warrior. Ishmael, never his equal as a killer of whales, supplies the civilized pleasures of domestic companionship, as Patroclus does for his friend. Ishmael, of course, is not killed as Patroclus is by Hector, but in a sense he departs from the epic narrative and enters the world of tragedy and comedy. Queequeg, both an island prince and a democratic hero, does not belong in the domain of Ahab's tragic sublimity or Ishmael's comic wit. He becomes, as Achilles does after the death of Patroclus, a wordless killer, less ferocious than Achilles but no less useful to the barbarous imperatives of his leaders. Emerging at moments like chapter 72, "The Monkey-Rope" or chapter 110, "Queequeg in His Coffin" to remind Ishmael of the world of epic comradeship and heroism, he then subsides.

His importance to the early chapters, however, which Harrison Hayford has argued Melville wrote after the rest of the novel to heighten the theme of bosom friendship,[3] suggests that Queequeg's role as epic hero is central to the novel, even though his presence in it diminishes. Perhaps Melville understood that close, erotic bonds between men could be treated with more latitude in epic than in classical drama or the social novel. Whether or not critics read the Ishmael-Queequeg relationship as a Homeric partnership, considerable scholarship has focused on the sexual and gender implications of Ishmael's role as Queequeg's "wife" (p. 25), of Ishmael's submissive sexuality in relation to Queequeg's glorious masculinity and phallicism.

Ishmael narrates these scenes comically, representing himself alternately as a sort of country bumpkin, a pedant, a sidekick, and a tyro, with Queequeg as cannibal savage, pipe-smoking confidant, magnificent and also terrifying tattooed body, and superb athlete. Yet at the same time, the genuine intimacy of these scenes weighs powerfully against the lack of close relationships elsewhere in the novel. And the language of this intimacy is some of the most compelling in the book:

> Upon waking next morning about daylight, I found Queequeg's arm thrown over me in the most loving and affectionate manner. You had almost thought I had been his wife. The counterpane was of patchwork, full of odd little parti-colored squares and triangles; and this arm of his tattooed all over with an interminable Cretan labyrinth of a figure, no two parts of which were of one precise shade – owing I suppose to his keeping his arm at sea unmethodically in sun and shade, his shirt sleeves irregularly rolled up at various times – this same arm of his, I say, looked for all the world like a strip of that same patchwork quilt. Indeed, partly lying on it, as the arm did when I first awoke, I could hardly tell it from the quilt, they so blended their hues together; and it was only by the sense of weight and pressure that I could tell that Queequeg was hugging me. (p. 25; chapter 4, "The Counterpane")

When Ishmael describes waking up in bed with Queequeg, he achieves an astonishing range of images that at the same time sharply delineate ("odd little parti-colored squares and triangles," "sun and shade") while also blending seeming opposites, so that Queequeg's distinct tattooings, "an interminable Cretan labyrinth of a figure," merge with the counterpane and look "for all the world like a strip of that same patchwork quilt." As with his other images of mixing and blending, like the chowder or the mutual joint-stock company of cannibals and Christians (p. 62), Ishmael's insight makes comic sense of what might otherwise be a disturbing conjunction of conflicting elements: Queequeg's outlandish tattooing and the domestic quilt, Queequeg's savage body and his affectionate, conjugal hug. These disturbing mixtures and conjunctions supply the fabric of Ishmael's narration and Melville's book. Here the images of patchwork quilt and patchwork body suggest that the artistic attempt to make a unity from many disparate parts carries with it a certain unsettling "weight and pressure," along with the ecstasy of oneness.

Although Queequeg largely disappears from the story, like Bulkington he remains a "sleeping-partner" (p. 16) even after he stops sharing Ishmael's bed. For the vision of epic heroism and masculinity as well as generous intimacy he brings into the book remains as witness to the lives of men whom Ahab and, surprisingly, Ishmael too, often view as an unreasoning mass. Starbuck, Stubb, Flask, Daggoo, Tashtego, Fleece, Pip, and Fedallah often seem more props than characters. Each represents a certain racial or national identity, a certain set of associations convenient for the narrative, much as the sailors in chapter 40, "Midnight, Forecastle" represent a global panoply of whaling nations rather than individuals. Yet as Queequeg does in the opening chapters, each also emerges for a moment into a heroism that partakes of the epic: Pip contemplating the infinite in chapter 93, "The Castaway," Fleece soberly correcting Stubb's voracity as he sermonizes to the sharks, Tashtego nailing the flag upon the sinking *Pequod*'s mast. Even more *as* a mass, the men represent a world of epic labor, a democratic "Spirit of Equality" lodged in the multiracial and multinational forecastle, a vision of masculine solidarity and heroism that is not always evident in Ahab's quarter-deck speeches or Ishmael's mast-head visions.

"Tributary Items": Gospel, the Whale, and the Discontinuous Text

We have considered the roles of major characters – Ahab, Ishmael, and Queequeg – and of influential genres – tragedy, comedy, epic – that make up the patchwork of Melville's richly various and hybrid text. Two other kinds of source-texts might seem quite distinct from each other: cetology (or natural history) and gospel. In the view of many scholars, *Moby-Dick*'s use of cetology, the study of whales, bespeaks the secular and encyclopedic strain in Melville's reading. His reliance, on the other hand, on a wealth of biblical references to Job, Jonah, Adam, Cain, and Christ manifests a theological drift utterly apart from, even opposed to, the world of science and classification represented by cetology. Yet when in "Extracts" Melville identifies his book as "veritable gospel cetology," he seems to blend the religious and the secular, the biblical and the encyclopedic in one. If we are to take him seriously here, we must ask how he pulls off such a remarkable feat.

The simplest and most straightforward answer is that Melville makes the whale divine. Hence any facts about the whale, any science or natural history, partake of the spiritual nature of his subject. We get an early sense of this logic in chapter 32, "Cetology," where Ishmael devises and at the same time mocks an elaborate taxonomy of species. Breaking them down by size, he organizes the whales like so many volumes in his library into folios, octavos, and duodecimos. Listing an impressive range of authorities – ancient historians like Pliny, early scientists like Sir Thomas Browne, taxonomists like Linnaeus, comparative anatomists and zoologists like Cuvier and Owen, explorers and whaling men like Scoresby, Beale, and J. Ross Browne, even a novelist ("the Author of Miriam Coffin," p. 135) – he then proceeds to question their knowledge of "living whales" and to criticize their efforts. Yet, as in chapter 55, "Monstrous Pictures of Whales," when he concludes that "the great Leviathan is that one creature in the world which must remain unpainted to the last" (p. 264), here he acknowledges that "the sperm whale, scientific or poetic, lives not complete in any literature. Far above all other hunted whales, his is an unwritten life" (p. 135).

The joke is that even as Ishmael more and more minutely anatomizes the whales, they elude his grasp. Acknowledging his unfitness for the undertaking, he suggests that it lies far beyond human ken: "But it is a ponderous task; no ordinary letter-sorter in the Post-office is equal to it" (p. 136). Likening his "task" to that of making a covenant with God, Ishmael suggests that the whale *is* God, "the unspeakable foundations, ribs, and very pelvis of the world" (p. 136). After performing his taxonomy of whales, he returns to the idea of the whale's divinity when he speaks of his "cetology" as a cathedral: "But I now leave my cetological System standing thus unfinished, even as the great Cathedral of Cologne was left, with the crane still standing upon the top of the uncompleted tower. For small erections may be finished by their first architects; grand ones, true ones, ever leave the copestone to posterity" (p. 145). For this whale-god, a proper cathedral is always under construction.

Ishmael comes back to the notion of the whale's divinity again and again. The whale's spout "seemed some plumed and glittering god uprising from the sea" (p. 232). In chapter 54, "The "Town Ho's Story" Moby Dick's intervention into the tale of Steelkilt and Radney "seemed obscurely to involve with the whale a certain wondrous, inverted visitation of one of those so called judgments of God which at times are said to overtake some men" (p. 242), as if the whale acted directly in accord with God's will. The sperm whale's head partakes of the divine: "this high and mighty god-like dignity inherent in the brow is so immensely amplified, that gazing on it, more in that full front view, you feel the Deity and the dread powers more forcibly than in beholding any other object in living nature" (p. 346). The priests in the Bower of the Arsacides treat the skeleton whale as their god and evict Ishmael from the premises when he ventures to measure him (chapter 104, "A Bower in the Arsacides"). On the first day of the chase, Moby Dick appears like Jupiter ravishing Europa, and rising from the water, "the grand god revealed himself, sounded and went out of sight" (p. 549). In countless ways Ishmael associates the whale with deities from Judaic, Christian, Hindu, Persian, Greco-Roman, and Egyptian traditions. And so, by implication, his natural history of the whale is also a witness to divine presence in the world.

In the "Agatha" correspondence, Melville told Hawthorne the plot of the story and then moved quickly to the "tributary items," those details, ideas, and symbols he had collected on his travels and that he thought gave meaning to the tale. As we see in *Moby-Dick*, he often considered "tributary items" to be as important as central facts and narratives. "Tributary" means that which flows into a river from other streams. We might think of the tributary items in *Moby-Dick* as those secondary materials that lend significance to the whole, and *Moby-Dick* is full of them. All the cetology, and the practical information on whaling too, might seem less important, and the book is often read in classrooms without the whaling material. A second meaning of "tributary," though, is that which pays tribute to an awesome power. The tribute may be an enforced payment, as when Midas of Crete required Athens to render up youths and maidens to his military might and political dominance. Or the tribute may consist of voluntary homage to divine authority. In either case, tributary items are critical for the maintenance of power. If the whale Moby Dick is divine, then

Ishmael's homage to him in the form of a cetological "System" is an essential act of reverence, though offered in a comical spirit. Indeed Ishmael's notion of divinity *is* comic, in the sense that the great god ever renews himself. And if the text *Moby-Dick* is named in honor of this endlessly regenerative divine whale, then it must partake of the whale's powers, must be, in the fullest possible sense, a sacred text. Its tributary items, then, are not secondary but primary in establishing that the book is "veritable gospel cetology."

The science of *Moby-Dick* is gospel in yet another way, namely as what Peter Stallybrass has identified as a discontinuous text. In his study of the history of European bibles, he discusses the ways in which early printers began to break up the unvarying flow of the original narrative, first by dividing it into chapters and verses. Once they could identify specific lines by number, ministers could search the text quickly and assemble clusters of quotations around a central verse or theme. Authors also produced concordances that allowed lay readers to search their bibles for themselves. Eventually different editions organized the sections and sometimes published certain books, such as the Psalms, separately for specific uses in church services. Lavish illustrations and maps made them visual texts as well, and with pages that allowed people to record births, deaths, and weddings, the family bible became a repository of individual as well as theological events. One could experience the Bible, then, not as a continuous narrative but as a discontinuous text which one could navigate at will.

The Bible, however, was not the only example of a discontinuous text in Melville's period. Another major publishing innovation of the eighteenth and nineteenth centuries was the encyclopedia, which often took forms almost unrecognizable to those schooled in the reference room Britannicas of the twentieth century, not to mention the online encyclopedias and wikipedia of the digital age. These popular nineteenth-century works, again often lavishly illustrated, seemed to follow a logic of their own, placing fact and fable, science and popular culture side by side. Sir Thomas Browne's compendium of *Vulgar Errors* provides an early example of miscellaneous lore that fascinated Melville, but the *Penny Cyclopedia* of his own day, which he consulted often, might now seem to readers no more accurate than a medieval book of fables. Indeed Melville ridicules the popular encyclopedias as much as he consults and borrows from them himself.

The joy of reading a discontinuous text, as anyone who has surfed the internet can attest, lies in the freedom of choice it offers. Quite a different kind of pleasure resides in a gripping narrative, to which the reader surrenders as to an unstoppable force. Melville depended on the linear logic of fictional plot in his early books. From the beginning of *Typee*, his narrators promise the delight of capitulating to a sensational adventure. At the same time, as Melville was later to say in *Billy Budd*, his books offer the satisfaction of stepping off the linear path of their own plots:

> In this matter of writing, resolve as one may to keep to the main road, some by-paths have an enticement not readily to be withstood. I am going to err into such a by-path. If the reader will keep me company I shall be glad. At the least we can promise ourselves that pleasure which is wickedly said to be in sinning, for a literary sin the divergence will be. (p. 56)

In *Moby-Dick*, Melville dared to suggest that such by-paths were not sinful but rather, like the tributaries he loved to explore, routes to virtue or worship.

Thus the idea of whales and whaling in *Moby-Dick* constituting a sacred text runs counter to the notion of Ahab's story as blasphemous and broiling in hellfire, as Melville told Hawthorne in his letter of June 29, 1851 (*L* 196). But the notion of the book as sacred text is just as daring and audacious as the ways in which Melville reconceived other literary forms and texts like tragedy, comedy, and epic. For his new gospel rests on earthly matter, and its secular tributaries are as significant as the divine center. If he offers human heroes in Ahab, Ishmael, and Queequeg, in the whale Moby Dick he creates the divine inspiration for a text that can be read backwards as well as forwards, in pieces and as a whole.

"Poetic Reference": *Moby-Dick* as Lyric

As lofty as the aim of writing veritable gospel cetology might seem, Melville knew it could end in disaster: "Though I wrote the Gospels in this century, I should die in the gutter" (*L* 192), he told Hawthorne. He knew that his gospel might well be other people's blasphemy and that ultimately he had other fish to catch. "Leviathan is not the biggest fish; – I have heard of Krakens" (*L* 213), he wrote to Hawthorne in another letter. Although he had written a book full of great heroes – Ahab the tragic king, Ishmael the comic mediator, Queequeg the epic warrior, Moby Dick the divine avatar – he reserved for himself another role even greater: that of poet. The poetic language of *Moby-Dick* is as heroic as its characters: seeking new forms of action and expression, saving characters from despair, inviting readers to a romance with words themselves. In the "Agatha" letters, Melville spoke of an image in the story as having "poetic reference" to its most meaningful events. Much of *Moby-Dick* is filled with "poetic reference" to the pathos and depth of human experience.

Thinking of *Moby-Dick* as a kind of poem allows us to understand its textual innovations in different ways. For one thing, it helps us to see Melville's career as more continuous than has generally been thought. Melville has been viewed as novelist first, short story writer second, and poet only occasionally and only late in his life, after the prose masterpieces. Yet *Mardi* includes several lyrics, and *Moby-Dick* contains extensive passages that, readers have found, scan like Shakespeare's speeches. By 1860, not too long after his last novel, *The Confidence-Man* (1857), Melville had written enough poems to collect them into a volume that did not find a publisher. Biographers and scholars have speculated that at the point when Melville first publicly published his poems in *Battle-Pieces* (1866), he had in fact been reading poets, writing poems, and experimenting with different poetic forms for a long time. *Moby-Dick* can be seen as part of that long gestation.

Melville did not think of himself as only a private poet. His aims in *Moby-Dick* are often explicitly national, as when he pays tribute to the Nantucket whalers in chapter 24, "The Advocate," or associates the ship, the *Pequod*, with the nation: "its wood could only be American!" (p. 571). The literary modes that interested him and that he associated with the world's greatest authors – tragedy, comedy, epic, sacred text – were also traditionally poetic modes (or, in the case of comedy and satire, adaptable to lyric). Even with Emerson, Whittier, or Bryant already in place, as he said in "Hawthorne and His Mosses," America needed its own Shakespeare, a poet who could speak to the nation's peculiar concerns and energies. Chief among these is what he called American "genius" and what we might call, and I have already identified as, American inventiveness. American poetry would not imitate the past, but would, as Emerson also believed, show originality. "It is better to fail in originality, than to succeed in imitation" (*PT* 247), Melville declared in "Hawthorne and His Mosses," and in *Moby-Dick* he set out to "write those sort of books which are said to 'fail'" (*L* 139), as he told his father-in-law Lemuel Shaw after finishing *Redburn* and *White-Jacket*. Writing a novel that would fail, he also created a great American poem that would certainly not be recognized as such. But his invention of a deeply lyrical prose work, a hybrid of different modes and genres written in a sinewy new language, surpassed many previous efforts in American poetry.

We see Melville's aims displayed in Ishmael's attitude to lyric throughout the novel. Appointing himself the whalemen's advocate, for example, he avers that "this business of whaling has somehow come to be regarded among landsmen as a rather unpoetical and disreputable pursuit" (p. 108). *Moby-Dick*, then, will restore the poetry to whaling, even if, as Melville wrote jestingly to Richard Henry Dana, "blubber is blubber you know; tho' you may get oil out of it, the poetry runs as hard as sap from a frozen maple tree" (*L* 162). When Ishmael lays out his cetology, he does so as much in the service of poetry as of science: for "the sperm whale, scientific or poetic, lives not complete in any literature" (p. 135). Speaking of the whale's anatomy, Ishmael assumes the mantle of poet: "Other poets have warbled the praises of the soft eye of the antelope, and the lovely plumage of the bird that never alights; less celestial, I celebrate a tail" (p. 375). When he speaks of having tattooed his arm with the "valuable statistics" of the whale skeleton's measurements, he "wished the other parts of my body to remain a blank page for a poem I was then composing" (p. 451); what poem could that be but *Moby-Dick* itself? As poet of whales and whaling, Ishmael hopes to take his place among the "ancient authors generally, as well as the poets here appearing" in his own opening "Extracts" and among "what has been promiscuously said, thought, fancied, and sung of Leviathan, by many nations and generations, including our own" (p. xvii). The most glorious form for that expression is poetry, and *Moby-Dick* may be thought of as Melville's first and, until *Clarel*, most ambitious poem.

All the passages I have considered so far in this chapter provide excellent evidence of Ishmael's poetic power and Melville's commitment to lyric. One might turn, then, to Melville's ending (chapter 135,

"The Chase, Third Day," before the Epilogue) for only a final, not necessarily the greatest, example of his poetic writing in *Moby-Dick*:

> But as the last whelmings intermixingly poured themselves over the sunken head of the Indian at the mainmast, leaving a few inches of the erect spar yet visible, together with long streaming yards of the flag, which calmly undulated, with ironical coincidings, over the destroying billows they almost touched; – at that instant, a red arm and a hammer hovered backwardly uplifted in the open air, in the act of nailing the flag faster and yet faster to the subsiding spar. A sky-hawk that tauntingly had followed the main-truck downwards from its natural home among the stars, pecking at the flag, and incommoding Tashtego there; this bird now chanced to intercept its broad fluttering wing between the hammer and the wood; and simultaneously feeling that etherial thrill, the submerged savage beneath, in his death-gasp, kept his hammer frozen there; and so the bird of heaven, with archangelic shrieks, and his imperial beak thrust upwards, and his whole captive form folded in the flag of Ahab, went down with his ship, which, like Satan, would not sink to hell till she had dragged a living part of heaven along with her, and helmeted herself with it. Now small fowls flew screaming over the yet yawning gulf; a sullen white surf beat against its steep sides; then all collapsed, and the great shroud of the sea rolled on as it rolled five thousand years ago. (p. 572)

The beauty and complexity of the images in this lyrical passage immediately call attention to themselves, with the grotesque juxtapositions of screaming sky-hawk and dying Tashtego's insistent hammer, of heavenly sky and demonic ship. The language is similarly evocative. The steady beat of the gerunds and participles – "whelmings," "streaming," "coincidings," "destroying," "fluttering," "yawning" – mimics the waves rolling over the sunken ship, and at the same time the contrasting rhythm of percussive and sibilant sounds – "sunken," "erect," "sky-hawk," "pecking," "death-grasp," "archangelic shrieks" – disrupts any sense of unity or harmony in the scene. Intense physical conflict – the drowning harpooner's hammer nailing a shrieking bird of heaven to the sinking mast – gives way to a flood of vowels that smooth out and "shroud" all tumult: "Now small fowls flew screaming over the yet yawning gulf; a sullen white surf beat against its steep sides; then all collapsed, and the great shroud of the sea rolled on as it rolled five thousand years ago."

These special effects of language produce a scene of immense and disturbing power. At the heart of the passage lies a significant pun that suggests Melville's particular sensitivity to the rich and plastic capacities of language: "at that instant, a red arm and a hammer hovered backwardly uplifted in the open air, in the act of nailing the flag faster and yet faster to the subsiding spar." Tashtego works to nail the flag "fast," that is tightly to the mast; and he also acts "fast," to complete his final task quickly before he dies. In an earlier chapter ("Fast Fish and Loose Fish," chapter 89), Ishmael had discoursed wittily on the meaning of the flags that the whaling men attach to their catch and that declare it to be a "fast fish" or a "loose fish." Here, Tashtego nails down the flag, but the ship is sinking, and no effort, no matter how fast, can hold it fast and secure. Melville's characteristic and here noticeably excessive use of verbal forms – vivid "-ing" words (both participles and gerunds) in abundance, with only a few seemingly insignificant verbs ("poured," "hovered, "chanced," "kept") – shows the language too seeming to act fast and yet being held fast. The verbs appear trapped in nouns and adjectives rather than being released to act upon their subjects. Only when this deadly conflict ends, a conflict that is at the same time a deadly stasis, can the verbs return: "flew," "beat," "collapsed," "rolled."

In contrast, in the Epilogue verbs ("step," "survive," "tossed," "dropped," "revolve," "burst," "shot," "sailed," "found") regain their natural function once again, in more harmonious balance with the suspended actions implied by gerunds and participles: "floating," "drawn," "contracting," "liberated," "rising," "sheathed": "Till, gaining that vital centre, the black bubble upward burst; and now, liberated by reason of its cunning spring, and, owing to its great buoyancy, rising with great force, the coffin-life-buoy shot lengthwise from the sea, fell over, and floated by my side" (p. 573). In the Epilogue, the potential for action that has been held fast in the final moments of the novel bursts forth once again and helps to heal Ishmael and reunite him with his kind.

As this brief example suggests, the language of *Moby-Dick* works heroically, showing a beauty, suppleness, and power like that of the whale and associated with the whale's survival at the end of the book, when all but one of the men have died. In relation to the book's many modes and genres, then, the lyrical strain threads through them all – tragic, comic, heroic, satiric, melodramatic, sentimental, philosophic, mystical, encyclopedic – while at the same time evading generic defini-tions and boundaries. Like the great whale, the book's lyricism is everywhere and nowhere at once, endlessly inventive, tricky, infuriat-ing, and ennobling. In *Moby-Dick* Melville reveled in the pathos and depth of the written word.

CHAPTER 6

"All Tender Obligations": *Pierre*

Like Taji before him and Pierre after, Ishmael is in love with language. But Pierre is also a lover of women and men, and in the novel following closely on *Moby-Dick* Melville experimented with something entirely new for him, a story of love, or of what he called in the "Agatha" correspondence the many "tender obligations" to which humans may be bound. As obsessed with genius and invention as *Moby-Dick*, *Pierre* (1852) also concerns romantic themes untried in Melville's earlier work – with hardly a whiff of the sea until Pierre steps on board a ferryboat at the end of the book.

Scholars have puzzled over this decision, which resulted in one of Melville's "botches" (*L* 191), a book nearly universally condemned by critics. As Melville's letter to Sophia Hawthorne seemed to reveal, however, he worked hard and aimed high to reach new readers in this book. Comparing *Pierre* to *Moby-Dick*, he told her it was eminently suitable for women: "But, My Dear Lady, I will not again send you a bowl of salt water. The next chalice I shall commend, will be a rural bowl of milk" (*L* 1219). Yet the subject of domestic life and romantic love seemed an odd choice for an author closely identified with nautical themes. Some have speculated that the failure of *Moby-Dick* to win the recognition that Melville felt it deserved galled him and drove him to write a book that ends in destroying its romantic hero and the whole field of romantic authorship along with him. Others have imagined that Melville wanted to exorcise certain family secrets and legends in a book that took on forbidden sexual themes. *Pierre* has been seen as imitating Hawthorne and successful female authors like Catherine Maria Sedgwick, Fanny Fern, Harriet Beecher Stowe, and Susan

Warner in a bid for popularity and also as an ambitious attempt to map out new psychological and philosophical terrain for an author still growing and developing his art.[1]

In the simplest sense, however, the book explores the power of love. Surprisingly, that subject brought Melville to state his frustrations and aims as a writer even more directly and, one might argue, inventively than his nautical works had. *Pierre* is the only one of Melville's full-length narratives to take a writer as its protagonist and to show him battling inner demons as violent and threatening as the white whale.

"The Omnipotence of Love"

Its story concerns a young American aristocrat and heir, Pierre Glendinning, who lives in a rural paradise similar to Melville's Berkshires. The son of a much-revered father now dead, he enjoys a blissful, almost fraternal intimacy with his youthful mother, Mary Glendinning. His love for an angelic young woman named Lucy Tartan lifts him to giddy heights of rapture. Into this world of celestial delight comes a terrifying letter from a stranger, Isabel Banford, who makes a mysterious claim upon him. When they meet over the course of several evenings, he discovers a dark-haired beauty who tells a tale of woe and neglect. After growing up orphaned, illiterate, and nearly inarticulate in a European madhouse, she has found her way to a farm near Pierre's abode where she earns her living through sewing and other menial work. Living in obscurity in Pierre's neighborhood, she hears a series of hints and legends, culminating in mysterious meetings with Pierre's father before his death. Through this contact she learns, or assumes, that she is his illegitimate daughter and hence Pierre's unacknowledged sister.

On reflection, Pierre recalls a shadowy story of his father's long-ago interest in an indigent but beautiful French émigré who later disappeared. The main evidence for this affair appears in a portrait of his father, painted during the time of the elder Glendinning's involvement with the French woman, that reveals a rakish character not hinted at in the more official portrait hanging in Mrs. Glendinning's room. Pierre, who inherited this earlier "chair-portrait" from his aunt, studies it now, and it seems to confirm Isabel's wild story. Seduced by her beauty and the haunting power of her guitar-playing, Pierre plans to save Isabel, his apparent half-sister, from obscurity and infamy by pretending to marry her and by taking her to New York City to escape the censure of his neighbors and family.

This heroic decision does indeed save Isabel, but it also violently ruptures Pierre's intimate relations with his mother and Lucy. Mrs. Glendinning orders him from the house, and Lucy wilts in despair. He flees to New York feeling like a murderer, like Taji, who has wreaked havoc in order to save a beautiful woman. Once arrived, he and Isabel settle in an old Church of the Apostles that has been converted to tenement housing. Here he resurrects his juvenile writing career and determines to write a novel that will revolutionize literature and win him acclaim. His attempts at literary greatness, however, earn him nothing, and his meager savings dwindle. At a critical juncture, Lucy, who has escaped from her mother, her brother Frederic, and Pierre's cousin, Glendinning Stanly (who has fallen in love with her), joins this thrifty household, asking to be treated as a "nun-like cousin" and to earn her bread by creating charcoal portrait drawings. Isabel grows jealous and suspicious, and Pierre, poised between the two women he loves, becomes increasingly frantic. On an excursion to an art exhibit in the city, Isabel sees a portrait that she is convinced is of her father; commenting on the coincidence of resemblance, Pierre reflects that Isabel may not be his sister after all and that he may have needlessly sacrificed himself and the ever patient Lucy. At last he receives an insulting rejection letter from his publishers and at the same time a deadly challenge from Glen and Fred. Stealing a pair of pistols, he rushes out and kills both men, thus ending up in the Tombs prison. Lucy and Isabel visit him there; hearing Isabel declare herself Pierre's sister, Lucy dies of shock, and Isabel administers a fatal poison to Pierre and herself. Isabel has the last spoken words of the book: "All's o'er, and ye know him not!" (p. 362).

Many of Melville's first readers considered the book, with its suggestions of mother–son and brother–sister incest, offensive. Many others have found it melodramatic, verbally excessive, and incoherent as well. If we are to take seriously, however, Melville's statement in the "Agatha" correspondence that he saw "the omnipotence of love" as a central motivation and theme, then we might well study his treatment of love in *Pierre*, the work immediately preceding his projected "Agatha" story. The first innovation Melville makes on the theme is that "omnipotence" does not necessarily imply pleasure or delight; in fact, the omnipotence of love proves fatal. And the second is that omnipotent love appears in numerous guises in *Pierre*. Melville seizes on the erotic vein in familial intimacy, same-sex friendship, and even love of self to suggest that romantic love makes up only a small part of the human emotional universe, with all its troubling crosscurrents and eddies. Uncovering the murky world of love and desire threatens the peace, sanity, and even lives of the main characters, with disastrous results.

In speeches that, like Ahab's, borrow their rhythms from Shakespeare, the Bible, and the Romantic poets, Pierre speaks as intensely of love as Ahab does of hatred. But whereas in *Moby-Dick* Ishmael's voice provides a certain comic (and sane) equilibrium with Ahab's, in *Pierre* the unnamed narrator often echoes Pierre's rhetoric, even when he seems to mock him. Both use language that is excessive to the point of grotesquerie.

Hence Pierre, for example, declaring his love to Lucy, speaks in ardent hyperbole:

> "The audacious immortalities of divinest love are in me; and I now swear to thee all the immutable eternities of joyfulness, that ever woman dreamed of, in this dream-house of the earth. A god decrees to thee unchangeable felicity; and to me, the unchallenged possession of thee and them, for my inalienable fief. – Do I rave?" (p. 36)

Pierre raves long and often throughout the novel, but so, in equal measure, does the narrator. Thus, describing Pierre's emotions earlier in the chapter, the narrator raises a paean to love itself:

> Man or woman who has never loved, nor once looked deep down into their own lover's eyes, they know not the sweetest and the loftiest religion of this earth. Love is both Creator's and Saviour's gospel to mankind; a volume bound in rose-leaves, clasped with violets, and by the beaks of humming-birds printed with peach-juice on the leaves of lilies. (p. 33)

Whereas one might expect such romantic language in a description of young love, the narrator uses the same elevated and passionate rhetoric to describe the love between Pierre and his mother: "In a detached and individual way, it seemed almost to realize here below the sweet dreams of those religious enthusiasts, who paint to us a Paradise to come, when etherealized from all drosses and stains, the holiest passion of man shall unite all kindreds and climes in one circle of pure and unimpairable delight" (p. 16). Such rhetoric also characterizes the narrator's description of the young love between Pierre and his cousin Glendinning Stanly:

> the friendship of fine-hearted, generous boys, nurtured amid the romance-engendering comforts and elegancies of life, sometimes transcends the bounds of mere boyishness, and revels for a while in the empyrean of a love which only comes short, by one degree, of the sweetest sentiment entertained between the sexes. Nor is this boy-love without the occasional fillips and spicinesses, which at times, by an apparent abatement, enhance the permanent delights of those more advanced lovers who love beneath the cestus of Venus. (pp. 216–17)

Eventually Pierre learns, primarily from Isabel, that his early experiences of love with his mother, cousin, and fiancée Lucy have poorly prepared him for the depths of emotion he encounters in his sister's mournfulness and misery. As he matures in his emotional range and confronts the challenges of living and working in New York, love merges with despair in his utterances and in the narrator's descriptions. When Pierre receives the news of his mother's death, for example, memories of their love become mingled with grief and guilt:

> This recalling of innocence and joy in the hour of remorsefulness and woe; this is as heating red-hot the pincers that tear us. But in this delirium of his soul, Pierre could not define where that line was, which separated the natural grief for the loss of a parent from that other one which was born of compunction. He strove hard to define it, but could not. He tried to cozen himself into believing that all his grief was but natural, or if there existed any other, that must spring – not from the consciousness of having done any possible wrong – but from the pang at what terrible cost the more exalted virtues are gained. (p. 286)

With the minute attention to detail that Ishmael lavishes on whale lines and harpoons, the narrator analyzes an emotion that includes love, guilt, and sorrow. Later, when Pierre receives the letter from Glen and Fred challenging him to a duel, love and hate become one: "Oh,

Glen! oh, Fred! most fraternally do I leap to your rib-crushing hugs! Oh, how I love ye two, that yet can make me lively hate, in a world which elsewise only merits stagnant scorn!'" (p. 357). Pierre's "scorn" for the world that would reject his novel – a book with which he intimately identifies himself – shows equally harsh and agonizing emotion. Love is never simple in *Pierre*.

Most complex of all are Pierre's relationships with Isabel and Lucy when they live together at the Apostles. Pretending to be Isabel's husband in front of Lucy, Pierre finds his pure worship of angelic womanhood, embodied in Lucy, coexisting uneasily with the apparently more physical bond he shares with Isabel. When Isabel tells him she would like to help the family by giving guitar lessons, he is overwhelmed with love and pity; what begins as spontaneous emotion develops into a scene laden with other conflicting desires:

> "My poor poor, Isabel!" cried Pierre; "thou art the mistress of the natural sweetness of the guitar, not of its invented regulated artifices; and these are all that the silly pupil will pay for learning. And what thou hast can not be taught. Ah, thy sweet ignorance is all transporting to me! my sweet, my sweet! – dear, divine girl!" And impulsively he caught her in his arms. While the first fire of his feeling plainly glowed upon him, but ere he had yet caught her to him, Isabel had backward glided close to the connecting door; which, at the instant of his embrace, suddenly opened, as by its own volition. Before the eyes of seated Lucy, Pierre and Isabel stood locked; Pierre's lips upon her cheek. (p. 334)

Melville captures the proximity and intermixture of erotic feelings in a moment that may have owed something to his own situation of living closely with wife, mother, and sisters in a not overly large Berkshires farmhouse. Of course, little in his previous work would have prepared his readers for such sexual and emotional complications. Nor had he attempted a character like Isabel, who in this scene manages a moment of intense mortification for her rival while at the same time enrapturing the ardent hero.

Pierre is the first of Melville's books to concern women centrally, to include forceful female characters, and to show a man as the slave of his romantic and sexual passions.[2] It would be easy to assume that he satirizes these passions in the way his characters submit to and are destroyed by the omnipotence of love. But the psychological complexity of the relationships speaks to Melville's serious investigation of the dynamics of domestic life and romantic love. They become as charged with significance as the relationships – between man and whale, man and other men – that he explored in *Moby-Dick*.

"The Post Falls": The Demise of Letters

A second and critical theme in *Pierre* is the inner life of the writer. As in *Mardi*, where Melville devotes considerable space to the travails of a romantic author named Lombardo, in *Pierre* the protagonist struggles to find himself as an author. The story of Pierre as author has received particular attention in relation to Melville's own professional crisis, when *Moby-Dick* appeared to fail (in part because reviews from abroad, where the Epilogue was by some unaccountable neglect not printed, criticized its abrupt ending with the apparent death of the narrator – an absurdity). Composing the later sections of *Pierre* during the months when damaging reviews surfaced in New York as well, Melville wrote his own frustrations into the book. Pierre, who has had some early success as a poet, as the writer of minor sonnets of impeccable taste, defies public opinion by embarking on a philosophical work inspired by his iconoclastic reading and rebellious beliefs. Melville's narrator seems to mock the figure of Pierre as author:

> Now look around in that most miserable room, and at that most miserable of all the pursuits of a man, and say if here be the place, and this be the trade, that God intended him [Pierre] for. A rickety chair, two hollow barrels, a plank, paper, pens, and infernally black ink, four leprously dingy white walls, no carpet, a cup of water, and a dry biscuit or tow. Oh, I hear the leap of the Texan Camanche, as at this moment he goes crashing like a wild deer through the green underbrush; I hear his glorious whoop of savage and untamable health; and then I look in at Pierre. If physical, practical unreason make the savage, which is he? Civilization, Philosophy, Ideal Virtue! behold your victim! (p. 302)

At the same time as this humiliating portrait, however, Melville's narrator presents Pierre heroically in a moving vision of the fallen Titan Enceladus, a god cast out of heaven and struggling to find his calling and his birthright:

You saw Enceladus the Titan, the most potent of all the giants, writhing from out the imprisoning earth; – turbaned with upborne moss he writhed; still, though armless, resisting with his whole striving trunk, the Pelion and the Ossa hurled back at him; – turbaned with upborne moss he writhed; still turning his unconquerable front toward that majestic mount eternally in vain assailed by him, and which, when it had stormed him off, had heaved his undoffable incubus upon him, and deridingly left him there to bay out his ineffectual howl. (p. 345)

Seeing himself as likewise maimed and burdened, Pierre identifies with the struggling demigod: "on the Titan's armless trunk, his own duplicate face and features magnifiedly gleamed upon him with prophetic discomfiture and woe" (p. 346).

Reflecting perhaps on these turbulent emotions while composing the first "Agatha" letter to Hawthorne, Melville indicated his skepticism about the fate of the writer in America. The image of the mailbox in his letter symbolizes Agatha's despair as she goes each day hoping to find letters from her departed husband. But it also suggests the despair of an author whose "letter to the world" (as in Emily Dickinson's phrase) produces no response. In his detailed description of the mailbox's decay – "As her hopes gradually decay in her, so does the post itself & the little box decay. The post rots in the ground at last" – Melville envisions the decline of his career in lamentable terms. In 1852, as the country faced an election in which Hawthorne's college friend Franklin Pierce offered a lackluster alternative to his opponent Winfield Scott, and in which tensions over the Compromise of 1850 and the Fugitive Slave Act split the nation over issues of abolition and the extension of slavery into new territories, it may not be surprising that Melville considered authorship a doomed enterprise. His pessimism about writing made a compelling case against his own novel, maiming his achievements in *Pierre* as severely as Enceladus' struggle had maimed him.

"This Wrecked Ship": Gospelizing Anew

Pierre has struck many readers as a radical departure from *Moby-Dick*, but in at least one vital respect they are closely aligned. Both speak passionately of the necessity for a new gospel text in a fallen world. That gospel emerges, in fact, from the wreck of the writer's hopes. We have seen how the destruction of the *Pequod* brings Ishmael forth – "Because one did survive the wreck" (p. 573) – to tell his story. For Ishmael, no one kind of narrative can do justice to such a monumental event, and he reaches for a new "veritable gospel cetology" to make his account a sacred text. That text, being in a sense the printed version of the whale's life (as *Moby-Dick* is the book about a whale called Moby Dick), partakes of the divine nature of its subject and thus ranges far beyond the conventional boundaries of fiction. As "gospel cetology" the book can thus be a discontinuous text, in Peter Stallybrass's sense of a work that can be read linearly or extralinearly, as the occasion demands.

No such sacred being seems to invest *Pierre* with divine power. The characters are mysterious but ultimately fallible humans, and the story does not seem to call for the reverence accorded a mighty whale. But the narrative does end in wreckage as cataclysmic as that created by Moby Dick, and the narrator mourns the demise of a great spirit. Though not himself divine, Pierre seeks divinity in omnipotent love and in the heady ether of literary art. His projected book partakes of the divinity of his subject and requires of him a new gospel, even if it appears blasphemous in the world's eyes:

> "Ah! now I catch glimpses, and seem to half-see, somehow, that the uttermost ideal of moral perfection in man is wide of the mark. The demigods trample on trash, and Virtue and Vice are trash! Isabel, I will write such things – I will gospelize the world anew, and show them deeper secrets than the Apocalypse! – I will write it, I will write it!" (p. 273)

Earlier the narrator has declared love its own gospel: "Love is both Creator's and Saviour's gospel to mankind" (p. 34). And Isabel has declared his actions a gospel too: "'Thou art a visible token, Pierre, of the invisible angel-hoods, which in our darker hours we do sometimes distrust. The gospel of thy acts goes very far, my brother'" (p. 156). According to the logic of these statements, if love is a gospel and if Pierre's heroic, though seemingly iconoclastic, actions are another kind of gospel, then the book Pierre is writing about love and heroic action, and by extension the book *Pierre* about the same things, are gospel too.

Granted that the sacred looks very different in *Moby-Dick* and *Pierre*, the first showing a whale that is godlike, the second making a somewhat less convincing case for godlike aspirations in Pierre, it seems clear that Melville is preoccupied in both with the challenge of writing a new gospel. If the gospel comes forth in a text that is discontinuous, that escapes the linear demands of fiction and invites browsing at will, then *Pierre* is discontinuous in ways that differ remarkably from *Moby-Dick*. *Pierre* has a unified plot, one that moves from youth to maturity and death, from innocence to experience, from love to tragic knowledge and despair. But in other ways it includes radical discontinuities: between Pierre's pastoral boyhood and his urban maturity, for example, and between his youthful efforts in conventional poetry and his mature struggles with revolutionary prose. Pierre slashes his way out of one existence, as the privileged heir of his parents' expansive domains and narrow prejudices, and into another where he struggles to keep body alive and soul soaring aloft.

Even on the level of structure and language, the novel contains disturbing discontinuities. The author-plot conflicts with the love-plot. The narrator's language in the first half of the book generally glorifies Pierre; in the later sections it appears more and more to mock him and his heroic efforts. In many passages, conflict seems to erupt from within the words themselves to threaten the integrity of the text's surface. So, for example, in a passage describing Pierre's novel and its meaning in terms of his new interior development, Melville's narrator cuts ironically into his own assertions until they can no longer stand on their own:

> Ten million things were as yet uncovered to Pierre. The old mummy lies buried in cloth on cloth; it takes time to unwrap this Egyptian king. Yet now, forsooth, because Pierre began to see through the first superficiality of the world, he fondly weens he has come to the unlayered substance. But, far as any geologist has yet gone down into the world, it is found to consist of nothing but surface stratified on surface. To its axis, the world being nothing but superinduced superficies. By vast pains we mine into the pyramid; by horrible gropings we come to the central room; with joy we espy the sarcophagus; but we lift the lid – and no body is there! – appallingly vacant as vast is the soul of a man! (p. 285)

The tone oscillates between respect for and mockery of Pierre's aspirations. To "unwrap this Egyptian king," to "come to the unlayered substance" of reality seems a heroic endeavor. But the discovery of vastness at the heart of the pyramid is not uplifting in the end but deflating and ridiculous: "appallingly vacant as vast is the soul of a man!" The soul that Pierre has been mining for inspiration turns out to be an empty coffin – not a coffin-lifebuoy, like Queequeg's magic totem, but an image of unfathomable emptiness and horror.

Melville called his book *Pierre: Or, the Ambiguities*, and this passage and many others like it do model a persistent verbal and philosophical ambiguity. Later critics spoke of Melville's method in *Pierre* as essentially ironic, using ambiguity to create multiple significances and evade confining definitions. As much as generating irony and ambiguity in his language, Melville also creates a discontinuous text, one that can be read straight through but that also requires frequent pauses for reconsideration. In those pauses, where the reader steps off the linear track of the story, one may find unexpected wells of meaning, and Melville appears to have used these to resist the story's forward drive.

Pierre might be thought of, then, as "veritable gospel romance," a taxonomy of passion rather than of whales, and a book made sacred by its devotion to a divine and immutable power. Its failure in the literary marketplace ensured that Melville would not attempt such an ambitious work again for a very long time.

PART IV

Turning a New Leaf: Short Fiction, *Israel Potter*, and *The Confidence-Man*

CHAPTER 7

"A Leaf From Professional Experience": Short Fiction of the 1850s

By the summer of 1852, when he proposed the "Agatha" story to Hawthorne, Melville had written seven books. In the same time period in which he established his career, the nation had moved from an era of exuberant Jacksonian democracy and expansionism, culminating in the Mexican War (1846–8), to a period of increasing sectional tension and controversy over slavery, women's rights, and social reform. Melville married Elizabeth Shaw, fathered four children, moved to the Berkshires, enjoyed an intense friendship with Hawthorne, raised potatoes and corn, struggled with debt, and applied unsuccessfully for a civil service position in the Pierce administration. For the nation and for one writer, it was a time of turbulent change and rapid growth.

In the same interval, Melville's publications reflected his development from novice sailor-author to aspiring artist and romantic rebel. They show the imprint of his extensive reading in poetry, philosophy, history and natural history, theology, and popular culture. As much as he might have at one time resisted the idea, Melville was educating himself as a writer and becoming a professional. No longer simply the spinner of yarns or the ingenious skrimshander, he was testing his skills in new and various spheres. He would not, it appeared, succeed where women novelists dominated the field. He would, however, turn magazine author and travel writer, re-inventor of other people's works and creator of new ones to entertain and delight.

By the time he met John Henry Clifford, the New Bedford lawyer who told him the "Agatha" story, Melville had become someone whom Clifford thought of as an experienced author: "You will perceive by the gentleman's note to me that he assumed that I purposed making literary use of the story." The transfer of the "Agatha" story resembles a business transaction. Clifford offers Melville a "leaf from his professional experience." Melville takes up the leaf, making it a leaf from *his* professional experience. Likewise – in the stories he wrote for *Harper's New Monthly Magazine* and *Putnam's Monthly Magazine of American Literature* between 1853 and 1856, some of which appeared in a volume called *The Piazza Tales* (1856); in *Israel Potter* (1855), his rewriting of Henry Trumbull's *Life and Remarkable Adventures of Israel R. Potter*; and in *The Confidence-Man* (1857), his account of a journey on a Mississippi River steamboat – Melville's narrators present themselves not as sailors but as middle-class professionals or practiced writers. The narrator of "Bartleby, the Scrivener: A Story of Wall-Street" is a lawyer, and the narrator of "The Tartarus of Maids" a seller of seeds, but most other narrators identify themselves either explicitly or implicitly as literary men. The tellers of "Benito Cereno" and *Israel Potter* borrow from pre-existing texts (Amasa Delano's *Narrative* of his voyages, Trumbull's life of Potter); the narrator of "The Encantadas" lards his sketches with literary references; the speaker in *The Confidence-Man* includes several chapters that discuss his own work as author; and narrators of stories like "The Piazza," "Cock-A-Doodle-Doo!," "I and My Chimney," and "The Apple-Tree Table" indicate that they belong to the professional class, even if they do not specify the narrator's occupation. Except for the narrators of the "The Encantadas," "The 'Gees," and possibly "Benito Cereno," there's hardly a sailor in the bunch.

Of course, *Moby-Dick* and *Pierre* have professional narrators too. Long before Ishmael tells us in chapter 104 ("The Fossil Whale") that he is "penning my thoughts of this Leviathan" – "Give me a condor's quill! Give me Vesuvius' crater for an inkstand! Friends, hold my arms!" (p. 456) – he has indicated in numerous ways that he is no longer a sailor. *Pierre*, as we have seen, makes authorship a central theme. But Ishmael and Pierre deliberately defy professional obligations. Ishmael makes it wittily clear that he favors tattooing a poem on his arm, or telling the Town-Ho's story "in the style in which I once narrated it at Lima" (p. 243) – that is, as a drinking story – over publishing in "your insular city of the Manhattoes" (p. 3). Pierre, while writing at the heart of insular Manhattan, finds publishing in the popular market unthinkable. In his experience publishers are little more than tailors (like Wonder and Wen, fitting up fashionable works in tasteful editions) or blackguards (like Steel, Flint, & Asbestos, charging him for the proofs of a book they have decided to reject). While being passionate readers and obsessed writers, neither Ishmael nor Pierre seems to take the professional side of authorship seriously.

With invitations to submit stories to *Harper's* and *Putnam's*, however, Melville certainly did so himself. He had indeed been steering his books through the literary market for some time. The difference in the mid- to late 1850s was that professional concerns begin to enter the narratives themselves. Perhaps, as biographers have suggested, his financial woes and family obligations pressed heavily upon him. Perhaps, alternatively, he responded to the creative challenges of writing in new forms – the tale, the sketch, the short travel narrative.[1] He may have enjoyed writing for different audiences in the company of a wider range of authors,[2] and he may also have been influenced by stimulating changes in the literary market in New York.[3]

Melville's critics have sometimes seen his development into a literary professional as a lamentable concession to economic pressures, limited readers, and narrow familial expectations. What would have happened if *Moby-Dick* and *Pierre* had received rave reviews? Would even greater novels have emerged? Writing for magazines and in briefer, more entertaining forms, this logic suggests, a bitterly frustrated Melville must have been forced to curtail his genius. Reading the "Agatha" correspondence, however, one sees a writer fully confident of his powers and quite ready, when Hawthorne withdraws, to carry on himself. In 1852 Hawthorne finished his *Blithedale Romance* and a campaign biography of Franklin Pierce; but except for some tales, he moved away from literary projects and devoted himself to his job as the American consul in Liverpool, until 1864, when he produced *The Marble Faun*. Melville, just as exhausted by writing and just as disheartened by a culture that seemed fatally divided over issues of slavery and abolition, rampant urbanization and capitalism, and ineffectual leadership in both political parties, nevertheless embarked with considerable energy on a new phase in his career.[4]

And he was prolific. In 1853 he wrote "Cock-A-Doodle-Doo!" (published in *Harper's*, December 1853); "The Happy Failure" (*Harper's*, July 1854); "The Fiddler" (*Harper's*, September 1854); and "Bartleby, the Scrivener," his debut publication (*Putnam's*, November and December 1853). Later in the winter of 1853–4, he began work on "The Encantadas" (*Putnam's*, March, April, and May 1854), and wrote "Poor

Man's Pudding and Rich Man's Crumbs" (*Harper's*, June 1854); "The Two Temples" (rejected by *Putnam's* in May 1854 and never published); and "The Paradise of Bachelors and the Tartarus of Maids" (*Putnam's*, April 1855). In June of 1854 he began work on *Israel Potter*, which was first serialized (*Putnam's*, from July 1854 to March 1855) and then published as a book in 1855. He also wrote and published "The Lightning-Rod Man" (*Putnam's*, August 1854) and in the fall possibly wrote "Jimmy Rose" (*Harper's*, November 1855) and "The 'Gees" (*Harper's*, March 1856). In late 1854 and early 1855 he wrote "Benito Cereno" (*Putnam's*, October, November, and December 1855), followed in spring 1855 by "The Bell-Tower" (*Putnam's*, August 1855), "I and My Chimney" (*Putnam's*, March 1856), and "The Apple-Tree Table" (*Putnam's*, May 1856). In early 1856 he collected five of his previous stories ("Bartleby," "Benito Cereno," "The Lightning-Rod Man," "The Encantadas," and "The Bell-Tower"), wrote a new sketch, "The Piazza," to introduce the collection, and published the work as *The Piazza Tales* in 1856. He began *The Confidence-Man* in early 1856 as well, submitting it to Dix, Edwards & Co. in the fall before embarking on his trip to Europe and the Levant. It came out on April 1, 1857 (*PT*, "Historical Note").[5]

Hence by the time Melville was reunited with Hawthorne in Liverpool, in the winter of 1856 (their first meeting after the November 1852 visit in Concord), he had written two serials ("The Encantadas" and *Israel Potter*) and sixteen tales in all, and had published a collection (*The Piazza Tales*) and two novels (*Israel Potter* and *The Confidence-Man*). Far from being depleted by the failure of *Pierre* he appears to have been energized, and even though the efforts of those five years exhausted him, they produced some of his richest and most provocative works.

In many of these he presents himself as taking "a leaf from his professional experience," introducing a professional narrator who, in the course of his rambles about the city or the countryside, meets unusual specimens of humanity: Bartleby the scrivener, or Merrymusk the woodcutter, a lightning-rod salesman, the bachelor lawyers of London and the factory workers of the Berkshires, the poor country woman of "Poor Man's Pudding," and the haughty beadle of "The Two Temples," the comical uncle of "The Happy Failure," or Hautboy, "The Fiddler." In his correspondence with editors and publishers, Melville occasionally spoke of his stories as "articles" (see *L* 248, 275), and they do sometimes resemble journalistic sketches, entertaining meditations on the varieties of human experience encountered in a working man's day.

With "Benito Cereno," parts of "The Encantadas," and *Israel Potter*, however, Melville takes up another kind of leaf, that is, someone else's narrative, and rewrites it in his own idiom. Sometimes he acknowledges his appropriation of another author's work, as in the case of *Israel Potter*, but just as often he does not. As a professional writer, he seems to say, one casually encounters all kinds of books and can make of them something pleasant and entertaining for the general public. As he puts it in the preface to *Israel Potter*, "From a tattered copy, rescued by the merest chance from the rag-pickers, the present account has been drawn, which, with the exception of some expansions, and additions of historic and personal details, and one or two shiftings of scene, may, perhaps, be not unfitly regarded something in the light of a dilapidated old tombstone retouched" (p. vii). He calls *Israel Potter*, as the lawyer-narrator of "Bartleby" calls his work, a biography; "Benito Cereno," with its appended deposition, might be viewed as history or, in part, legal testimony. As inventive as Melville's use of these materials turns out to be, he frequently presented himself as a mere observer or recorder of events.

Yet within the framework of these "re-touched" sketches, Melville explored new dimensions of human emotion and experience, new latitudes of fiction. In this sense he may have followed the lead of Agatha's husband, the man to whom he attributed the "latitudinarian notions" of a sailor. Like this ex-mariner, the narrator-protagonist of many of Melville's tales of the 1850s is a wanderer, someone with hasty passions and brief alliances. While presenting himself as a gentleman and a professional writer, Melville's narrator frequently acts as a Robertson, falling in love with strong women, admiring strange and savage men, and generally flouting convention in every possible way.

"Patience, & Endurance, & Resignedness": The *Povertiresque*

We might divide Melville's stories into two groups, according to their aesthetic and thematic concerns. One might be called by the term that

Pierre uses ironically to describe a genteel taste for descriptions of human misery:

> If the grown man of taste, possess not only some eye to detect the picturesque in the natural landscape, so also, has he as keen a perception of what may not unfitly be here styled, the *povertiresque* in the social landscape. To such an one, not more picturesquely conspicuous is the dismantled thatch in a painted cottage of Gainsborough, than the time-tangled and want-thinned locks of a beggar, *povertiresquely* diversifying those snug little cabinet-pictures of the world, which, exquisitely varnished and framed, are hung up in the drawing-room minds of humane men of taste, and amiable philosophers of either the "Compensation," or "Optimist" school. They deny that any misery is in the world, except for the purpose of throwing the fine *povertiresque* element into its general picture. (pp. 276–7)

Pierre identifies a particularly obnoxious use of the picturesque, namely to throw over the spectacle of want and oppression the mantle of aesthetic beauty. Yet, to often humorous effect, Melville's protagonists do much the same thing in stories where the characters' woes produce a salutary response in the narrator: in, for example, "The Happy Failure," "The Fiddler," "Cock-A-Doodle-Doo!," "Jimmy Rose," and "The 'Gees." A similar effect, but more troubled and less humorous, appears in "Bartleby, the Scrivener," "The Encantadas," "Poor Man's Pudding and Rich Man's Crumbs," "The Paradise of Bachelors and the Tartarus of Maids," and "The Piazza." In most of these stories, Melville chooses a narrator who sees the woe but cannot resist the temptations of the *povertiresque*, retreating to a position of benign but helpless sympathy.

The comic examples of the *povertiresque* are among the slightest and least regarded of Melville's stories, and none appeared among his choices for inclusion in *The Piazza Tales*, but they nevertheless contain considerable interest. In each a figure of undoubted distress endures his discomfort with enviable ease. Thus, in "The Happy Failure," the narrator's uncle, unsuccessful inventor of the "Great Hydraulic-Hydrostatic Apparatus for draining swamps and marshes and converting them, at the rate of one acre the hour, into fields more fertile than those of the Genessee" (p. 255), collapses when the device fails. Yet in spite of his defeat, he resignedly concludes, " 'Praise be to God for the failure!' " (p. 260). This saving recognition is good for the uncle, but even better, it appears, for the nephew: "If the event made my uncle a good old man, as he called it, it made me a wise young one. Example did for me the work of experience" (p. 261). The story, while mocking both men's self-consoling postures (shown, through the perspective of the uncle's faithful Dutch African servant Yorpy, to be ludicrous), nevertheless comically exposes the self-blindness that appears in many of Melville's other narrators.

In "The Fiddler" and "Jimmy Rose," failure also sits lightly upon men of buoyant optimism who instruct the narrator in patience and stoicism. The narrator of "The Fiddler" meets a music instructor, Hautboy, who appears unselfconsciously happy, honest, and good-natured. A friend tells him that Hautboy is "an extraordinary genius," a former child prodigy who toured Europe playing his violin and winning universal acclaim (p. 265). Hautboy has chosen, however, to live in obscurity, assured of a greater happiness " 'with genius and without fame' " (p. 267). The narrator, an aspiring poet, is chastened by Hautboy's resignation to anonymity and casts away his own ambitions, tearing his manuscripts into pieces. His rather wordy final exclamation suggests that Hautboy's loss is his gain: " 'If Cicero, traveling in the East, found sympathetic solace for his grief in beholding the arid overthrow of a once gorgeous city, shall not my petty affair be as nothing, when I behold in Hautboy the vine and the rose climbing the shattered shafts of his tumbled temple of Fame?' " (p. 267). In rhetoric that subtly draws attention to Hautboy's phallic and ruined shafts, images Melville also used in *Pierre* and "Bartleby," the picturesque vine and rose obscure the character's tumbled temple in an aesthetically pleasing way.

Similarly, in "Jimmy Rose," the rose of the eponymous hero's name and of his bright cheeks throws a pleasing hue over his poverty, alcoholism, and distress. The old man, once a prosperous and generous host to multitudes of courtiers, has failed in his business and finds himself an outcast among the very people who sought his favors before. He goes cheerfully among them, trading charming conversation for tea and toast. The narrator, himself an old man, remembers seeking out the ruined Jimmy and getting no response. Delivering a repeated sigh – "Ah, poor, poor Jimmy – God guard us all – poor Jimmy Rose!" (p. 342) – he imagines the old man's declining years, his lonely and bitter death. Sitting in the house where Jimmy enjoyed his early life of wealth and pleasure, the narrator melancholically "bethinks" himself "of those undying roses which bloomed in ruined Jimmy's cheek" (p. 345). Transfigured by suffering, they become emblems of an undying courage: "Transplanted to another soil, all the unkind past forgot, God grant that Jimmy's roses may immortally survive!" (p. 345).

One of the most obscure of Melville's sketches, "The 'Gees," also casts a rosy glow over a despised group, the descendants of Portuguese and African sailors from the Cape Verde islands. In fact, the narrator says the " 'Gees" stand in relation to other Portuguese as "attar of roses does to rose-water" (p. 347), an ironic and disturbingly racist reference to the strength of their odor and a declaration of the intensity with which " 'Gees" are detested by sailors. In this sketch, the narrator does not indicate any distress on the part of the " 'Gees," as in Melville's other comic tales. Instead he makes snide fun of their insensibility, their animal brutishness. This sketch, then, lacks the sentimentality of the other stories, implying no sympathy with its degraded subject. Few scholars have known what to make of it, except Carolyn L. Karcher, who has shown that it parodies the writings of such scientific racists as Josiah C. Nott and George R. Gliddon. With its curiously unsettling and jocular tone, "The 'Gees" invites the reader to participate in the crudest racism and to join in the exposure of the brutish " 'Gees," as if in a coarse jest – a most disquieting effect.

The most substantial, perhaps, of Melville's comic *povertiresques* is "Cock-A-Doodle-Doo!," a story that like the others of this group ironically presents a spectacle of miserable destitution as elevating to the depressed narrator's spirits. Here the subject of his sympathy is the indigent Merrymusk family – a woodcutter with his ailing wife and children. The largest part of the tale concerns the narrator's search for a magnificent cock whose glorious crow he has heard in the woods. Looking for it high and low, he finds the cock crowing exuberantly amidst the Merrymusks' unbearable poverty, seeming to cheer them into life, warmth, and happiness. The narrator would like to buy the cock to cheer himself, but Merrymusk will not part with this splendid source of his vitality and potency. In the end, however, the cock's crows fail, and the family succumbs to disease, dying with the cock's beautiful plumage in their eyes and his inspiriting calls in their ears: "Far, deep, intense longings for release transfigured them into spirits before my eyes. I saw angels where they lay" (p. 288). With one final "supernatural note" the cock too dies. But the narrator, inspired by his immortal cry, takes it up himself: "I buried them, and planted the stone, which was a stone made to order; and never since then have I felt the doleful dumps, but under all circumstances crow late and early with a continual crow. COCK-A-DOODLE-DOO! – OO! – OO! – OO! – OO!" (p. 288). The narrator, then, rather than buying the cock *becomes* the cock, although the story suggests that he is certainly deceived about his own potency.[6]

"Cock-A-Doodle-Doo!" is a good deal longer and more complex than the other comic sketches, and it suggests more disturbingly than they do the odd co-dependency between the disabled narrator and his suffering subjects. Each tale is a fable of the power of aesthetic enchantment to blind even a well-meaning observer to the world's realities. In more melancholy versions of the *povertiresque*, though, Melville overtly condemns the damage done by such benevolent intentions and refined sensibilities. The first and most celebrated of these, "Bartleby, the Scrivener," presents the New York lawyer-narrator with a puzzling figure, a silent man who applies to copy legal documents at so many pennies per page. The lawyer finds him an eminently satisfactory employee, more steady and reliable than his only partly successful office workers, Turkey and Nippers, each of whom executes but half a day of productive labor apiece. When called upon to read his copy with the others, Bartleby responds with the memorable phrase, "I would prefer not to" (p. 20). To the lawyer's annoyance, he repeats this response at every request and eventually withdraws from his work altogether, retreating behind the screen that keeps him invisible to his employer. The lawyer oscillates between blind fury and tender sympathy but never succeeds in understanding the opaque Bartleby. Eventually, after trying every kind of blandishment to get Bartleby to leave, the lawyer moves his offices, and the police remove Bartleby to the Tombs prison. Here the lawyer goes to visit him but discovers him lying in the yard curled up near looming prison walls, reminiscent in their dismal grandeur of the fortress-like landscape of Wall Street. Touching him, he finds him dead.

The story fills the dry lawyer with considerable emotion, especially when he reveals that Bartleby may previously have worked in the Dead Letter Office, the graveyard of undeliverable mail:

Dead letters! does it not sound like dead men? Conceive a man by nature and misfortune prone to a pallid hopelessness, can any business seem more fitted to heighten it than that of continually handling these dead letters, and assorting them for the flames? For by the cart-load they are annually burned. Sometimes from out the folded paper the pale clerk takes a ring: – the finger it was meant for, perhaps, moulders in the grave; a bank-note sent in swiftest charity: – he whom it would relieve, nor eats nor hungers any more; pardon for those who died despairing; hope for those who died unhoping; good tidings for those who died stifled by unrelieved calamities. On errands of life, these letters speed to death.

    Ah Bartleby! Ah humanity! (p. 45)

    The allusions to dead letters, as a number of critics have recognized, seem to emerge in part from the image of the decayed mailbox in the "Agatha" correspondence and to refer to Melville's frustrated hopes as a writer. The story has also been viewed as critical of the lawyer's sentimental vision of suffering; the *povertiresque* in Bartleby elicits a philosophical sigh but no effective action. On the other hand, many readers find Bartleby's behavior unaccountable and sympathize with the lawyer's attempts to help and understand him. These biographical and psychological readings arrive at a similar dead end, or wall, in that Melville does not offer enough information to make complete sense of his own intentions, not to mention the lawyer's motives or Bartleby's secrets. The realistic and to some extent comic rendering of the lawyer's predicament leads one to expect a rational explanation of the story's meaning, but in fact the realism arrives at a silence as vast and illegible as the whale's brow in *Moby-Dick*'s chapter 79, "The Prairie": "Read it if you can" (p. 347). In the unfathomable space between human beings, Melville seems to say, one must recognize the insufficiency of mere language to address their suffering and create an adequate ethical response.

    In another sense, Melville may be searching for an aesthetic to believe in, a version of the *povertiresque* that works. For while "Bartleby" seems to mock the narrator's efforts to reach his recalcitrant employee, recording the failure of human communication, it also celebrates the power of storytelling to convey the misery of someone whom the reader cannot possibly understand. Melville shows how the narrator's reflections on Bartleby's sadly scanty life unveil a vast significance and stir the depths of his somewhat limited imagination:

For the first time in my life a feeling of overpowering stinging melancholy seized me. Before, I had never experienced aught but a not-unpleasing sadness. The bond of a common humanity now drew me irresistibly to gloom. A fraternal melancholy! For both I and Bartleby were sons of Adam. I remembered the bright silks and sparkling faces I had seen that day, in gala trim, swan-like sailing down the Mississippi of Broadway; and I contrasted them with the pallid copyist, and thought to myself, Ah, happiness courts the light, so we deem the world is gay; but misery hides aloof, so we deem that misery there is none. These sad fancyings – chimeras, doubtless, of a sick and silly brain – led on to other and more special thoughts, concerning the eccentricities of Bartleby. Presentiments of strange discoveries hovered round me. The scrivener's pale form appeared to me laid out, among uncaring strangers, in its shivering winding sheet. (p. 28)

Melville displays here not only the volatility of the narrator's emotions, as he ranges from sympathy to terror, but also the full spectrum of his own (Melville's) creative use of images, moving from the vivid plumage of fashionable crowds on Broadway to the violently contrasting picture of Bartleby's lonely death. Only such an exercise of the imagination can address the poverty and emptiness of Bartleby's existence. The passage argues forcefully for the vital importance of an aesthetic response to suffering, for it can imagine and find meaning in the vast and horrifying depths of misery.

Indeed, the story suggests that the same aesthetic frame that demeans human suffering and is revealed in the lawyer's sentimental and insufficient attempts to understand Bartleby can also transcend its own limits. The "fraternal melancholy" that proves inadequate in the lawyer can make a reader overcome his or her resistance to the copyist's remote and puzzling behavior. So then, oddly, the *povertir-esque* both fails and succeeds in "Bartleby, the Scrivener," for in sensing the lawyer's moral bankruptcy readers have their own chance to repair the damage. Hence the multiple valences of the concluding exclamation, "Ah Bartleby! Ah humanity!" It exposes the lawyer's generalizing tendency to swallow up Bartleby's individual story in the mass of human experience, thus producing a "not-unpleasing sadness." At the same time it calls on "humanity" to receive Bartleby as one of its own, to acknowledge Bartleby as a brother in "fraternal melancholy."

Melville experimented with many different versions of the melancholy *povertiresque* in other stories of the 1850s: "The Encantadas," "Poor Man's Pudding and Rich Man's Crumbs," "The Paradise of Bachelors and the Tartarus of Maids," and "The Piazza." In each the narrator comes close enough to the object of his sympathy to feel touched. But he generally fails the story's ethical tests, lacking the will or compassion to save the characters from suffering. Nevertheless, the story has a forceful emotional and aesthetic impact, acting upon the narrator in powerful ways. Acting as well upon readers who can detect the narrator's ethical limitations, the story's effects can produce an ethical response beyond the boundaries of the narrative.

Not surprisingly for the author who reacted so strongly to Agatha's tale, the locus of suffering in most of these stories is a woman: Hunilla, or the Chola widow, in "The Encantadas," Martha Coulter in "Poor Man's Pudding and Rich Man's Crumbs," the factory women in "The Paradise of Bachelors and the Tartarus of Maids," and Marianna in "The Piazza." In each case, although men populate the story, a mostly silent, poor, and cheerless woman captures the moral heart of the sketch and carries its social and ethical point.

"The Encantadas" seems unusual among Melville's works, gathering ten descriptive and narrative sketches connected loosely by the geography and history of the Galápagos Islands. But it is also a discontinuous text, like *Moby-Dick*, and a collection, like the later *The Piazza Tales* and Melville's volumes of poetry (*Battle-Pieces, John Marr, Timoleon*). Like those works it resists linear narrative and formal unity, aiming for dramatic backdrops and spotlights instead. Among the vivid descriptions of the islands and their flora and fauna – the tortoises being among the most memorable – Melville includes richly evocative tales of the buccaneers of Barrington Isle, the Creole "Dog-King" of Charles's Isle, and the vicious hermit Oberlus of Hood's Isle. Their stories call up the history of European colonialism in South America and the Pacific, recounting a chronicle of violence and bloodshed, piracy, slavery, and warfare.[7]

The longest and most fully considered story appears in the eighth sketch, "Norfolk Isle and the Chola Widow," and concerns a "lone island" where the characters live in dreamy and ultimately fatal isolation from the world's cataclysmic events (p. 151). Hunilla, a Peruvian native or Chola, has come to the island with her Spanish husband Felipe and brother Truxill, to catch tortoises and refine their oil. The captain who delivered them to the isle sails off and forgets about them, the two men are drowned at sea, and Hunilla, a female Robinson Crusoe, lives on in desolate solitude with a number of fluffy little dogs, offspring of her pets, for companionship. A prey, the narrator implies, to sailors who stop at the island and may have raped her and moved on – "unnamed events which befell Hunilla on this isle" (p. 158) – she survives until the narrator's ship appears and responds to her signal, a waving handkerchief. Tearing herself from her buried dead and her beloved dogs, Hunilla sails away with the ship, which brings her to Payta; here she is last seen making her way into town, "riding upon a small gray ass; and before her on the ass's shoulders, she eyed the jointed workings of the beast's armorial cross" (p. 162). The image of the cross serves as a moving reminder of both her Christian faith, tested by adversity, and her grief, symbolized by the memorial cross planted upon her dead husband's grave.

Not surprisingly, critics have seen Hunilla as a literary reincarnation of Agatha and her story as perhaps the tale Melville wrote and called "Isle of the Cross," and was later "prevented" from publishing at Harper & Brothers (*L* 250). In any case, the parallel themes of wreckage, loss, memory, female patience, and bottomless suffering are striking. The effect is less than it was in "Bartleby" to move the narrator to a "not-unpleasing sadness" and more to silence him, as Hunilla has been silenced by her grief. Of course, the narrator cannot literally be silenced, since he is telling the story, but he uses dramatic breaks in the narrative to signal the collapse of his own efforts.[8] Thus, when he comes to tell of Hunilla's violation by the passing sailors, he stops himself:

> When Hunilla – –
> Dire sight it is to see some silken beast long dally with a golden lizard ere she devour. More terrible, to see how feline Fate will sometimes dally with a human soul, and by a nameless magic make it repulse a sane despair with a hope which is but mad. Unwittingly I imp this cat-like thing, sporting with the heart of him who reads; for if he feel not, he reads in vain. (p. 156)

The extra-long pause after Hunilla's name and the eerie evocation of a "feline Fate" suggests not only the fate that plays with her but also the narrator's feline power to violate the reader's helpless "human soul," even as he demurs. In a similarly dramatic pause, the narrator cedes his power to an even greater one, that of Hunilla's God:

> Braced against her woe, Hunilla would not, durst not trust the weakness of her tongue. Then when our Captain asked whether any whale-boats had – –
>
> But no, I will not file this thing complete for scoffing souls to quote, and call it firm proof upon their side. The half shall here remain untold. Those two unnamed events which befell Hunilla on this isle, let them abide between her and her God. In nature, as in law, it may be libellous to speak some truths. (pp. 157–8)

Again, the curious punctuation and the narrator's scruples against intervening in Hunilla's story advertise his self-restraint in ways as dramatic and conspicuous as Hunilla's silence.

In "The Encantadas," Melville relocates the *povertiresque* to the Pacific, where the melancholy pleasures of American versions of the mode become intensified. In Hunilla's story, female suffering has the power of the divine, as before invested in the whale Moby Dick or the unearthly Isabel, to arrest the narrator's loquacious sentimentality. Melville plays out this pattern repeatedly with female characters in his other stories of the 1850s. In "Poor Man's Pudding," for example, the pregnant wife of a woodcutter silently rebukes the wealthy philanthropist Blandmour and the compliant narrator with her poverty. Serving the narrator a "pudding" made of old rice and rancid salt, Martha Coulter turns the narrator's stomach with her wretched food and at the same time corrects his ill-informed and misplaced benevolence. He turns away in an odd mixture of sympathy and moral repulsion. Recoiling at her loving descriptions of her dead children, he laments: "I could stay no longer to hear of sorrows for which the sincerest sympathies could give no adequate relief. . . . I offered no pay for hospitalities gratuitous and honorable as those of a prince. I knew that such offerings would have been more than declined; charity resented" (pp. 295–6). The narrator's refusal to give alms pays tribute to the Coulters' independence but clearly falls short of true charity.

The companion piece, "Rich Man's Crumbs," pairs the spectacle of independent American poverty with the misery of starving beggars in London. The narrator attends a public display of municipal charity, where the city's officials give the remnants of a great feast away to its most indigent citizens. Against the image of patient Martha Coulter the narrator presents a different kind of suffering woman: " 'See that pasty now, snatched by that pale girl; I dare say the Emperor of Russia ate of that last night.' " In images that combine imperial conquest with sexual depredation – " 'it looks as though some omnivorous Emperor or other had had a finger in that pie,' "; " 'I don't doubt it,' murmured I, 'he is said to be uncommonly fond of the breast' " (p. 299) – Melville mocks wealth and privilege. The ending suggests a tidy moral: " 'Now, Heaven in its kind mercy save me from the noble charities of London,' sighed I, as that night I lay bruised and battered on my bed; 'and Heaven save me equally from the "Poor Man's Pudding" and the "Rich Man's Crumbs" ' " (p. 302). But the violence, of both the charitable feast and the contrast between the two forms of poverty, proves unsettling and leaves the speaker "bruised and battered."

Melville used contrast to dramatic effect in his other paired sketches, "The Two Temples" and "The Paradise of Bachelors and the Tartarus of Maids." In both, a traveling narrator plays off Europe against America in contrasting vignettes of class and gender differences. "The Two Temples" brings the narrator first into the wealthy Grace Church of Manhattan, where he observes a showy display of wealth and snobbery in what is meant to be a place of humble worship. Then he attends a play in a working-class London theater where by a kind of reverse magic the site of display and performance turns out to provide more real fellowship and human kindness than the New York church did. In "The Paradise of Bachelors," the narrator attends a dinner at London's Inns of Court, the dwelling of numerous unmarried barristers who grow progressively garrulous and bibulous as the lavish meal goes on. In contrast, "The Tartarus of Maids" presents a scene of unutterable misery, as the narrator, a seedsman seeking paper for his envelopes at a paper mill in the mountains, encounters the "maids," or factory workers, all women. Here the production of paper offers an obscene version of the women's reproductive functions turned awry. In a series of suggestive bodily metaphors, Melville implies that the maids' biological and sexual vitality has become absorbed into the manufacture of paper for bachelors like the lawyers far away, and of course authors like Melville, to write on.

As in "The Encantadas," women carry the burden of the story's ethical and aesthetic meaning in "Paradise/Tartarus." Like Hunilla, they labor in silence, and like Martha Coulter they see their reproductive labor come to nothing. The narrator comes away chastened by the spectacle of female "patience, & endurance, & resignedness," as in the "Agatha" story. At the end of "Tartarus," struck by the women's hopelessness, the narrator feels "some pained homage to their pale virginity [that] made me involuntarily bow" (p. 334). Beyond suggesting his ethical intuitions, which make him keenly aware of the women's suffering but unable to do more than depart all the more closely "wrapped in furs and meditations" (p. 335), the story also creates a vivid image of the female body under intense duress. Melville's representation of the menstrual flow of the "Blood River" (p. 329), the "abdominal heat" of the womb-like vats of "albuminous" pulp, and the "nine minutes" (p. 331) of gestation during which the pulp becomes paper and is sheared and dropped from the machine like a newborn babe, competes violently with the narrator's "meditations" and moral reflections on the women's misery. This imagery speaks powerfully for the silent women, who cannot speak for themselves and who, like Isabel, forlornly and futilely seek the narrator's compassion: "Slowly mournfully, beseechingly, yet unresistingly, they gleamed along, their agony dimly outlined on the imperfect paper, like the print of the tormented face on the handkerchief of Saint Veronica" (p. 334). In the face of the narrator's summary conclusions, the story weaves a disturbing tapestry of the women's enslavement and oppression.

Such images of female servitude and oppression saturate Melville's sketch "The Piazza" as well. Here the narrator views a picturesque landscape from his porch or piazza, a structure similar to the addition Melville built on to his own farmhouse, Arrowhead. From his perch amid the glorious Berkshires scenery, the narrator thinks he sees a little "spot of radiance" on the mountainside, a place he imagines as enchanted: "Fairies there, thought I; some haunted ring where fairies dance" (p. 5). Betaking himself to this supposed fairy land, he finds only a lonesome cottage where a young woman called Marianna sits forlornly sewing until her brother returns from cutting wood. Her only consolation is that from her window she can see a beautiful house that seems to her "King Charming's palace": a place where "some happy one" (p. 9) must live. Her vivid imagination makes the view a fairy tale to her, but looking from her window the narrator sees that the house she has taken to be King Charming's palace is his own farmhouse. She cries, "'Oh, if I could but once get to yonder house, and but look upon whoever the happy being is who lives there!'" (p. 12). Without revealing himself as the King Charming of her dreams, the narrator slips away, returning to the piazza and his "box-royal" view of the countryside. Marianna's mournful story haunts him, however, and he cannot shake it away: "But, every night, when the curtain falls, truth comes in with darkness. No light shows from the mountain. To and fro I walk the piazza deck, haunted by Marianna's face, and many as real a story" (p. 12).

Beginning as a deeply satirical term in *Pierre*, the *povertiresque* becomes a flexible mode for Melville, allowing him to range from comic effects in some of his stories to more deeply challenging and unsettling ones in others. Fitting only somewhat comfortably into the framework of the magazine sketch, these tales also contain disquieting energies, and Melville found ways to let those energies come into fuller play in stories of more open conflict.

"Air . . . Suppressedly Charged": Slumbering Volcanoes and the Aesthetic of Suspense

Quite a different aesthetic effect emerges in a second group of Melville's stories, where the spectacle of misery may engage the viewer in picturesque musings, but the characters' actions violently disrupt that aesthetic distance. In what I would like to call an aesthetic of suspense, characters in stories like "Benito Cereno," "The Bell-Tower," "The Lightning-Rod Man," "I and My Chimney," and "The Apple-Tree Table" manage to shake the protagonist out of his *povertiresque* sensibility, often not by acting on him in any direct way but through action suspended and frozen in deadly *inaction*. The ironic result of this quiet, or sometimes not so quiet, resistance, this suspended action, is to unsettle the narrator by a confrontation with the unexpected violence of a seemingly tranquil scene. Rather than retreating to a pleasing melancholy, the narrator assumes a more militant or embattled posture, standing his ground in the face of the unspeakable.

Melville described this aesthetic of suspense in the "Agatha" correspondence when he set the opening scene:

> The afternoon is mild & warm. The sea with an air of solemn deliberation, with an elaborate deliberation, ceremoniously rolls upon the beach.

> The air is suppressedly charged with the sound of long lines of surf. . . . –
> Filled with meditations, she [Agatha] reclines along the edge of the cliff
> & gazes out seaward. She marks a handful of cloud on the horizon,
> presaging a storm thro' all this quietude.

Agatha appears here, not as the solitary suffering woman of Judge Clifford's sentimental characterization, but as a thoughtful and watchful mind. Her awareness of sea and sky bespeaks a sensitive imagination, and her "meditations" show alert intelligence. Above all, she appreciates the troubling presence of the unseen and unknown. The air is "suppressedly charged" with the sounds of surf, the sea stretches away to a continent she cannot see, and the wind and water have invisibly worked their influence upon the landscape. The tension presaging the storm and the shipwreck proves terrifying, but at the same time is almost welcome to her.

Such an awareness and appreciation of suspense characterizes some of the most disturbing and elusive of Melville's stories. In "Benito Cereno," borrowing a phrase (the "slumbering volcano") from one of Frederick Douglass's speeches, Melville has his protagonist Amasa Delano wonder if the slave ship, the *San Dominick*, carries pirates or other disruptive elements in its hold: might not "the San Dominick, like a slumbering volcano, suddenly let loose energies now hid?" (p. 68). Douglass was speaking of the "slumbering volcano" of racial violence, and Melville does too, although Delano cannot conceive of such a possibility.[9] But like Agatha, Delano seems to have some awareness of the power of the unseen and to be wrapped in "meditations" upon its meaning. In the suspense that precedes the letting loose of slumbering energies, Melville creates an unsettling effect. The tension in "Benito Cereno" builds its power from the *avoidance* of action, from sustained but ultimately untenable stasis. As in a number of other stories Melville wrote, the release of tension brings little relief except to reveal how compromised the characters' notions of their own security really are.

The suspense in "Benito Cereno" derives from an intricate structure of plots held in uneasy competition and equilibrium with one another. For "Benito Cereno" tells several stories at once, stories that conflict with each other and prevent the full story from being told, holding the reader in deadly suspense, as if enslaved, until the end. In the first narrative, a Yankee sea captain, Amasa Delano (modeled after the man who wrote the original account on which Melville based his story), encounters a strange ship called the *San Dominick* off the coast of Chile in 1799 and goes aboard to investigate. He finds an ailing Spanish captain, Benito Cereno, who tells a horrifying story of storms that have reduced the ship to its present debilitated condition. His crewmen have mostly sickened and died while his "cargo," a large number of African slaves, now move freely over the ship. Their leader, Babo, proves a devoted servant and has supported him throughout the crisis with uncommon fidelity. Delano, while entertaining numerous doubts about what he sees, especially after Cereno asks him pointed questions about whether his own ship (the *Bachelor's Delight*) is properly manned and armed, nevertheless charitably gives food and water to the starving crew and slaves. At a critical moment, as Delano leaves the ship to return to his own, Cereno unaccountably leaps into the boat after him. Delano, taking him for a murderer, believes that his previous suspicions have been justified, until he sees Babo leap after him and aim a dagger, not at Delano's but at Cereno's heart. In a "flash of revelation" (p. 99), Delano realizes that the slaves have taken over the ship and that what he thought was weak command on Cereno's part turns out to be a risky charade of white control and African servitude. After a judicial investigation in Lima, for which Melville provides Cereno's deposition giving his version of the facts, the story ends with the captains conversing together. In a gruesome final image, Babo is executed, and his severed head, "that hive of subtlety" (p. 116), stands on a pike in the Plaza in Lima.

In a second story, one that the reader and later Delano must imagine happening before and around these events, the African slaves belonging to Cereno's friend Alexandro Aranda rebel and take over the ship. Killing Aranda and many of the whites, the former slaves prepare Aranda's corpse by stripping it of its flesh – cannibalism is implied but not spelled out – and nail it to the prow, removing the previous figurehead, a representation of Christopher Columbus. When they spy Delano's ship and realize that he can help them, Babo covers the skeleton as if for repairs, writing beneath it in Spanish the words "Follow your leader," as a warning to the white sailors, and instructing everyone on the ship to maintain the fiction of white control over the Africans. As the day goes on, Babo plans to take Delano's ship as well, which is small and lightly armed. He also uses various ruses to distract Delano's attention from the obvious lapses in Cereno's story and the serious breaches in shipboard discipline. At the height of these maneuvers, Babo invites Delano into the cuddy, claiming that it is time to shave his master but using the razor to reduce Cereno to quivering terror. Cereno, paralyzed by fear for himself as well as Delano and the other sailors, remains in this abject state until the moment of Delano's departure, when he summons his remaining energy and springs into the boat. As a result the elaborate masque is exposed, the ship taken, a number of Africans killed, and Babo tried and executed.

Since Babo never tells his story overtly, we might say that these two stories represent what Delano knows (the first) and what Cereno knows (the second). But there is a third story in "Benito Cereno," and that is the story of the reader. This is the story that holds the others in suspension and prevents them from making themselves fully known, as the reader inhabits different characters' narratives in turn. Although we cannot generalize for all readers, we might say that the typical reader enters the story much as Delano does – mystified by the ship's movements and appearance, baffled by the behavior of the captain and his slave, appalled by the glimpses of violence among the other slaves and truculence of the crew. Like Delano, the reader struggles to make sense of the confusing events of the day until, at the climax, hidden terrors become revealed in a "flash of revelation." Cereno's deposition follows and supplies the names and facts that clarify the *San Dominick*'s strange history; now the reader can perceive the cruelty of Babo and his confederates fully revealed. But a final section returns the reader to the main characters, casting a new light on their actions. It confirms that Cereno trembled for his guest's safety and behaved heroically in maintaining the fiction so as to protect him as long as he could; and that Delano, though enlightened about the true workings of the plot, remains preternaturally cheerful in the face of Cereno's deep gloom. "'What has cast such a shadow upon you?'" asks Delano; "'The negro,'" Cereno replies (p. 116), ending the conversation and retreating into silence.

But then Babo too reappears in the ending and likewise refuses speech, implying that "since I cannot do deeds, I will not speak words" (p. 116). Even more eloquently than Cereno, his severed head speaks of the horrors of his experience, reproaching the whites in the Plaza and the systems of government and church that have condemned him, and significantly having the last word in the story, in that his phrase, "Follow your leader," ends the narrative. Many readers, brought by

Melville's narrator to identify first with Delano, whose perspective dominates the largest portion of the story, and then with Cereno, whose deposition emerges at the climax, find themselves confronting Babo in the end and being reminded that, as violent as his actions have been, those of the whites are equally if not more horrific. While witnessing his grotesque demise, the reader is invited to admire the daring, brilliance, and artistry of Babo's scheme.

That, at least, is one reading narrative for the story. But it implies as "typical" a reader likely to identify with Delano in the first place, an assumption that raises several questions. What kind of reader identifies with Delano and why? Does the reader respond to Delano's authority as captain? Does one accept his "goodness" and "generosity," as Cereno repeatedly does, and assume he has moral authority in the story? Does one side with him because he is American or white or male, unlike the characters who are Spanish or African, female, or in other ways considered inferior? But then, how many readers really accept Delano's point of view? Or, to put the question another way, at what point does a reader begin to suspect that Delano's doubts point to a truth his presumed goodness and innocence cannot perceive? For many readers, Delano is not a trustworthy narrator. If he isn't, a new problem arises. Whom *can* one trust in the story? Is Cereno a hero? Is Babo? Does the narrator give enough access to any other character to make an alternative identification or judgment possible? And if not, then at a further level of questioning the reader must ask, if we cannot identify the true positions and motives of the story's characters, how do we judge the author's meaning and intentions? Does Melville endorse Delano's actions, or Cereno's, or Babo's? Does he support the slaves' actions or not? Is he on the side of the victims or the oppressors? But wait, who *are* the victims and oppressors in this story?

And this line of questioning represents only one part in the story of the reader. For now the reader is no longer the innocent who entered "Benito Cereno" at first but someone who knows what happened and can investigate the mechanisms of the narrative. At this point, the reader may give up entirely, or alternatively become a rereader at what we might call part two of the reader's story. This more experienced reader can study the details of Melville's narration, the verbal textures of the story that reveal early warnings of "shadows present, foreshadowing deeper shadows to come" (p. 46); that suggest that Delano's "singularly undistrustful good nature" does not necessarily imply "more than ordinary quickness and accuracy of intellectual perception" (p. 47). This reader will recognize that as much as Delano notices and comments on the irregularities on the *San Dominick*, he just as often silences doubt by falling back on his racist and sexist prejudices. He cannot see the masquerade in front of him because he believes the blacks incapable of intrigue. Hence he argues repeatedly that even though Cereno's behavior is unaccountable, his classic European profile proves that he is "a true off-shoot of a true hidalgo" (p. 65); the "slumbering negress" appears to him a "doe" (p. 73) and Babo a "a shepherd's dog" (p. 51) because he feels "genially" (p. 84) toward Africans, as if they were animals; it appears to him unlikely that the sailors are plotting with the slaves to deceive him because "who ever heard of a white so far a renegade as to apostatize from his very species almost, by leaguing in against it with negroes?" (p. 75); and in reviewing the clear signs that something is amiss on the ship, Delano reminds himself that "There is some one above" (p. 77) looking out for him. Even when the "play of the barber" unfolds and he dimly perceives that "in the black he saw a headsman, and in the white, a man at the block" (p. 85), even when he wonders if "for some unknown purpose, [Cereno and Babo] were acting out, both in word and deed . . . some juggling play before him," Delano views "the notion as a whimsy" (p. 87) and dismisses it.

For an experienced reader, these self-deceptions appear as dangerous as anything Babo has done. As later revelations make clear, Babo's plan succeeds as far as it does because it so brilliantly anticipates and exploits Delano's *povertiresque* blindness to the Africans' real characters and motives. The ending, then, must raise serious questions about the reader's own assent to Delano's views the first time through. From being shocked and surprised by the revolt, the reader moves to sympathizing with Babo's actions, even when Babo withholds an explanation and Melville makes Babo's interior as vast and unfathomable as the African continent appeared to many nineteenth-century Americans.

The aesthetic of suspense fixes the story's plots and actions at significant moments of inaction, tableaux that hint at the characters' true intentions. One of these occurs when Delano prepares to distribute the food and water his men have brought to relieve the sufferers on the *San Dominick*. As the Africans crowd around the food, he makes a "half-mirthful, half-menacing gesture" meant to enforce discipline. The crowd immediately arrests its movements: "Instantly the blacks paused, just where they were, each Negro and Negress suspended in his or her posture, exactly as the word had found them – for a few seconds continuing so – while, as between the responsive posts of a telegraph, an unknown syllable ran from man to man among the perched oakum-pickers." In their "suspended" postures, the Africans embody the way the story itself is suspended, while "an unknown syllable" (p. 79) runs from character to character beneath the verbal surface of the narrative. The tableau reveals the way action and gesture carry the story as much as language does and shows how the slaves' performance of deference actually controls and suspends the whites' intended actions.

In a similarly suspended posture, Babo's head stands on a pole at the end of the story, reminding the whites of his power over them:

> Some months after, dragged to the gibbet at the tail of a mule, the black met his voiceless end. The body was burned to ashes; but for many days, the head, that hive of subtlety, fixed on a pole in the Plaza, met, unabashed, the gaze of the whites; and across the Plaza looked toward St. Bartholomew's church, in whose vaults slept then, as now, the recovered bones of Aranda; and across the Rimac bridge looked toward the monastery, on Mount Agonia without; where, three months after being dismissed by the court, Benito Cereno, borne on the bier, did, indeed, follow his leader. (pp. 116–17)

Babo's gaze continues to fix Benito Cereno in his stare long after the charade is over, and the suspense of his *inaction* continues to act on others long after his capacity for action has ended. Suspense, then, turns out to be the one most effective mode the Africans can use to hold the white master narrative in their thrall.

This complicated use of suspense serves an important function. Neither the narrator nor the reader can avoid knowing on some level that a slumbering volcano is about to erupt, whether from the hold of the Spanish American *San Dominick*, from Babo's Africa, or from North America's plantations and cities. The brooding tension in the story makes any retreat to the picturesque or *povertiresque* impossible, and in the end, characters and readers confront the starkly terrifying image of Babo's severed head with no comforting screen of moral certitude.

Although "Benito Cereno" is the longest and most involved example of Melville's use of deeply layered and unbearable suspense, other stories use it too to give an "air . . . suppressedly charged" to events. In "The Bell-Tower," for example, the threat of insurrection haunts a story of arrogant power in ways reminiscent of Melville's methods in "Benito Cereno." Here the "slumbering volcano" is not a shipload of slaves but one iron vassal, the mechanical figure created to strike the bell in Bannadonna's medieval clock tower. Bannadonna, the prideful builder of this new Babel, kills one of his workmen in an "esthetic passion" (p. 176) for absolute perfection. As if in revenge, the mechanical figure, whom Bannadonna calls Haman, strikes him dead at the feet of Una, the first of twelve mechanical female hours who are meant to circulate through the tower. The death appears to be an accident, but later the tower collapses dramatically and in its fall seems also to deliver a fearsome message: "So the blind slave obeyed its blinder lord; but, in obedience, slew him. So the creator was killed by the creature. So the bell was too heavy for the tower. So that bell's main weakness was where man's blood had flawed it. And so pride went before the fall" (pp. 186–7). The violence of "esthetic passion" and pride turns back upon itself and kills the "lord"; the suspended posture of master and slave maintains itself in mechanical equilibrium, in what Ahab called the "iron way."

As in "Benito Cereno," though with as great an emphasis on class as on race, "The Bell-Tower" suggests a deadly tableau. The bell is literally hanging in the tower, the hours frozen in their positions, and the striker locked into place for a considerable and breathless stretch of time. The violent release of inevitable forces brings the story to its conclusion, but the conflict is not fully resolved, and the story confronts the reader with a spectacle of Bannadonna's "blind" enslavement to passion that cannot be wished away.

The salesman of "The Lightning-Rod Man" imports a similarly ominous threat into the story, represented by the lightning rod, which resembles one of Jupiter's thunderbolts and suggests a demonic power over the narrator. Although the story is brief, it escalates violently, with the two characters facing off, shouting their defiance at each other, and standing their ground on the narrator's hearth. Ironically, the narrator holds his own in the place where he feels safest, exactly where the salesman warns him he will most likely be hit by lightning. The violence of their quarrel matches the violence of the storm raging overhead and suggests that something more is at stake than the sales-man's lightning rods. Unleashing the fury of nature, as Babo lets loose the passions of the slaves and Bannadonna unlocks the mechanical violence of the clock, the salesman gives the narrator no safe place where he can retreat. The narrator seems to win the argument; when the salesman comes at him, lightning rod in hand, the narrator defends himself manfully: "He sprang upon me; his tri-forked thing at my heart. I seized it; I snapped it; I dashed it; I trod it; and dragging the dark lightning-king out of my door, flung his elbowed, copper scepter after him." He does not succeed, however, in having the last word: "But spite of my treatment, and spite of my dissuasive talk of him to my neighbors, the Lightning-rod man still dwells in the land; still travels in storm-time, and drives a brave trade with the fears of man" (p. 124). The narrator's humor cannot banish the unease of the lightning-rod man's challenge to his snug domesticity.

If "Benito Cereno" suggests that the volcano slumbering at the heart of American complacency is the threat of racial revolt, and if "The Bell-Tower" and "The Lightning-Rod Man" add class conflict to that terrifying vision, two other stories focus on the suppressed charge of female insurrection. In "I and My Chimney" and "The Apple-Tree Table," the narrator presents a spectacle not of suffering and silent victims but of powerful women, the wives and daughters of an aging, sardonic, but ultimately weak narrator. The protagonist of "I and My Chimney" loves his enormous old chimney as the narrator of "The Lightning-Rod Man" loves his spacious hearth, and it provides similar assurances of safety and potency. But his wife wants to improve the house and remove the chimney, seemingly taking with it her own husband. She consults with a mason, a Mr. Hiram Scribe, who asserts that the chimney contains a secret closet and is hence radically unsound. The narrator spots a plot against him and methodically proves Scribe in error. As a result he wins the quarrel but never succeeds in convinc-ing his wife. At the end, he stands guard over his chimney, condemned never to leave his house: "It is now some seven years since I have stirred from home. My city friends all wonder why I don't come to see them, as in former times. They think I am getting sour and unsocial. Some say that I have become a sort of mossy old misanthrope, while all the time the fact is, I am simply standing guard over my mossy old chimney; for it is resolved between me and my chimney, that I and my chimney will never surrender" (p. 377).

The story is in some ways a comic version of "Tartarus of Maids," in that it anatomizes a human body. Here, however, the body is male, the chimney's spine, smoke, and "ash-hole" (p. 372) identified with the narrator's aging and ailing flesh. The slumbering volcano, then, is not only the threat of female insurgency against declining male potency but the rebellious body itself, which refuses to serve its crippled master. The narrator must enslave his chimney, and in the end his body, in order to maintain his control. A more successful outcome occurs in "The Apple-Tree Table," where, as in Thoreau's *Walden*, a ticking beetle emerges from its place embedded in an old piece of furniture and makes its way into the light. The wife and daughters in this story take the ticking for the sound of spirits, such as those summoned by the Fox sisters and other "spirit-rappers" of the mid-nineteenth century. Here the narrator's skepticism about a mystical explanation for the mysterious sounds proves correct, and he triumphs over his foolish wife and daughters, but he also obliterates the enchantment of the spirits. The natural explanation, however, and the natural emanation, an insect "as beautiful as a butterfly" (p. 395) console the family and restore domestic harmony.

In Melville's domestic stories, as in "Benito Cereno," little happens. Instead sustained suspense ends in a dramatic confrontation that damages everyone involved, not fatally as in "Benito Cereno," but comically. The specter of hidden insurrection, however, threatens the stability advertised by the story's conclusion. For the most part in Melville's short fiction, the air remains "suppressedly charged" after the conflict ends and reminds the reader of tensions still simmering beneath the surface of middle-class American complacency and prosperity. The inventions of narrative, it would seem, even those conducted by the most professional of narrators, prove inadequate to calm the volcanoes boiling away beneath the earth's crust. In Melville's next novels, in the rapacious environments of cities and frontiers, the characters, like Agatha's husband Robertson, must resort to daring subterfuges and desperate measures to keep their wits about them.

CHAPTER 8

"Peculiarly Latitudinarian Notions": *Israel Potter* and *The Confidence-Man*

Many of Melville's stories might be described as tableaux, their characters fixed in certain ethical or social positions that create unbearable tension and suspense. Such a static pattern may seem uncharacteristic of the author who chose "Omoo," which he claimed was the Polynesian word for "rover," as a title and used his earlier novels to describe worldwide wanderings. In sketching for Hawthorne the character of Agatha's husband, the sailor he calls Robinson, Melville expressed considerable familiarity with and sympathy for his mobile and restless nature:

> The probable facility with which Robinson first leaves his wife & then takes another, may, possibly, be ascribed to the peculiarly latitudinarian notions, which most sailors have of all tender obligations of that sort. In his previous sailor life Robinson had found a wife (for a night) in every port. The sense of the obligation of the marriage-vow to Agatha had little weight with him at first. It was only when some years of life ashore had passed that his moral sense on that point became developed. And hence his subsequent conduct – Remorse &c. Turn this over in your mind & see if it is right. If not – make it so yourself.

Melville, taking a leaf from his professional experience as a sailor, makes sense of Robertson's "latitudinarian" morality, but he also models a latitudinarian attitude to writing when he invites Hawthorne to "[t]urn this over in your mind & see if it is right. If not – make it so yourself." This statement might stand as a motto for Melville's practice in the novels that grew out of and away from his short stories – *Israel Potter: His Fifty Years of Exile* and *The Confidence-Man: His Masquerade*. The characters in these novels come unmoored from the bonds that confine the magazine sketches and travel freely among the latitudes of Melville's fluid imagination. Less realistic and focused than the short fiction, these novels take considerable latitude in their telling as well, adopting more experimental modes of narration. Melville seems quite pleased to have a reader of his work "[t]urn this over in your mind & see if it is right. If not – make it so yourself." Indeed, Melville's making it "right" himself, a matter, often, of making the narrative his own even if it involves stealing from another author, becomes a central theme in both books. These novels, often ignored in favor of *Moby-Dick* and the short fiction, show remarkable developments in Melville's writing and concept of himself as author.

Stealing in *Israel Potter: His Fifty Years of Exile*

Like "Benito Cereno," *Israel Potter* owes its being to a previous text, *The Remarkable Adventures of Israel R. Potter*, originally published by Henry Trumbull in 1824. Melville was thinking about the story during his trip to London in 1849 and bought a map of the city, noting in his journal: "I want to use it in case I serve up the Revolutionary narrative of the beggar." He also collected local scenery that later appeared in the book: "While on one of the Bridges, the thought struck me again that a fine thing might be written about a Blue Monday in November London – a city of Dis (Dante's) – clouds of smoke – the damned &c. – coal barges – coaly waters, cast-iron Duke &c. – its marks are left upon you, &c. &c. &c" (*IP*, "Historical Note," 174, 176). After being serialized in *Putnam's*, the book was moderately successful but later received little critical attention, in part because it adheres so closely to its source as to seem an almost embarrassing case of Melville's professional laziness, and in part because its humor and its patriotic themes make it seem a light and entertaining concession to the popular market rather than a serious work by the great master.

Trumbull's original narrative tells the story of a soldier in the American Revolution who was captured and detained in England during the war and afterwards lived nearly fifty years in poverty and adversity before finally returning home. Trumbull published the story as part of a series on homespun American heroes (Daniel Boone, for one), hoping to raise funds for the indigent Potter, who had failed to win a pension. While borrowing liberally from Trumbull's book, Melville also elaborated freely, introducing a long central section in which Potter is no victim of historical fate but instead an energetic, mobile confidence man and trickster who engages in hair's-breadth escapes and lively adventures. Traveling through the English countryside in a number of disguises, Potter observes rural life and ends up as a gardener for the king, engaging George III in animated conversation. He serves as courier for American sympathizers in England and travels to Paris to deliver secret documents to Benjamin Franklin – and to deliver numerous shrewd and comic remarks about him. He also makes a fast friend of America's freebooter captain John Paul Jones, who has come to Franklin for aid.

Later, on Potter's return to England, his patron Squire Woodcock immures him in a closet hidden in a chimney. When the Squire unexpectedly dies, Potter frees himself from his cell and escapes the house dressed as the dead man's ghost, later trading clothes with a scarecrow. Through a series of other adventures, he ends up on John Paul Jones's *Bonhomme Richard* and fights in the battle with the *Serapis*, but afterward he accidentally finds himself on an English ship, where he pretends to be one of the crew and succeeds in passing himself off as an English sailor. Going ashore, he meets American rebel Ethan Allen, held in English custody, and then later takes flight once again for London, where he hopes to lose himself in the urban throng.

Melville collapses the rest of Potter's long life into a few chapters, called "Israel in Egypt" (when he works as a brickmaker outside London), "In the City of Dis," and "Forty-five Years," which describes Potter's marriage, poverty, occupation as a chair-mender, and old age. Finally, through the efforts of his last surviving son, he gains a passage home to America. Arriving coincidentally on the Fourth of July at the dedication of the Bunker Hill Monument (commemorating his first battle), he nearly gets run over by a "patriotic triumphal car" (p. 167). Neglected and alone except for the faithful son, he returns to his family's farm like an aged Rip Van Winkle, ending his days in obscurity: "He was repulsed in efforts, after a pension, by certain caprices of law. His scars proved his only medals. He dictated a little book, the record of his fortunes. But long ago it faded out of print – himself out of being – his name out of memory. He died the same day that the oldest oak on his native hills was blown down" (p. 169). Dying without a memorial, Potter nevertheless gains a written memorial in Melville's text, which is ironically dedicated to the Bunker Hill Monument.

The book's patriotic subject and plot-driven structure have made it seem a deviation from Melville's more subversive novels and short stories, a falling off from the intellectual and creative progress implied in his earlier works. In fact, however, *Israel Potter* signals an important development in Melville's growth as a writer. Just as Israel Potter, a wandering sailor, seems to have "latitudinarian notions" of his own, Melville takes considerable latitude with his borrowed plot and characters. In his magazine fiction, the satiric critique of American racism, social injustice, and aggressive capitalism often gets diffused through the screen of a mildly sentimental narrator or suspended in indeterminate action. In *Israel Potter*, an outspoken narrator makes more challenging utterances. For example, comparing the revolutionary freebooter John Paul Jones to a savage, the narrator declares of America: "Sharing the same blood with England, and yet her proved foe in two wars; not wholly inclined at bottom to forget an old grudge: intrepid, unprincipled, reckless, predatory, with boundless ambition, civilized in externals but a savage at heart, America is, or may yet be, the Paul Jones of nations" (p. 120). Describing the famous battle between Jones's *Bonhomme Richard* and the *Serapis*, Melville's narrator utters the kinds of political taunts that pepper *Typee* and *Moby-Dick*: "In view of this battle one may well ask – What separates the enlightened man from the savage? Is civilization a thing distinct, or is it an advanced state of barbarism?" (p. 130). Israel's suffering makes him as pitiable as the paupers and resigned women of Melville's short fiction, but instead of subsiding into melancholy reflections, the narrator openly condemns Potter's plight. He also satirizes American heroes like Benjamin Franklin, describing him ironically as one of those "labyrinth minded, but plainspoken Broadbrims, at once politicians and philosophers; keen observers of the main chance; prudent courtiers; practical magians in linsey woolsey" (p. 46); and the rakish John Paul Jones as "this jaunty barbarian in broadcloth; a sort of prophetical ghost, glimmering in anticipation upon the advent of those tragic scenes of the French Revolution which levelled the exquisite refinement of Paris with the bloodthirsty ferocity of Borneo; showing that broaches and finger-rings, not less than nose-rings and tattooing, are tokens of the primeval savageness which ever slumbers in human kind, civilised or uncivilised" (p. 63).

Indeed, in some respects the most latitudinarian of Melville's characters turn out to be not the far-ranging Israel Potter, who spends much of the book in physical, political, or economic bondage, but Franklin and Jones. Each in his own way is a pirate.[1] Franklin helps himself to the civilized comforts – brandy, sugar, cologne, and soap – in Potter's Parisian hotel room, so that (as Franklin self-interestedly explains) Potter will not be tempted or betrayed into an indiscretion. And Jones boards ships and sets fire to coastlines in random acts of maritime violence, seeming to fight as much for his own independence as that of his country. In the latitude these powerful figures take with Potter's life, they resemble the latitude Melville takes with Potter's life story. In appropriating Trumbull's text – some might call it stealing – Melville seems to have delighted in his own outlawry and written it into the text.

One moment dramatizes Melville's concern with theft, both as writer and as borrower of Israel Potter's story. When Potter steals away from the house of his English patron, Squire Woodcock, wearing the dead man's clothes, he also inadvertently steals the Squire's purse, with a good deal of money. His dilemma reflects on the ethics of both literal and literary theft:

> The grand moral question now came up, what to do with the purse? Would it be dishonest under the circumstances to appropriate that purse? Considering the whole matter, and not forgetting that he had not received from the gentleman deceased the promised reward for his services as courier, Israel concluded that he might justly use the money for his own. To which opinion surely no charitable judge will demur. Besides, what should he do with the purse, if not use it for his own? It would have been insane to have returned it to the relations. Such mysterious honesty would have but resulted in his arrest as a rebel, or rascal. (p. 78)

Melville seems to suggest that in stumbling upon Trumbull's book he has appropriated something, a literary property, that it would be "insane" to surrender. Perhaps he too felt that, like the original Potter, he "had not received . . . the promised reward for his services" in the literary market and that "he might justly use the money for his own." To respect Trumbull's authorship would be "mysterious honesty" indeed.

In many other ways – as a picture of rootless American identity, of American freedom turned to piracy, of a certain kind of American slavery – *Israel Potter* seems a striking and unsettling book.[2] Too often dismissed as a minor work, it reflects ironically on the issues of literary authority and textual piracy that plagued Melville's career. In its representation of America as a wandering Israel, it also takes up Ishmael's wandering spirit and foreshadows the peregrinations of the later Confidence Man and Clarel's pilgrim band. Its "latitudinarian notions" directly challenge the pious and patriotic self-image of mid-nineteenth-century America.

Borrowing and Lending in
The Confidence-Man: His Masquerade

The Confidence-Man, too, displays latitudinarian notions, subversive ideas coming not from a sailor-patriot but from someone more like the Benjamin Franklin of *Israel Potter*, a subtle "Machiavelli in tents" (*IP* 46). Melville's Confidence Man, also called "an impoverished Machiavelli," seems to assume many different forms, tricksters of one kind or another, who operate on a Mississippi River steamboat, bilking credulous travelers out of their cash, their faith, and their security. One of the victims, a Missourian named Pitch, muses on this unaccountable character:

> Was the man a trickster, it must be more for the love than the lucre. Two or three dirty dollars the motive to so many nice wiles? And yet how full of mean needs his seeming. Before his mental vision the person of that threadbare Talleyrand, that impoverished Machiavelli, that seedy Rosicrucian – or something of all these he vaguely deems him – passes now in puzzled review. . . . Analogically, he couples the slanting cut of the equivocator's coattails with the sinister cast in his eye; he weighs slyboot's sleek speech in the light imparted by the oblique import of the smooth slope of his worn boot-heels; the insinuator's undulating flunky-isms dovetail into those of the flunky beast that windeth his way on his belly. (p. 23)

Pitch sees the Confidence Man as a devil whose equivocal coattails and sly boots convey the full extent of his wickedness. At the same time he is attracted to his smooth-tongued proposals and air of liberal geniality. In this book Melville captures the allure of the seducer, just such a cosmopolitan, one supposes, as Agatha's husband Robertson might have been.

The Confidence-Man is perhaps the most puzzling of Melville's novels, one that has eluded readers and critics since its publication in 1857. Early readers saw it as an improvement over *Pierre*, a work of speculation and philosophy like *Mardi* and *Moby-Dick*, but not as entertaining as Melville's early sea-adventure novels. Based in part on Melville's journey with E. J. M. Fly to Galena in 1840, the story takes place on a Mississippi steamboat named the *Fidèle*. It is filled with crowds of passengers, "a piebald parliament, an Anacharsis Cloots congress of all kinds of that multiform species, man" – and woman too (p. 9). Early in the narrative, Black Guinea, "a grotesque negro cripple" (p. 10), entertains the passengers and begs for coins. When a skeptic in the crowd challenges his authenticity, he calls on various "ge'mmen" who can vouch for him:

> "Oh yes, oh yes, dar is aboard here a werry nice, good ge'mman wid a weed, and a ge'mman in a gray coat and white tie, what knows all about me; and a ge'mman wid a big book, too; and a yarb-doctor; and a ge'mman in a yaller west; and a ge'mman wid a brass plate; and a ge'mman in a wiolet robe; and a ge'mman as is a sodjer; and ever so many good, kind, honest ge'mmen more aboard what knows me and will speak for me, God bress 'em; yes, and what knows me as well as dis poor old darkie knows hisself, God bress him! Oh, find 'em, find 'em," he earnestly added, "and let 'em come quick, and show you all, ge'mmen, dat dis poor ole darkie is werry well wordy of all you kind ge'mmen's kind confidence." (p. 13)

After Black Guinea departs, the "man with a weed," a Mr. Roberts recently widowed, does indeed speak for the cripple, before turning to his new acquaintance and asking for his sympathy and some money. It would seem, then, that the various "ge'mmen" in the book are working together to cheat the public in different ways.

Indeed, as the novel progresses, a number of the gentlemen on Black Guinea's list appear, though never together, and ask various passengers for confidence, cash, or assistance. In some of these encounters, the confidence man works a classic game, duping some credulous fool out of his or her money. But as the novel proceeds, the cons become more subtle. A herb doctor, for example, promises health to a dying miser; a "ge-mman wid a brass plate" bearing the initials PIO (for "Philosophical Intelligence Office," a kind of meta-physical employment agency) tries to persuade the misanthropic Missourian Pitch to hire a young orphan boy; and finally a new kind of confidence man appears, a man who calls himself the Cosmopolitan and wears a coat of many colors. Rather than punish people for being fools, the Cosmopolitan seems to expose those who lack faith in human benevolence. A genial sort who loves to drink and talk, the Cosmopolitan admonishes first Pitch and then a series of other inter-locutors, two of whom seem based on Emerson and Thoreau, for being manhaters and cynics. At the end, the Cosmopolitan persuades a barber, William Cream, who has put up a sign outside his shop saying "NO TRUST," to give him a free shave. He then moves off into the darkness, helpfully leading a feeble old man who has decided to buy a money belt from a young scamp, who may or may not be acting in league with the Cosmopolitan, who may or may not be a devil. Casting any certainties to the winds in the final lines, Melville ends ambiguously: "Something further may follow of this Masquerade" (p. 251).

Along with the oddities of the plot, which requires us to accept a certain supernatural agency in the confidence man of many guises, the novel includes a number of other unsettling elements. It contains, first, several interpolated narratives that take up different varieties of human infidelity: sexual betrayal (the story of Goneril), murder and racism (John Moredock the Indian-hater), loss of friends and sanity (the gentleman-madman), and loss of friends and money (the story of China Aster). These build on the novel's themes but also interrupt its loosely episodic plot in complicating ways. Second, it also stops at three chapter-length points to comment on the author's making of the story and characters, and halts at other moments to reflect on the meaning of events. These interruptions have led critics to emphasize the novel's deconstructive impulses, as it seems to undo whatever premises it sets up, to suggest and then derail its various literary modes: comedy, satire, allegory, pilgrims' progress, or mystery play. Few readers can agree on a central theme or meaning for *The Confidence-Man*, and although it has aroused increasing respect and enthusiasm since the mid-twentieth century, it remains one of the lesser-known and lesser-read of Melville's works.

As a meditation on borrowing, however, it offers a "leaf from his professional experience" in more ways than one. Melville borrowed heavily from family friends to meet payments on loans he had taken out on his home, Arrowhead. His literary efforts owed a great deal to his ability to borrow from authors like Delano and Trumbull as well. Hence he might well identify with a character like the confidence man who makes his way in the world by telling stories and asking listeners to give him money in return. In a significant development about halfway through the novel, the confidence man becomes a Cosmopolitan who asks, not for a payment, like the herb doctor who hawks his wares, or a donation, like the solicitors of charity, but for a loan. In an extended experiment, he tries to show a character, Charlie Noble, how friends should lend freely to friends in need. Charlie Noble, who appears to be a confidence man himself, trying to wheedle the wealthy Cosmopolitan Frank Goodman by playing a kindly friend, undergoes a "metamorphosis more surprising than any in Ovid" when Frank tells him, " 'I am in want, urgent want, of money' " (p. 178). Charlie tells him to "go to the devil" (p. 179) until Frank displays a pocketful of gold coins and conjures him to return to his own ways. The Cosmopolitan then tells the story of Charlemont, a "gentleman-madman" who, like Jimmy Rose, withdraws from society when his fortune disappears and returns only when he has regained it, knowing that with no money he has no friends.

In another conversation with Egmont, the Thoreau-like disciple of the Emerson-like Mark Winsome, the Cosmopolitan once again uses a request for money to test the power of friendship. Here Egmont refuses the loan, saying, "I will transact no business with a friend" (p. 202). By way of illustration, Egmont tells a story, this one about China Aster, a poor man who borrows unwisely from the silken-tongued Orchis and then finds himself increasingly burdened with debt until he dies an ignominious death. His father's elderly friends, Old Plain Talk and Old Prudence, like Job's advisors, offer no consolation but instead consider their dire warnings vindicated by this outcome. The Cosmopolitan declares himself unsatisfied with this picture of humanity – " 'Enough. I have had my fill of the philosophy of Mark Winsome as put into action' " (p. 223) – and he dismisses Egmont, giving him a shilling. The elaborate charade of asking for a loan ends, then, with the Cosmopolitan giving money away.

This series of meditations on borrowing and lending reflects bitterly, perhaps, on Melville's own pecuniary distress, but it speaks cogently to his professional necessity. From the beginning of his career, Melville borrowed from other authors; at a certain stage in most of his early novels, he paused in spinning yarns and began weaving and splicing other people's texts into his own. Taking a leaf from his professional experience often required his taking a leaf from other books. In *The Confidence-Man*, he intriguingly constructs two kinds of writer. One, like the early confidence man, simply asks for the money outright. To be a professional writer, this model seems to suggest, is to sell one's stories or, viewed in a grimmer light, to ask for charity. The Cosmopolitan, though, is a borrower and as such invites the reader's greater investment in the literary transaction. The reader will not simply buy the story but will lend himself to the narrative until the original debt, the author's, is paid off. This charitable loan redeems the taint of literary borrowing (or, it may be, theft), while implicating the reader in the author's latitudinarian actions. Melville is asking for considerable latitude from his readers indeed.

He gives himself the latitude he needs by distinguishing subtly between borrowing and lending. The borrower acts from distress and perhaps shadier motives. The lender, however, can choose whether to give a loan or not, and in so doing can also decide whether to act in the spirit of friendship – a "friendly loan" – or in the cooler spirit of business. The lender can also decide how much interest to charge and what to accept as security. As the Cosmopolitan and Egmont negotiate their terms, Melville explores the many meanings of loan, interest, and security, playing off the business view of such transactions against a more charitable or literary one.

Ironically, in the end, the putative lender, Egmont, borrows the story of China Aster to make his point.

"I will tell you about China Aster. I wish I could do so in my own words, but unhappily the original storyteller here has so tyrannized over me, that it is quite impossible for me to repeat his incidents without sliding into his style. I forewarn you of this, that you may not think me so maudlin as, in some parts, the story would seem to make its narrator. It is too bad that any intellect, especially in so small a matter, should have such power to impose itself upon another, against its best exerted will, too. However, it is satisfaction to know that the main moral to which all tends, I fully approve. But, to begin." (p. 207)

Since Egmont cannot tell the story in his own words, he borrows those of the original storyteller. As he imposes his will and the story on his importunate friend the Cosmopolitan, however, he finds himself "tyrannized" over by the borrowed story. In a final twist, the tale of China Aster, a version of the *povertiresque* which Melville had so fully explored elsewhere, brings Egmont to a "main moral" which he can "fully approve." But he seems to have missed the meaning of the story he has borrowed, and like the narrators of Melville's *povertiresques*, he contemplates China Aster's poverty, which he has imaginatively created, without understanding it.

The Cosmopolitan is one of the most latitudinarian of Melville's characters, a man who travels widely, shifts shapes at will, and performs subtle varieties of magic. He and the text he represents impose themselves forcefully upon readers, asking for their confidence but also for the loan of time, money, and interest that a narrative demands. Writing this novel may have allowed Melville to experiment with considerable latitude, to borrow heavily on his readers' sympathies and patience. In the end, however, it may also have sickened him, as the persistent requests for loans seem to have sickened the Cosmopolitan. After finishing the book he decided, like Bartleby, that he would do no more writing for the present. And when he next took up his pen, he had stopped trading in fiction. Poetry would be next to follow from his Masquerade.

PART V

Melville's Later Career

CHAPTER 9

"Fulness & Veins & Beauty": *Battle-Pieces* and *Clarel*

Although Melville's Confidence Man is an inveterate borrower, seeming to depend on the support of others, the barber William Cream and his friends also see him as standing alone, "quite an original." In a chapter devoted to explaining this concept, Melville wryly distinguishes the "original" character from the merely odd one:

> As for original characters in fiction, a grateful reader will, on meeting with one, keep the anniversary of that day. True, we sometimes hear of an author who, at one creation, produces some two or three score such characters; it may be possible. But they can hardly be original in the sense that Hamlet is, or Don Quixote, or Milton's Satan. That is to say, they are not, in a thorough sense, original at all. They are novel, or singular, or striking, or captivating, or all four at once. (p. 238)

By "original," Melville means something more than "unique." He also has in mind the meaning of original "genius," as a spirit that originates or creates: "the original character, essentially such, is like a revolving Drummond light, raying away from itself all round it – everything is lit by it, everything starts up to it (mark how it is with Hamlet), so that, in certain minds, there follows upon the adequate conception of such a character, an effect, in its way, akin to that which in Genesis attends upon the beginning of things" (p. 239).

Although Melville may be speaking of literary characters in this chapter, he also reveals an interest in his own work as original author. This concern with originality seems a throwback to the romantic spirit of *Mardi* and *Moby-Dick*, where he aimed overtly and ambitiously to "create the creative." In later works, he seemed to jettison *ab ovo* originality in favor of inventive borrowing from, or even bold piracy of, other authors' texts. But Melville may be thinking of "original" in another sense here, suggesting what would be new and original for *him*. Two of the works he mentions, *Hamlet* (mostly) and *Paradise Lost*, are written in verse. For Melville, to be original might require him to become a poet. He had been reading and thinking about poets and poetry for some time; we might read this passage as announcing his decision to move in a new and unexpected direction that owed little to his earlier fiction-writing and would thus seem to his readers highly fresh and original.

Melville apparently took up the challenge of poetic originality in the years following his last published novel. He had written and published fiction for slightly over a decade (from *Typee* in 1846 to *The Confidence-Man* in 1857). He would devote himself next to a longed-for journey to Europe, Egypt, and the Holy Land, spend three winters giving lecture tours (1857–60), and then write poetry for the rest of his life: publishing poems over two dozen years, writing them, most likely, for over three decades. During that time his country was riven by civil war, he took a job in the New York Custom Office, his family foundered heavily amid its troubles and witnessed the deaths of two sons, and he moved into seemingly unbearable isolation.

But in spite of the considerable stresses of the second half of Melville's life, one important change may have proved a great relief. He had until 1857 been a professional: sailor first and writer second. After *The Confidence-Man* he had a job, in the Custom House, but he gradually ceased professional authorship. His writing increasingly became a private activity, pursued around the edges of other kinds of labor and supported, eventually, not by trade publication but by private presses and familial subventions. In a sense he became like the poets he admired, Shakespeare, Milton, and others, a recipient of patronage and hence, ironically, free from the demands of the market. For his "patrons" – Peter Gansevoort, Lemuel Shaw, his own wife – did not censor his writing, and his small and shrinking band of readers did not review his work. So, most remarkably, Melville no longer needed to borrow. His financial indebtedness lessened because of his job, and eventually family legacies freed him from the obligation to work for a salary. Freed as well from the pressure to write for publication, he seldom borrowed from literary sources either, at least not in the ways he had formerly done. He could be, himself, an original, and he chose to be an original poet.

Melville's poetry was not, of course, entirely original, and scholars have shown how thoroughly he studied other poets, especially Milton and Matthew Arnold, in honing his own technique.[1] We have also seen that the poetic impulse was not new for Melville in his later career. It had showed itself early in his writing, in the lyrical passages of his novels and in poems interpolated into them. Strikingly too, in the "Agatha" correspondence, Melville makes note of the story's "poetic reference," its significant symbols and lyrical possibilities. Although calling it a "regular story founded upon striking incidents," he also begs Hawthorne to consider that, "You have a skeleton of actual reality to build about with fulness & veins & beauty." As we have seen, the lyrical "fulness & veins & beauty" captured his imagination as compellingly as the "skeleton of actual reality."

The poems that occupied Melville's last thirty years show as much range and originality as his fiction, if not more. His first collection, *Battle-Pieces and Aspects of the War* (1866), commemorates the actors and cataclysmic events of the Civil War. *Clarel: A Poem and a Pilgrimage* (1876), a narrative poem based on his travels around and beyond Jerusalem, takes up the debates over world religions, faith and doubt, theology and science, that proved as divisive to American culture as the Civil War. His later collections included a variety of concerns: memories of long-gone sailors and scenes of the sea in *John Marr and Other Sailors* (1888), classical and aesthetic themes inspired by his travels in *Timoleon* (1891), and meditations on art and mortality in the unpublished "Weeds and Wildings, Chiefly: With a Rose or Two." He also wrote a number of uncollected lyrics, which he may have been revising and considering for publication right up to his death in 1891. Melville's devotion to writing poetry was entire and remarkable. As he noted of *Clarel*, it was "eminently adapted for unpopularity" (*L* 483). Yet, in spite of small editions and few sales, Melville persisted single-mindedly in his craft.

As Melville's poetry has become more significant to scholars and admirers of his other work, it has aroused tremendous respect, as well as controversy. Some critics have boldly begun to speak of him as a poet who wrote some prose, as a fit companion to Emily Dickinson and Walt Whitman, and as a radical innovator in metrics and style.[2] His poetic output has been seen both as a marked departure from his prose works and also as revealing certain thematic and stylistic continuities. It is certainly the area of his literary production about which there remains the least knowledge or consensus. For our purposes, the poetry should remind us, as Melville hinted in *Billy Budd*, that he is still, in a sense, "a writer whom few know" (p. 114).

"This Melancholy Monument": *Battle-Pieces and Aspects of the War*

Melville announces a straightforward aim in *Battle-Pieces*: to do justice to the Civil War as it would be remembered, not just by the historians, but by ordinary people on both sides who fought in it or witnessed it from a distance. His commitment to remembering the war and those who fought and died arises from the natural grief of survivors, and many of the poems are elegies. At the same time, he wanted to avoid political resentment and partiality. In the prose "Supplement" that follows the poems, he pleaded for moderation and especially for Northern patience with the South's bitterness. The task of memory, he suggests, is to refrain from taking sides, and thus in his preface he describes a method of listening to all points of view, one that would ensure fairness and moderation:

> The aspects which the strife as a memory assumes are as manifold as are the moods of involuntary meditation – moods variable, and at times widely at variance. Yielding instinctively, one after another, to feelings not inspired from any one source exclusively, and unmindful, without purposing to be, of consistency, I seem, in most of these verses, to have but placed a harp in a window, and noted the contrasted airs which wayward winds have played upon the strings. (p. 52)

Adopting the Romantic image of the Aeolian harp, Melville presents himself as a passive instrument of poetic memory, but his allusion to Coleridge is deceptively aesthetic; it carries a forceful political point as well. For he seems to say that speaking for the American nation requires not finding the one voice – and political persuasion – which will unify a shattered people but rather striking many notes, touching "moods variable, and at times widely at variance."

Melville has been criticized for the moderation, even conservatism, of his racial and political views expressed in the "Supplement," where he argues that, as much as the freed slaves deserve "the sympathies of every humane nature," the defeated Southerners deserve them even more: "such kindliness should not be allowed to exclude kindliness to communities who stand nearer to us in nature" (p. 184). But in making himself an Aeolian harp, recording the moods of the many minds affected by the war rather than a single and identifiable ideological position, Melville may have aimed for an inclusive politics and poetics of memory that he did not see elsewhere in the poetry and prose of the war.

We get some sense of what this poetics of memory meant to him in his description of the wrecked ship in the "Agatha" letter.

> This in course of time becomes embedded in the sand – after the lapse of some years showing nothing but the sturdy stem (or, prow-bone) projecting some two feet at low water. All the rest is filled & packed down with the sand. – So that after her husband has disappeared the sad Agatha every day sees this melancholy monument, with all its remindings.

The ship becomes a powerful image of the past, "with all its remindings," something that Agatha returns to again and again in different moods. But no official has raised this "melancholy monument" to the departed Robertson; it is something created by time and nature in the space between the significant object – the ship – and Agatha's abiding grief. In addition, it remains a physical and visual symbol, something that wordlessly embraces multiple meanings. So too with Melville's Civil War poems. As much as possible, he uses language to create the effect of a wordless monument of the wrecked ship of state, one that mobilizes feeling and gives a site for grief and memory, without identifying itself divisively with one individual meaning.[3] Poetry works to undo partisan rhetoric in *Battle-Pieces*.

This is not to suggest that the poems are aesthetic objects remote from the realities of the war. Melville read lengthy accounts of the different battles published in *The Rebellion Record* and included in his poems names, dates, and tributes to individual heroes and battles.[4] He also made no secret of his sympathy with the Union cause and his conviction that the Southerners were "zealots of the Wrong" (p. 97). But by reminding readers of a larger perspective within which the war can be remembered, he distances political rhetoric and focuses on immediate impressions. The reader we might imagine as an Agatha, daily passing the melancholy monuments of massive sorrow. The poems seem intended to respond to individual grief and, over time, to sink into the reader's consciousness as Robertson's ship eventually sinks into the sand.

Melville structured the collection in part thematically and in part chronologically. It opens with a brief series that introduces general feelings of foreboding in the early days of the war ("The Portent," "Misgivings," "The Conflict of Convictions," and "Apathy and Enthusiasm"). Forty-eight poems then follow the progress of the conflict through various battles, from the perspective of officers and ordinary soldiers, living and dead, witnesses in America and abroad. A final section, "Verses Inscriptive and Memorial," includes sixteen brief poems commemorating different dead soldiers and leaders. It concludes somewhat unexpectedly with two long narrative poems. "The Scout Toward Aldie," based in part on an expedition that Melville joined while on a trip to Washington during the war, tells the story of a Northern party sent out to find Mosby, a Southern resistance fighter, and his men.[5] Mosby is an outlaw and trickster who ensnares a brave but credulous Colonel and kills him. This long poem explores the hostile landscape of the South as a kind of Gothic nightmare world filled with duplicitous spies, lurking terrors, even mysterious women. Mosby escapes, and the poem ends somberly at the Colonel's graveside, with a statement about the inadequacy of poetic remembrance:

> Now halt the verse, and turn aside –
>   The cypress falls athwart the way;
> No joy remains for bard to sing;
> And heaviest dole of all is this,
>   That other hearts shall be as gay
>   As hers that now no more shall spring:
>   To Mosby-land the dirges cling. (p. 163)

Standing among other poems that mark the Union victory, this mournful reminder of a land of Mosbys, where dangers still lurk in the wake of the North's withdrawal, sounds a quiet, joyless note. The second narrative poem, "Lee in the Capitol," adopts a similarly somber tone, telling the story of Robert E. Lee's appearance before Congress and his plea, as in Melville's Supplement, for forbearance: "Push not your triumph; do not urge / Submissiveness beyond the verge" (p. 167). The section ends with "A Meditation," a Northerner's reflections on the courage exhibited on both sides of the war. With "Lee in the Capitol," "A Meditation" leads logically to the prose "Supplement," where Melville underlines the message of restraint and fraternal generosity.

The *Battle-Pieces* are primarily ballads, written often in stanzas with rhymes and meters that, though regular, often produce jarring and unexpected effects. Melville seems to exploit the reader's expectations of a patriotic song, that it will celebrate the victors and condemn the losers, but instead poetic form often tells a different story. For example, in the opening poem, "The Portent" (quoted here in full), brief, simple lines mimic the rhythms of hymns, but the mournful exclamation points, odd rhymes and assonances, dramatic breaks, and violent imagery undercut the consoling power of the hymn:

> Hanging from the beam,
>   Slowly swaying (such the law),
> Gaunt the shadow on your green –
>   Shenandoah!
> The cut is on the crown
> (Lo, John Brown),
> And the stabs shall heal no more.
>
> Hidden in the cap
>   Is the anguish none can draw,
> So your future veils its face,
>   Shenandoah!
> But the streaming beard is shown
> (Weird John Brown),
> The meteor of the war. (p. 53)

In this beautiful lament, the "cuts" and "stabs" on John Brown's body seem to break the poem in half and the stanzas into pieces. Yet rather than displaying what lies within the ruptured body, the cuts and breaks reveal only a further "veil" over it. And the beard that veils Brown's face becomes an ambiguous symbol of what might emerge from his death: a meteor, a portent of future catastrophe. As in the rhymed prophecies of *Macbeth*'s "weird" sisters, the poem uses enigmatic rhymes and ponderous rhythms to prophesy a hidden and ominous future.

In another example of unexpected auditory effects, "The March to the Sea," Melville's lines swing to the upbeat tempo of Sherman's triumphal progress:

> Not Kenesaw high-arching,
>   Nor Allatoona's glen –
> Though there the graves lie parching –
>   Stayed Sherman's miles of men;
> From charred Atlanta marching
>   They launched the sword again.
>   The columns streamed like rivers
>   Which in their course agree,
>   And they streamed until their flashing
>   Met the flashing of the sea:
>   It was glorious glad marching,
>   That marching to the sea. (pp. 115–16)

By the end of the poem, however, the rhythms of "glad marching" sustain a bitter dirge:

> For behind they left a wailing,
>   A terror and a ban,
> And blazing cinders sailing,
>   And houseless households wan,
> Wide zones of counties paling,
>   And towns where maniacs ran.
>   Was it Treason's retribution –
>   Necessity the plea?
>   They will long remember Sherman
>   And his streaming columns free –
>   They will long remember Sherman
>   Marching to the sea. (p. 118)

The oddities and varieties of verse forms throughout the collection advertise a poetic point of view that is similarly askew or, to use Emily Dickinson's word, "slant." Although Melville works directly from historical records and aims for completeness and accuracy, he reports events from peculiar angles, noting perspectives that the official records have missed. So, for example, in "The Old Stone Fleet," when describing the effect of scuttling a number of old ships to block the entrance to a harbor, he writes as an "old sailor," almost from the point of view of the ships themselves:

> I have a feeling for those ships,
>   Each worn and ancient one,
> With great bluff bows, and broad in the beam:
>   Ay, it was unkindly done.
>   But so they serve the Obsolete –
>   Even so, Stone Fleet! (p. 62)

A similar nostalgia for the wooden fleets that have given way to the ironclads infuses other ship poems. In "In the Turret," "The Temeraire," and "A Utilitarian View of the Monitor's Fight," his focus on the ships as much as the people fighting in them lifts the conflict out of a battle between opposed sides and reminds readers of the conflict between old and new styles of warfare (a theme he returns to in *Billy Budd*).

Other poems adopt equally disconcerting points of view. The speaker of "Battle of Stone River, Tennessee: A View from Oxford Cloisters," an Englishman, compares America's sectional conflict to the Wars of the Roses; Melville's choice of an unexpected, outside perspective is unsettling. The voice of "The House-Top: A Night Piece," which takes place during the New York City Draft Riots of 1863, comes from someone distanced from the action both physically (seeing the riots from the house-top at night) and socially (viewing the primarily Irish rioters as "rats – ship-rats / And rats of the wharves" [p. 94]). The speaker's distance makes it possible for him to condemn the rioters and praise the police, but at the same time he calls disciplinary efforts "cynic tyrannies," thus suggesting a further distance from the municipal officials as well as the unruly mob. A poem on the siege of Charleston, "The Swamp Angel," looks at the city from the mouth of a cannon (the "Swamp Angel" of the title), which Melville describes as a "coal-black Angel / With a thick Afric lip" (p. 105). The speaker associates the cannon both with the slaves who escaped into the swamp and with Northern power battering against the city. The effect is to suggest, in one sense, an uneasy alliance between Southern slaves and Northern soldiers, and in another to make the siege seem horribly menacing and unnatural: "The Swamp Angel broods in his gloom" (p. 105).

Melville's habit of viewing the war's battles from alien and unsettling perspectives registers in subtle ways the shock and impact of horrific events. In another disconcerting tactic, he describes the fallen dead in scenes where no human might logically view them.[6] In "Shiloh: A Requiem," for example (quoted here in full), the men lie on the field, their bodies mingled in the fellowship of "dying foemen," with only the birds to witness their fall:

> Skimming lightly, wheeling still,
>   The swallows fly low
> Over the field in clouded days,
>   The forest-field of Shiloh –
> Over the field where April rain
> Solaced the parched one, stretched in pain
> Through the pause of night
> That followed the Sunday fight
>   Around the church of Shiloh –
> The church so lone, the log-built one,
> That echoed to many a parting groan
>   And natural prayer
>   Of dying foemen mingled there –
> Foemen at morn, but friends at eve –
>   Fame or country least their care:
> (What like a bullet can undeceive!)
>   But now they lie low,
> While over them the swallows skim
>   And all is hushed at Shiloh. (pp. 81–2)

In the aftermath of unspeakable horror, the swallows can provide no comfort, and the suggestion of human community implied by the reference to the church (and to requiem) offers no consolation either. Even more disconcertingly, the bodies lie in indiscriminate disorder, so that the rationale for the battle has been fatally undermined: "Foemen at morn, but friends at eve." The men, who have surrendered their concern about "fame or country," seem to have lost all comforting myths: "What like a bullet can undeceive!" What, then, might a mourner say? In this scene, mourners, who cannot know what the dead know, do not belong. Only the swallows can be present at such a vista of carnage and the terrible knowledge that it brings. At moments like this, Melville reminds the reader of Ahab's conviction of the "malignity of the sea," the indifference of nature.

A similarly foreboding spirit presides over "The Armies of the Wilderness," where Melville claims that "None can narrate that strife in the pines, / A seal is on it – Sabaean lore!" (p. 104). The battlefield is a place only for the dead, who form a grisly, almost domestic community:

> In glades they meet skull after skull
>   Where pine-cones lay – the rusted gun,
> Green shoes full of bones, the mouldering coat
>   And cuddled-up skeleton; (p. 102)

Here men die alone, out of sight of their fellows and of any priest or other sign of human fellowship:

> Pursuer and pursued like ghosts disappear
>   In gloomed shade – their end who shall tell?
> The crippled, a ragged-barked stick for a crutch,
>   Limp to some elfin dell –
> Hobble from the sight of dead faces – white
>   As pebbles in a well.
>
> *Few burial rites shall be;*
>   *No priest with book and band*
> *Shall come to the secret place*
>   *Of the corpse in the foeman's land.* (p. 103)

The task for the commemorative poet, then, is fatally complicated. He must write what is unspoken and unspeakable. The poem "An Uninscribed Monument" speaks from the point of view of just such a paradoxical memorial:

> Silence and Solitude may hint
>   (Whose home is in yon piney wood)
> What I, though tableted, could never tell –
> The din which here befell,
>   The striving of the multitude.
> The iron cones and spheres of death
>   Set round me in their rust,
>   These, too, if just,
> Shall speak with more than animated breath
>   Thou who beholdest, if thy thought,

Not narrowed down to personal cheer,
Take in the import of the quiet here –
  The after-quiet – the calm full fraught;
Thou too wilt silent stand –
Silent as I, and lonesome as the land. (pp. 136–7)

This poem argues that the only suitable memorial is a silent one, even though the "tablet" has witnessed the war. Ironically, the story may get told in the meaningless "din" of battle, but its truer "import" emerges in the silence after conflict. The poem, however, imposes silence on the viewer, who may be the author visiting the scene, or the reader viewing it vicariously through the poem. In either case, the voice of the monument cancels out the voice of the poet, even as the poem gives speech to an uninscribed stone. These paradoxes hold the poet to an impossible task – both to tell and to be silent – and also hold him in inevitable solitude: "lonesome as the land."

Although many of the *Battle-Pieces*, like the poems mentioned above, meditate quietly on death and grief, others concern heroic action by magnificent (and controversial) leaders like Grant, McClellan, Lincoln, Sherman, Sheridan, Jackson, and Lee. One can chart the development of the war through the topical references in the poems to achieve a kind of blow-by-blow history. Melville's more remarkable achievement, however, may be the way his poems reflect on the means and media by which that history gets told. "Donelson" recreates a long, bloody winter siege by showing how the news gets read in local newspapers at some distance from the battle. Imitating the language of the newspapers, with headlines and journalistic commonplaces, Melville mimics the excruciating effect of getting the news in irregular dispatches: "About the bulletin-board a band / Of eager, anxious people met, / And every wakeful heart was set / On latest news from West or South" (pp. 63–4). The poem is deliberately long and detailed, showing villagers reading reports in real time and reacting with sickening emotional dips and shifts. When the battle turns, giant headlines take over the poem:

GLORIOUS VICTORY OF THE FLEET!

FRIDAY'S GREAT EVENT!

THE ENEMY'S WATER-BATTERIES BEAT!

WE SILENCED EVERY GUN!

THE OLD COMMODORE'S COMPLIMENTS SENT

PLUMP INTO DONELSON! (p. 68)

The story is not over, however. The lengthy report must follow, then the news of "VICTORY!" and finally another event: the anxious waiting until families receive the death list. The agony of *reading* about the battle substitutes for the soldiers' suffering and produces the poem's exhausted conclusion:

> Ah God! may Time with happy haste
>   Bring wail and triumph to a waste,
>   And war be done;
>   The battle flag-staff fall athwart
>   The curs'd ravine, and wither; naught
>   Be left of trench or gun;
>   The bastion, let it ebb away,
>   Washed with the river bed; and Day
>   In vain seek Donelson. (p. 76)

Melville shows considerable interest in the different media of war throughout *Battle-Pieces*. Hence one poem explores photography – "On the Photograph of a Corps Commander" – and two examine paintings – "The Coming Storm" and " 'Formerly a Slave' " – as ways to capture the effects of the war suggestively. As we have seen, cannon mouths or uninscribed monuments become unwitting media too. Melville seems uncommonly alert to the way information circulates through the theater of war and emerges in unexpected forms.

Battle-Pieces reflects Melville's discoveries of new lyric potentialities as much as it reveals his attitudes to the war. Although its lukewarm reception might have led him to doubt his future as a poet, he must have found its composition tremendously rewarding. In spite of its seeming failure, not to mention frustrations in his marriage and the death of his son Malcolm, he turned to a decade of steady writing of a poem such as he had never seen in America before: a religious epic, his *Clarel*.

"Liberal Play": *Clarel: A Poem and a Pilgrimage*

Battle-Pieces in many ways concerns what cannot be said about war. Although Melville represents such explicit texts as newspapers and reports, as well as implicitly written histories, laws, and constitutions, he often meditates on how poetry must somehow say the unsayable, speak of an unspeakable grief, and make utterance the province of ordinary people, rather than of cultural texts or large political entities with abstract ideologies. *Clarel*, on the other hand, keeps large texts and utterances centrally in view. In particular, it focuses obsessively on sacred texts, testing their age-old meanings against the experience of modern travelers in the Holy Land. By addressing the central question of what holy texts mean to contemporary nineteenth-century readers, Melville also asks what any text, including his own novels and poems, can mean and how it means. His poem is an epic consideration of the Book, understood as religious bible, or alternatively as archive of a culture's thoughts, words, and traditions in print. " 'The books, the books not all have told' " (1.1: 83), says the young theological student, Clarel, in the poem's opening lines.

Melville based *Clarel* on his own journey to Jerusalem and its environs in 1857, on a lengthy study of poets and philosophers who matched his skeptical mood, and on the extended period of reflection that followed his intense career as novelist, the Civil War, and the loss of Malcolm. What faith, what consolation could fill the void left by these troubling events? No holy book, it would seem, could address the depths of the nation's suffering and his own. At an earlier stage of his career, he could have his authorial characters Ishmael and Pierre speak of writing new gospels, even if he mocked such hubris. Now he might well wonder how apostles in an earlier age and ordinary humans in his own could write at all. But he tried anyway, and he chose verse – not just verse but five hundred pages of narrative verse.

Clarel is written in iambic tetrameter lines, with a varying rhyme scheme – some couplets, others alternating rhymes, some more irregular. The volume is divided into four parts, identified by geographical locations: "Jerusalem" (where Clarel travels alone and then meets other travelers with whom he will take a three-day trip outside the city), "The Wilderness" (where the so-called pilgrims journey through Jericho to the Dead Sea), "Mar Saba" (continuing through the desert to a monastery at Mar Saba), and "Bethlehem" (ending in a return to Jerusalem). Each part contains from thirty to forty-odd cantos of varying lengths, divided not so much into stanzas as into verse paragraphs. The poem tells a narrative of Clarel's journey, as he meets in Jerusalem the family of Nathan, an American converted to Zionism, and falls in love with Nathan's daughter Ruth; Nathan is murdered, and so Ruth and her mother go into seclusion; Clarel, grieving for his lost love and also suffering from a crisis in faith, joins a group of other seekers; the pilgrim band engages in lengthy dialogues between characters who represent a variety of religious and philosophical positions – Rolfe the freethinker, Vine a Hawthorne-like aesthete, Derwent a liberal but limited Anglican, Nehemiah the saintly and literal reader of the Word, Margoth a geologist, Mortmain an embittered Swede, Ungar a Civil War veteran, Djalea a Druze guide, and others they meet along the way. Their travels bring them to Mar Saba, where the main characters contemplate a palm tree that, like the doubloon in *Moby-Dick*, seems endlessly symbolic; Clarel returns to Jerusalem no more certain about his faith than before but learns that Ruth is dead; and in the final scene, during an Easter procession winding its way along the Via Crucis, he disappears into the crowd, leaving the narrator to speculate that he may yet find salvation: "Emerge thou mayst from the last whelming sea / And prove that death but routs life to victory" (4.35: 33–4). Within the simple outlines of the story, Melville, as in his novels, includes a wide field of other authors, plots, and genres, while also introducing a number of individual stories that enliven the philosophical dialogue among the characters.

A central issue in *Clarel* for Melville is the debate over faith among believers and nonbelievers of all kinds. This debate is theological in nature, as adherents of different Christian, Jewish, Islamic, Greek, and other systems try out their ideas against the backdrop of a landscape that Melville describes as inhospitable to faith. At a typical moment, Clarel struggles to reconcile what he sees with what his studies have taught him. Looking through his window at the Mount of Olives, where Christ delivered the Sermon on the Mount, he cries:

> The nature and evangel clashed,
> Rather, a double mystery flashed.
> Olivet, Olivet do I see?
> The ideal upland, trod by Thee? (1.2: 136–9)

In this dusty and forbidding landscape, at sites crowded with annoying tourists, peddlers hawking their wares, and confused pilgrims, it seems impossible to believe that Christ ever lived and walked. The discussions that arise from and flow out of this central question, however, are not only theological but also social and cultural. *Clarel* provides a rich canvas of teeming human activity, within which people from every conceivable region, religious background, and racial and cultural identity converge at the world's most cosmopolitan city, lending it the diversity of their many voices and opinions. Such a vision of all humanity on display rises to a kind of rapture in the last canto, where Clarel watches the Easter procession: "As 'twere a frieze, behold the train!" (4.34: 26). Like *White-Jacket* and *Moby-Dick*, the book contains multitudes.

As much as it concerns a global range of religious and cultural identities living in sometimes contentious proximity with one another, *Clarel* also takes up another tension that preoccupied Melville throughout his career: between continuity and discontinuity, between a given text and the "liberal play" with which one might dance around it. That phrase appears in the "Agatha" correspondence, when Melville advises Hawthorne that he must interpret John Henry Clifford's reading of the character of Agatha's husband with some flexibility: "In estimating the character of Robinson Charity should be allowed a liberal play." The same wording also appears in *Clarel*, in 3.11 at the Mar Saba monastery, when the pilgrims meet a merchant from Lesbos, who festively sings and urges the company to drink. The Anglican minister Derwent contemplates his actions with some ambivalence:

> Derwent a little hung behind –
> Censorious not, nor disinclined,
> But with self-querying countenance,
> As if one of the cloth, perchance
> Due bound should set, observe degree
> In liberal play of social glee. (3.11: 121–6)

In both moments Melville pits a given text – Clifford's diary in one, religious strictures in another – against the "liberal play" of a creative, inventive, or festive imagination. In both, liberality may carry with it connotations of moral error, but it also releases the imagination into a freer zone.

The given text in *Clarel* is the Judeo-Christian Bible, a book that within its own covers carries on a dialogue between story and history, God's word and human interpretation, type and antitype, sacred writ and liberal play. On the one hand, the Bible is the work of many writers over centuries of human history. It belongs to more than one religion. It presents conflicting testimonies and discontinuous narratives. It is an archive, a repository, a motley collection. In another sense it is a single book written by God, and to a Christian believer, the diverse stories of the Old Testament resolve themselves into the single narrative of the New, with Judaic prophets preparing the way for one revealed Messiah. So, as we have seen in our consideration of gospel in *Moby-Dick* and *Pierre*, the Christian Bible is both a continuous narrative of the revelation of God's word and Christ's life and also a discontinuous cultural document that can be read in multiple directions and through varying lenses. It encourages both literal absorption and liberal play.

As a model for Melville's *Clarel*, the Bible works in different ways. On the one hand, it is the Word, a fixed text, the unquestioned record of faith, and the unyielding standard of religious creed and history. Nehemiah carries his Bible as a literal guidebook to Jerusalem. Clarel tests what he sees against what he has read. In contrast with the Bible as literal text, *Clarel*, might be seen as the liberal play of a secular author, the discontinuous counterpart to a rigorously unified and continuous narrative. At the same time, *Clarel* has a tight structure and contained narrative of its own. Although the dialogues carry the story off its track, the pilgrims remain on a predetermined physical and spiritual itinerary. Compared to *Clarel*, the Bible might seem a discontinuous text, one that can be read as open and fluid, not closed and fixed.

So – literal and liberal readings can take place with both the biblical text and Melville's poem. Melville, in making a reader aware of these textual concerns, opens up profound questions about why and what humans believe, about how they interpret central religious texts and literary traditions, and about how history influences what many see as eternal truths. These questions appear throughout *Clarel*, but perhaps the most striking example of literal and liberal readings appears in the poem's use of palm imagery, culminating in a striking series of cantos on an actual palm tree.

The image of the palm appears early in the poem and sets up the later cantos in intriguing ways. In the canto "Abdon," for example, Clarel reads a poem in which the "World" asks a "Palmer," or pilgrim, what he has brought from the Holy Land. The Palmer replies: "These palms I bring – from dust not free / Since dust and ashes both were trod by me" (1.2: 121–2). The palm leaves coated in dust and ash contrast with the "Sychem grapes" or "garlands" one might expect from the precincts of "Sharon's rose" (1.2: 110–15), but they seem apt emblems of a land of ashes, the desolate landscape of "Christ's tomb" (1.2: 120). They also serve, as Whitman's leaf of grass does, as emblems of poems, the lyrical gifts of this desert land. Clarel finds the image of palm first in a poem printed on cheap paper lining his trunk. Melville had joked in 1862, in a letter to his brother Thomas, that the poems he wrote before sailing with him to San Francisco had found their way into trunk linings too: "You will be pleased to learn that I have disposed of a lot of it [his "doggerel"] at a great bargain. In fact, a trunk-maker took the whole stock off my hands at ten cents the pound. So, when you buy a new trunk again, just peep at the lining & perhaps you may be rewarded by some glorious stanza stareing you in the face & claiming admiration" (*L* 377). The Palmer's poem stares Clarel in the face and reminds him of the kind of poetic leaf he might bring back from his journey.

Palm trees and palm leaves appear often in *Clarel* as an inescapable feature of the landscape in and around the city and as a reminder of the early European pilgrims, Templars, and crusaders who brought palm leaves back from Jerusalem as a sign that they had completed their pilgrimages. Melville also plays upon the association of Christ with the palm, on Palm Sunday (2.1), and he associates the tropics with the palm when he speaks of the Southern palm and Northern pine: "– the palm and pine / Meeting on the frontier line" (3.13: 116–17).[7] The palm imagery peaks in the cantos surrounding the Mar Saba palm. Here, as in "The Doubloon" in *Moby-Dick*, different characters read a particularly prominent and impressive palm according to their various lights. In severally recognizing its symbolic power, they testify to a central human habit of reverence that Melville seems to indicate is essential to both religious worship and thoughtful skepticism, or what Robert Milder has called "agnostic spirituality".[8]

As the pilgrims wander and lounge around the environs of the Mar Saba monastery, several find themselves attracted to the magnificent palm, high on a ledge, seeming to defy the barren desert landscape outside the monastery's walls. Vine sees it first and thinks of it as a remnant of Eden:

> "Witness to a watered land,
> Voucher of a vernal year –
> St. Saba's Palm, why there dost stand?
> Would'st thou win the desert here
> To dreams of Eden? Thy device
> Intimates a Paradise!" (3.26: 30–5)

Associating the Hebraic tree with a Hellenic one – "'Worshipped on Delos in the sea – / Apollo's Palm?'" (3.26: 41–2) – Vine wonders at the common roots of different religious archetypes. For him, the power of the archetype can be understood as aesthetic in its meaning:

> "Thou that pledgest heaven to me,
> Stem of beauty, shaft of light,
> Behold, thou hang'st suspended
> Over Kedron and the night!
> Shall come the fall? shall time disarm
> The grace, the glory of the Palm?" (3.26: 44–9)

Even if the palm should lose its grace and glory, should undergo a fall, Vine urges it to retain its beauty: "'But braid thy tresses – yet thou'rt fair'" (3.26: 55). Even if some force should plot its overthrow, the palm, he says, will "'Still bear thee like the Seraphim'" (3.26: 63).

Vine's aesthetic admiration of the palm seems powerful and genuine, but Melville plays it off against other views that suggest the anxious equivocations of Vine's love of beauty. Mortmain the cynic may not be able to see the beauty in the palm, but the intensity of his bitterness proves ironically to show more grasp of its significance than Vine's refined appreciation. Seeing the palm as a version of the Cross, Mortmain reflects bitterly that Christ's teachings have failed: "the true lore / Is impotent for earth" (3.28: 7–8). As a result, Christ's story "Me it makes a misanthrope" (3.28: 14). Nevertheless he turns to the palm hoping for a sign of salvation, in defiance of his despair:

> "Envoy, whose looks the pang assuage,
> Disclose thy heavenly embassage!
> That lily-rod which Gabriel bore
> To Mary, kneeling her before,
> Announcing a God, the mother she;
> That budded stalk from Paradise –

Like that thou shin'st in thy device:
And sway'st thou over here toward me –
Toward *me* can such a symbol sway!" (3.28: 56–64)

Comforted by the vision of the tree as a healing lily, Mortmain lapses into a trance and, as the pilgrims find the next day, dies, "With eyes still feeding on the Tree" (3.28: 96).

For Rolfe, the former sailor, world traveler, and agnostic, the palm arouses no such aesthetic or metaphysical passions. Instead it reminds him of his early visits to the Marquesas, and he wonders what has become of the island paradises he once enjoyed. Do they remain the abode of peace and plenty he once knew, with their siren song?

Remembering the Pacific islands' invitation to linger in Paradise, Rolfe wonders why he ever left their Edenic shores:

"But who so feels the stars annoy,
Upbraiding him, – how far astray! –
That he abjures the simple joy,
And hurries over the briny world away?
    "Renouncer! is it Adam's flight
Without compulsion or the sin?
And shall the vale avenge the slight
By haunting thee in hours thou yet shalt win?" (3.29: 72–9)

Could he be that Adam fleeing Paradise? And does the "vale" haunt him in revenge? Characteristically, Rolfe asks questions but has no answers.

Clarel is the palm's last visitor and the only one who sees the others and hence is aware that the palm may suggest different meanings to different interpreters.[9] He has just come from a disturbing encounter with a celibate monk who implicitly reproves his sensuality and love for a woman, Ruth. Clarel is drawn to the monk's purity but nevertheless feels compelled to ask why women may not enter the monastery grounds. By way of an elliptical answer, the monk opens his book to a page that records misogynistic views of biblical women and hopes for their eventual disappearance: "The rib restored to Adam's side / And man made whole, as man began" (3.30: 113–14). After the monk leaves, Clarel views the palm and notices Vine, to whom he had made an emotional "advance" earlier in the poem: "His glance / Rested on

Vine, his reveries flow / Recalling that repulsed advance" (3.30: 142–4). He wonders if desire for man can compete with love of woman: "Can be a bond / (Thought he) as David sings in strain / That dirges beauteous Jonathan / Passing love of woman fond?" (3.30: 149–52). As with Rolfe, his questions lead him only to further questions: "Can time teach? / Shall all these billows win the lull / And shallow on life's hardened beach?" (3.30: 154–6).

Without settling his uncertainties about sexuality and love, Clarel turns his questions about the palm's meaning to thoughts of Christ, the man of palms, with a renewed sense of his divine power:

> while anew,
> From chambers of his mind's review
> Emerged the saint, who with the Palm
> Shared heaven on earth in gracious calm,
> Even as his robe partook the hue. (3.31: 15–19)

He wonders if Christ would demand celibacy of him. Does love of God require sexual purity? Are women only a snare? Or can one derive some intimation of heavenly love from love below?

> But if Eve's charm be not supernal,
> Enduring not divine transplanting –
> Love kindled thence, is that eternal?
> Here, here's the hollow – here the haunting! (3.31: 43–6)

Clarel's questions challenge the foundation of religious feeling, suggesting that love of God may partake of the erotic nature of human love. If so, then may one love cancel out the other? Caught in this logical and spiritual vise, Clarel considers himself "suspended 'twixt the heaven and hell" and as such cut off from "Truth, truth cherubic!" (3.31: 64, 60).

The Mar Saba palm serves as the locus for longings that are aesthetic, religious, philosophical, and erotic, yet it seems to escape them all, refusing to be a text that can be read sequentially or with a given meaning. Each seeker finds himself baffled by the palm, and Mortmain dies contemplating its significance, "The filmed orbs fixed upon the Tree." In a remarkable development, however, Melville makes the palm serve as another kind of symbol, one as rich and evocative as the Mar Saba palm. When an old sailor named Agath (a possible echo of Agatha) joins the group, he reveals an elaborate tattoo on his arm that includes yet another image of the palm:

> Upon the fore-arm did appear
> A thing of art, vermil and blue,
> A crucifixion in tattoo,
> With trickling blood-drops strange to see.
>
> Above that emblem of the loss,
> Twin curving palm-boughs draping met
> In manner of a canopy
> Over an equi-limbed small cross
> And three tri-spiked and sister crowns:
> And under these a star was set:
> And all was tanned and toned in browns. (4:2: 49–59)

The palm that waved its fronds over the Mar Saba monastery in succeeding images of mobility and variety appears here etched into Agath's skin as part of what Rolfe calls an "ensign." As Rolfe explains, the image has an ancient history as a symbol of the pilgrim's journey to Jerusalem:

> Washed in with wine of Bethlehem,
> This Ensign in the ages old
> Was stamped on every pilgrim's arm
> By grave practitioners elect
> Whose calling lacked not for respect
> In Zion. Like the sprig of palm,
> Token it was at home, that he
> Which bore, had kneeled at Calvary. (4.2: 102–9)

In later times, Rolfe further explains, the sign of pilgrim's quest and crusader's venture has become a good-luck charm, a protective device, among superstitious mariners:

> "conjecture fair,
> These [crusaders] may have borne this blazon rare,
> And not alone on standard fine,
> But pricked on chest or sinewy arm,
> Pledged to defend against alarm

His tomb for whom they warred? But see,
From these mailed Templars now the sign,
Losing the import and true key,
Descends to boatswains of the brine." (4.2: 116–24)

The "ensign," or logo of the Templars has become popular art among sailors who borrow freely from both Christian imagery and Polynesian tattooing.

When Agath appropriates, though unknowingly, the pilgrim's palm for his tattooed charm, he performs the sort of creative borrowing that characterizes many of Melville's earlier works and that earned him both disdain, for novels like *Israel Potter*, and acclaim, when, in "Benito Cereno," his theft appeared the work of an artist. When is the writer a scrivener, a copyist like Bartleby, and when is he an inspired genius whose inventions dazzle the reader and obscure what they owe to other texts? The palm in *Clarel* is one of the poem's most potent images, seeming to spring from the slopes of Mar Saba like a fresh new birth, but in the succeeding cantos Melville shows it as a text circulating through the poem, taking on new meanings and associations, degenerating, seemingly, in its significance, and taking up its residence, finally, in an old sailor's skin.

Clarel's journey, too, seems to leave him not higher but rather lower than where he began. He returns to Jerusalem on Palm Sunday, with Melville bringing the palm imagery full circle too from its beginnings in the poem. Ruth is dead, Clarel has lost his friends, and he "vanishes" into the crowds on the Via Crucis. The palm, though, seems to triumph in spite of Clarel's fall into obscurity. Once again, in this celebration of Palm Sunday, it signifies Christ's glory and the pilgrims' devotion. As the harbinger of Easter, where the poem ends, it also suggests the poem *Clarel*'s own death and rebirth as text, its endless circulation through Melville's mind and the minds of readers. The image of the palm is the leaf on which Melville has inscribed his text, and like the palm, his text is both perennially green and subject to decay, fixed and fluid, continuous and discontinuous, original and borrowed, literal and liberal, ancient and ever new.

CHAPTER 10

"Different Considerations": Late Poetry

In his first "Agatha" letter, Melville spoke of the lawyer's perception of Melville's intentions as a writer: "You will perceive by the gentleman's note to me that he assumed that I purposed making literary use of the story; but I had not hinted anything of the kind to him, & my first spontaneous interest in it arose from very different considerations." So, John Henry Clifford thought that when he told the "Agatha" story to Melville, he would make "literary use" of it, namely write it as a fictional narrative. Melville told Hawthorne, however, that he appreciated the story because of "different considerations" and did not at first think of writing "a regular story." What "different considerations" did he have in mind? Is it possible that he thought of writing a poem instead? When, later in life, during his long period of noncommercial authorship, Melville had the liberty to write as he wished, he wrote poems. But his poems often included stories and even prose narratives, and he seems to have been looking for a new way to tell stories that was neither wholly prose nor wholly lyric. *Clarel* develops a long story in verse; it is undeniably a poem, but it borrows many elements from prose narrative. Melville's shorter poems, gathered into two published volumes – *John Marr and Other Sailors* (1885) and *Timoleon, Etc.* (1891) – and one unpublished collection – "Weeds and Wildings, Chiefly: With a Rose or Two" – as well as a number of other uncollected poems, experimented with prose and narrative elements too. They suggest the many "different considerations" of an author innovating in the available literary forms and creating new ones.

"A Man of the Sea": *John Marr and Other Sailors*

In *John Marr*, Melville indicates in several ways that he is experimenting with poetic form and stretching its generic boundaries. Although the poems seem like occasional lyrics, individual pieces inspired by themes of memory, loss, nature, and death, he organized the volume carefully so that, as in *Battle-Pieces*, each part of the whole reflects upon the others.[1] The first section, called "John Marr and Other Sailors," presents sailors from a heroic past during the age of sail, before the invention of ironclad ships and steam engines. The poems, "John Marr," "Bridegroom Dick," "Tom Deadlight," and "Jack Roy," in different ways eulogize sailors and together form a group, a "chorus," of voices from the past. A second section, "Sea-Pieces," contains one long narrative poem, "The Haglets," and a shorter lyric, "The Aeolian Harp." Both describe shipwrecks, scenes of desolation placed in the context of, in "The Haglets," indifferent nature (the haglets, birds who follow the craft as it sinks, resemble fate) and, in "The Aeolian Harp," equally indifferent art – reminders, again, of similar themes in *Moby-Dick* and *Battle-Pieces*. This section provides a transition as well – from stories of individual sailors to scenes of impassive nature – and moves to the third section, called "Minor Sea-Pieces." "Minor" may refer to the length of these twelve poems, some of which are indeed brief. But it also identifies their tone, written in a minor key and speaking to the melancholy themes of loss, death, and nature developed earlier in the collection. With occasional references to sailors like those in the "John Marr" section (Melville's brother Thomas, in "To the Master of the Meteor," or, "To Ned") and with images of death in "The Maldive Shark," and "The Berg," this group underlines the elegiac tone of the earlier sections. A final set of brief stanzas, called "Pebbles," invokes once more the "implacable Sea" (p. 299) and speaks to themes that unify the whole collection.

John Marr shows Melville's innovative uses of prose. The headnote to "John Marr" tells the story of an old sailor retired from the sea and removed inland, where he lives in dreary isolation and yearns for his long-dead comrades. Like Agatha's father, "a man of the sea . . . subdued & quiet & wise in his life," he has seen much. In solemn rhythms, Melville describes the old sailor's grief after he buries his wife and child and turns for consolation to people who share none of his experiences:

> They were a staid people; staid through habituation to monotonous hardship; ascetics by necessity not less than through moral bias; nearly all of them sincerely, however narrowly, religious. They were kindly at need, after their fashion; but to a man wonted – as John Marr in his previous homeless sojournings could not but have been – to the free-and-easy tavern-clubs affording cheap recreation of an evening in certain old and comfortable seaport towns of that time, and yet more familiar with the companionship afloat of the sailors of the same period, something was lacking. That something was geniality, the flower of life springing from some sense of joy in it, more or less. (p. 264)

The people surrounding John Marr, in other words, staid, kindly, religious, seem to live in the world of prose; the free-and-easy, genial sailors inhabit that of poetry. The contrast is necessary for Melville's task of showing the poetic meaning of the sailors' reckless, "homeless" existence.

A briefer prose headnote introduces "Tom Deadlight," and Melville's use of the device here suggests an organic relationship between prose and poetic narrative, as the prose explains, frames, but also gives way to the poem. Melville seems to have grown fascinated by this relationship between narrative and lyrical language. Indeed, many scholars agree that *Billy Budd* likewise began as a prose headnote to the ballad "Billy in the Darbies," and then grew into the novella over the course of several years. Like "John Marr," *Billy Budd* mourns a world in which the sailors seem to live in a lost poetic era, "a less prosaic time" (*BB* 43) than the era of steamships. Melville's prose in *John Marr* works to situate the poems within a narrative of this lost time and to suggest a vision of unity for the collection against which the individual poems, often concerning loss and the rupture of human ties, seem to "strain, / Parted" (p. 267).

Although *John Marr* contains a variety of poetic styles and concerns, it presses a central point, namely to contrast the vision of sailor geniality and community with the inhuman nature of the sea. The narrative poems are saturated in emotion and might be called sentimental invocations of the speaker's shipmates. In "John Marr," for example, the speaker writes openly of his longing for departed comrades. Mourning their youth and beauty, he describes them in intimate and erotic terms:

> Twined we were, entwined, then riven,
> Ever to new embracements driven,
> Shifting gulf-weed of the main!
> And how if one here shift no more,
> Lodged by the flinging surge ashore?
> Nor less, as now, in eve's decline,
> Your shadowy fellowship is mine.
> Ye float around me, form and feature: –
> Tattooings, ear-rings, love-locks curled;
> Barbarians of man's simpler nature,
> Unworldly servers of the world.
> Yea, present all, and dear to me,
> Though shades, or scouring China's sea. (pp. 267–8)

Thinking of his heart as a drumbeat summoning the sailors to their posts in his memory, and his poetic meters as another kind of beat, he ends with an emotional call to his shipmates:

> A beat, a heart-beat musters all,
> One heart-beat at heart-core.
> It musters. But to clasp, retain;
> To see you at the halyards main –
> To hear your chorus once again! (p. 268)

The sailors are associated with the rhythms of poetry, the music of their "chorus," as well as the beating heart of friendship and fellowship. The succeeding sailor poems, "Bridegroom Dick," "Tom Deadlight," and "Jack Roy," sound similar notes in mourning the bluff, often untutored, and dashing heroism of the men: "Heroic in thy levity wert thou, Jack Roy" (p. 283).

The nature poems, by contrast, emphasize the brooding desolation of the sea in images of shipwreck and death. The tone is less that of the longing shipmate and more that of the remote observer meditating on inhuman fate. Thus, "The Haglets" ends with a vision of a dead admiral in a sunken ship that emphasizes immense reaches of time and space:

Embedded deep with shells
And drifted treasure deep,
Unfathomable sleep –
His cannon round him thrown,
His sailors at his feet,
The wizard sea enchanting them
Where never haglets beat.
On nights when meteors play
And light the breakers' dance,
The Oreads from the caves
With silvery elves advance;
And up from ocean stream,
And down from heaven far,
The rays that blend in dream
The abysm and the star. (pp. 289–90)

As in the concluding lines of *Clarel*, human figures disappear, leaving a terrifying image of "the last whelming sea" (*C* 499) against which human strength is helpless. In its solemn beauty, however, the same image offers an odd consolation, a "dream" of "the star" rising from "the abysm."

Melville's interest in the "abysm" accompanies a commitment to "the Real" explored in his poems about the "implacable" sea. A stanza in "The Aeolian Harp" makes his intentions clear:

Listen: less a strain ideal
    Than Ariel's rendering of the Real.
What that Real is, let hint
    A picture stamped in memory's mint. (p. 290)

He identifies his poems as coming out of his own past, "memory's mint," rather than the bookish sources he consulted for his novels.[2] The Aeolian harp functions less here as the image of the Romantic poet, as in Coleridge's or Wordsworth's conceptions of the poet capturing the strains of nature, than as an instrument of truth. Shakespeare's Ariel, of *The Tempest*, may be a fairy sprite, but he also causes shipwrecks that can send the sailors "full fathom five," where they lie in their final beds: "Those are pearls that were his eyes." "Ariel's rendering of the Real" promises a terrible beauty, not comfort. In "The Aeolian Harp," Melville tells of a shipwreck that drifts about the sea until other ships wreck themselves upon it in turn. The vessel of sailor camaraderie and joy becomes an engine of death, killing other sailors as it pursues its murderous way: "Saturate, but never sinking, / Fatal only to the other!" This vision of unspeakable horror requires a different kind of poetry from the elegies of the first section:

> O, the sailors – O, the sails!
> O, the lost crews never heard of!
> Well the harp of Ariel wails
> Thoughts that tongue can tell no word of! (p. 291)

Ariel's verse gives melancholy music to stories that cannot be told in words.

A number of the remaining poems seem to be sung in this key. "The Maldive Shark" describes the "phlegmatical one, / Pale sot of the Maldive sea," within whose bloodthirsty jaws the "little pilot-fish" swim unharmed. Never seeming to understand the shark's menace, they serve as "Eyes and brains to the dotard lethargic and dull, / Pale ravener of horrible meat." Death is a "dotard" in this poem (pp. 294–5), and in "The Berg," where the great iceberg threatens the ships with destruction, it is "a lumbering one – / A lumbering lubbard loitering slow." Like the shark, the iceberg confronts its victim with "dead indifference" (p. 297).

This is the theme of "Pebbles," a collection of brief lyrics that speak of the resistless power of the sea:

> Implacable I, the old implacable Sea:
>   Implacable most when most I smile serene –
> Pleased, not appeased, by myriad wrecks in me. (p. 299)

Yet at the same time, oddly, that the sea grinds the rocks of ages into poetic pebbles, it inspires the poet's praise:

> Healed of my hurt, I laud the inhuman Sea –
> Yea, bless the Angels Four that there convene;
> For healed I am even by their pitiless breath
> Distilled in wholesome dew named rosmarine. (p. 299)

In these, the concluding lines of "Pebbles" and of *John Marr* as a whole, the poet blesses the gods of the sea who have "healed" his pain.

The ocean's watery depths yield up a precious distillation, an essence he calls "rosmarine." The name puns, as he will do later in "Weeds and Wildings," on roses and attar of rose, the precious distillation of the flower, and also plays on the name of rosemary, which, with rue, means remembrance to Shakespeare's Ophelia and is associated with death. But "rosmarine" also suggests the rose of the sea and serves as a fittingly poetic name for Melville's verse, a fragrant distillation of the bitter water of the sea and the implacable truth that it tells.

"Rounded & Beautified & Thoroughly Developed State": *Timoleon, Etc.*

If *John Marr* reveals its seams in disjunctions between images of sailor fellowship and an implacable sea, between lyric and prose, Melville's next collection focuses on the more seamless world of an ideal, of art itself. In one poem, "The Great Pyramid," he describes this creation of human hands as seeming to owe little to earthly influences: "Your masonry – and is it man's? / More like some Cosmic artisan's" (p. 339). Its "strata" seem untouched by time: "Shall lichen in your crevice fit? / Nay, sterile all and granite-knit" (p. 339). The subjects of many of *Timoleon*'s poems seem like what Melville in the "Agatha" letter to Hawthorne described as a finished form: no longer a motley collection of "material furnished by the New Bedford lawyer" but something complete, "in its rounded & beautified & and thoroughly developed state."

Timoleon, printed, like *John Marr*, in a private edition of twenty-five copies, was dedicated to an artist, Elihu Vedder (1836–1923). As *John Marr* pays tribute to the tradition of sea fiction by acknowledging the author of *The Wreck of the Grosvenor*, William Clark Russell, in its introduction *Timoleon* asserts its allegiance to the world of art embodied in Vedder's paintings, one of which had inspired Melville's poem in *Battle-Pieces*, "Formerly a Slave." The themes of *Timoleon* hark back to Melville's encounters with art, architecture, and the ancient world in his travels to Europe, Greece, Egypt, and Jerusalem, and they reflect as well his intensive reading in art and aesthetics as well as philosophy. They also show him returning to his journal from 1857 for words and details.

The collection does not seem as unified as *John Marr*, adopting a more intuitive structure. An opening section of twenty-three poems, headed by the title poem "Timoleon," takes up a variety of different inspirations, from ancient history ("Timoleon," "The Age of the Antonines") to religion ("Buddha," "The New Zealot to the Sun"); from love and loss ("After the Pleasure Party," "Monody") to the making of art ("In a Garret," "Art"); from painters like Teniers ("The Bench of Boors") and writers like Coleridge and Shelley ("C – 's Lament," "Shelley's Vision") to wine and tobacco ("Magian Wine," "Herba Santa"); from architecture ("The Ravaged Villa," "Lone Founts") to nature ("The Garden of Metrodorus," "Lamia's Song"). A second section of nineteen poems, "Fruit of Travel Long Ago," pays homage to, among others, "Venice," "Pisa's Leaning Tower," "Pausilippo," "The Attic Landscape," "The Parthenon," "The Archipelago," "Syra," and "The Great Pyramid." A final section, "L'Envoi," contains one love poem, "The Return of the Sire de Nesle," about a traveler coming home in "A.D. 16 –" to embrace his beloved. The collection combines sober, almost scholarly treatments of the ancient world and its philosophy, vivid images of sun-drenched Mediterranean landscapes, penetrating treatments of aesthetics, and poems that seem to break away from Melville's earlier themes into something new and unexpected.

Among the most unexpected for this writer, supposedly, of the sea, is "After the Pleasure Party." This monologue à la Robert Browning bursts forth passionately from a female astronomer named Urania, who regrets her repressed sexuality when she encounters frolicking young men and women at a picnic. A mature woman, she rages at the god "Amor," who has senselessly aroused her, as if in revenge for her intellectual pursuits. Suddenly she encounters a power she cannot fathom:

> Desire,
> The dear desire through love to sway,
> Is like the Geysers that aspire –
> Through cold obstruction win their fervid way.
> But baffled here – to take disdain,
> To feel rule's instinct, yet not reign;
> To dote, to come to this drear shame –
> Hence the winged blaze that sweeps my soul

Like prairie fires that spurn control,
Where withering weeds incense the flame. (p. 311)

Interestingly, although she has been watching a young man cast his amorous glances upon a "peasant girl" (p. 312), she describes the young woman far more minutely than the man. She also compares herself to Sappho, the great Lesbian poet, and calls herself Urania, the name adopted by Victorian poets and scholars from Plato's *Symposium* for idealized homoerotic desire.[3] The astronomer, then, seems to be looking for a love that, if not homosexual, transcends heterosexual attraction. At the end of the poem, she ponders a choice between two versions of militant womanhood, each an "armed Virgin": the Christian Mary and the Greek Athena. She asks Athena to strengthen her against the assaults of love, but as the poet reminds her, her request is a "Fond [i.e. foolish] appeal":

> For never passion peace shall bring,
> Nor Art inanimate for long
> Inspire. Nothing may help or heal
> While Amor incensed remembers wrong.
> Vindictive, not himself he'll spare;
> For scope to give his vengeance play
> Himself he'll blaspheme and betray.
>
> Then for Urania, virgins everywhere,
> O pray! Example take too, and have care. (p. 314)

Besides offering a remarkable view of complex female sexuality, the poem suggests that art is no match for passion. Such an argument, in a collection that elsewhere emphasizes the enduring power of art, appears anomalous.

Indeed Melville's poem "Art" has been taken as his poetic manifesto. This short lyric, much revised in multiple drafts, suggests that art is a form of divine struggle:[4]

> In placid hours well pleased we dream
> Of many a brave unbodied scheme.
> But form to lend, pulsed life create,
> What unlike things must meet and mate:
> A flame to melt – a wind to freeze;
> Sad patience – joyous energies;

> Humility – yet pride and scorn;
> Instinct and study; love and hate;
> Audacity – reverence. These must mate
> And fuse with Jacob's mystic heart,
> To wrestle with the angel – Art. (p. 322)

The moving image of Jacob wrestling with the angel suggests the depth and intensity of Melville's extraordinary exertion as poet, and with its balanced yet contending phrases, broken with dashes, the verse seems to do battle with itself. The concluding line, rather than resolving this internal conflict, raises a new question. Does the final dash suggest a pause leading to a new unity? Is the angel, then, Art, created from the poem's conflicts in a kind of Hegelian dialectic? Or does the pause indicate an "abysm," an alien space between the Jacob-and-angel conflict, and Art, which still exists above and beyond the struggle? As in "After the Pleasure-Party," some mischievous spirit disturbs any settled understanding of the truth.

Focusing only on the poems that thematize Melville as artist, however, robs the reader of the diverse pleasures of *Timoleon*. His reflections on landscape, culture, and history reveal a discerning eye and elastic mind. One less discussed poem, "In the Desert," gives a sense of the range of his vision:

> Never Pharaoh's Night,
> Whereof the Hebrew wizards croon,
> Did so the Theban flamens try
> As me this veritable Noon.
>
> Like blank ocean in blue calm
> Undulates the ethereal frame;
> In one flowing oriflamme
> God flings his fiery standard out.
>
> Battling with the Emirs fierce,
> Napoleon a great victory won,
> Through and through his sword did pierce:
> But, bayoneted by this sun
> His gunners drop beneath the gun.
>
> Holy, holy, holy Light!
> Immaterial incandescence,
> Of God the effluence of the essence,
> Shekinah intolerably bright! (pp. 338–9)

In this brief lyric, Melville lends the physical landscape a wide range of historical, religious, and cultural associations. The Egyptian desert brings to mind oppressive Pharaoh and proud Thebes but also Napoleon's armies, the fierce "Emirs," and the god of Christians and of Jews. This god, Melville noted in his journal of 1857, was pitiless. Speaking of the blasted landscape around Jerusalem, he wrote: "No country will more quickly dissipate romantic expectations than Palestine – particularly Jerusalem. To some the disappointment is heart sickening. &c. Is the desolation of the land the result of the fatal embrace of the Deity? Hapless are the favorites of heaven" (*J* 91). His invocation of "Holy, holy, holy Light!" imparts heartfelt worship, but paired with "Shekinah intolerably bright," it suggests the "fatal embrace" of a divinity as merciless as Pharaoh and Napoleon.

Melville generally adopts a solemn tone throughout the collection. The opening poem, "Timoleon," concerns a Corinthian prince whose brother, Timophanes, is a tyrant. Timoleon, acting against his mother's wishes and violating his natural love of his brother, takes the people's side and arranges for Timophanes to be killed. The fraternal struggle calls to mind America's Civil War and the grief it caused, even if "Right in Corinth reassumes its place" (p. 308) and order has been restored. With a similar sense of great forces and issues at stake, *Timoleon* grapples with angels throughout. It ends, however, with a pilgrim's return to his "lasting love" in "L'Envoi." His journey has filled him with a grim knowledge: "For terrible is earth!" Yet like the speaker of "Pebbles" who calls himself "Healed of my hurt," the Sire de Nesle finds solace in his homecoming:

> But thou, my stay, thy lasting love
> One lonely good, let this but be!
> Weary to view the wide world's swarm,
>   But blest to fold but thee.

The poem ends the collection with an image of love and union. Characteristically, though, Melville sprinkles the verse with "buts." The "lasting love" is "but" a "lonely good"; the pilgrim is "blest to fold but thee" – and no other? The questions raised in this seemingly forthright declaration of love emerge even more problematically in Melville's last poetic collection, a gift to his wife.

"Breathe a Fair Wind": "Weeds and Wildings, Chiefly: With a Rose or Two"

John Marr and *Timoleon* represented years of planning, arrangement, and multiple drafts of many poems. Publishing them in small private printings to be distributed among friends, Melville had complete authorial and editorial control over his work. They are personal texts in many ways, products of his complete absorption and dedicated attention. Even more personal seem his collected but unpublished poems, "Weeds and Wildings, Chiefly: With a Rose or Two." Dedicated to his wife Elizabeth under her pet name, "Winnefred," these poems include flowers, children, small animals, and the influences of pastoral scenes and narratives, far from the "implacable Sea" of *John Marr* or the grand and often baroque world of *Timoleon*. They exhibit wit, affection, and charm. As in Melville's phrase in his last "Agatha" letter to Hawthorne, they seem to "breathe a fair wind" after the stormy weather of a long and arduous career. Yet, like earlier poems, they are not without subtleties and complications.

On the surface, at least, they do seem less fraught with conflict than Melville's published collections. An opening section called "The Year" includes nineteen brief lyrics on nature, the seasons, children, and mostly pastoral scenes of weeds and wildflowers. In Part II, "This, That, and the Other," he placed four poems, some with more serious themes of mortality and reputation. "The American Aloe on Exhibition" suggests the public's lack of interest in a plant (or poet) that blooms only once in a hundred years. Part III, "Rip Van Winkle's Lilac," containing a long prose narrative before the poem, describes Rip Van Winkle's house and a legendary lilac bush. A later section, "A Rose or Two," groups fourteen poems under the title "As They Fell," and two under another title, "The Rose Farmer." All the last poems play upon various puns and conceits surrounding roses, their poetic associations, and the problem of art: should one treasure the fleeting pleasures of the blossoming rose or gather the flowers to make essences for attar of rose? The roses, grown for their beauty, raise complicated issues that seem out of place with the weeds and wildings. The collection as a whole balances the theme of nature against art, the unaffected clover, buttercup, or apple blossom against the cultivated rose.

Some readers have seen these poems as autobiographical reminiscences, with implicit references to Herman, Elizabeth, and their children ("Madcaps," "The Chipmunk"), their pastoral years at Arrowhead, and a simpler, childlike existence evoked in references to Irving's "Rip Van Winkle" and "The Legend of Sleepy Hollow." Some scholars have read the collection as Melville's apology and tribute to Lizzie in the later, calmer years of a long and turbulent marriage.[5] Other readers have noted more troubling strains in the poems that characterize the marriage as frustrating to the end.[6] The inclusion of Rip Van Winkle, for example, suggests the bitter comedy of an unhappy marriage, and the rose poems, if intended as a marital bouquet, contain many disconcerting assertions of the passing of beauty and the death of love.

Perhaps the contention among critics arises because it is hard to recognize or locate the Melville many readers know in these seemingly charming ditties and musings on flowers. The rose poems, however, give evidence of the wry sensibility and ironic wit of Melville's prose writing, and his concern with immortality, represented most fully in "The Rose-Farmer," has been taken as evidence of the elder poet's late reflections on his reputation. This poem concerns a dialogue between the farmer and a visitor who would make attar from the roses. The farmer, however, passionately defends the rose *au naturel*:

> "This evanescence is the charm!
> And most it wins the spirits that be
> Celestial, sir. It comes to me
> It was this fleeting charm in show
> That lured the sons of God below . . . (p. 308)

> "But now, sir, for your urgent matter.
> Every way – for wise employment,
> Repute and profit, health, enjoyment,
> I am for roses – *sink* the Attar!" (p. 309)

The poet likewise concludes that destroying the rose's beauty in order to capture its essence commits a serious wrong. Somewhat mixing his metaphors (textiles with horticulture), he adopts a profound gravity:

> But here arrest the loom – the line.
> > Though Damask be your precious stuff,
> Spin it not out too superfine:
> > The flower of a subject is enough. (p. 310)

Melville's nature poems do not, however, concern only aesthetic issues or leave his earlier political and social concerns behind. "The Cuban Pirate," about a humming bird, packs not only intense feeling but also complex political thought into its tiny frame:

> Buccaneer in gemmed attire –
> Ruby, amber, emerald, jet –
> Darkling, sparkling dot of fire,
> Still on plunder are you set?
>
> Summer is your sea, and there
> The flowers afloat you board and ravage,
> Yourself a thing more dazzling fair –
> Tiny, plumed, bejewelled Savage!
>
> Midget! yet in passion a fell
> Furioso, Creoles tell.
> Wing'd are you Cupid in disguise
> Now flying spark of Paradise? (pp. 275–6)

Reminiscent of Emily Dickinson's poem on a hummingbird ("A Route of Evanescence"), the lines flash with the impact of a vivid visual effect: the brilliant, jewel-like colors and furious speed and intent of the tiny bird. The second stanza, however, develops a more political image of a sea-pirate, using terms of boarding and ravaging that recall John Paul Jones of *Israel Potter* and his savagery. In fact, the original final line read "little Paul Jones of Paradise?"[7] The reference to Cuba further suggests that the real pirate is not a Cuban buccaneer, but an America bent on ravaging its neighbor to the south. A reviewer of *Israel Potter* recognized in Melville's piratical John Paul Jones the spirit of the Ostend Manifesto of 1854, in which America declared that if Spain did not sell Cuba to the US, Americans would be justified in seizing it for themselves (*IP*, "Historical Note," 217). The poet of "The Cuban Pirate" might well ask the "John Paul Jones of nations" if "Still on plunder are you set?" Thus, although the last stanza associates the hummingbird's passion with love, suggesting the vengeful Amor of "After the Pleasure Party," the reference to Creoles and Cuba emphasizes a more predatory passion for colonial territory.

But although the poem makes its political point, it may also remind us of Melville the literary pirate. Here the man who plundered other authors' texts throughout his literary career ridicules the small though intense ambitions of a "Midget!" Mocking the hummingbird still set on plunder, Melville suggests that he himself no longer raids other people's flowers. Perhaps he has found "a thing more dazzling fair" – the "flying spark of Paradise" in his own poetic flights.

Melville's pattern of publishing his poems in private editions or, in the case of "Weeds and Wildings" and a number of uncollected poems, not publishing them at all suggests that, like Emily Dickinson, he favored having authorial control over his poetic works instead of giving them over to publishers. To see him as a private or unprofessional poet is to understand that, rather than shrinking from public recognition of his poems, he "preferred not to" publish. It is hard to know whether this decision caused him the anguish of the neglected poet or conferred on him the freedom to write, as he said of Pierre, "precisely as I please" (p. 244). Certainly, by not publishing through the commercial presses that had controlled, often in damaging ways, his works and reputation, he attained a certain anonymity for himself as poet. That anonymity has dropped away as readers in more recent times have come to appreciate his poetic innovations and search out his lyrical inventions.

CHAPTER 11

"Instinct with Significance": *Billy Budd*

Billy Budd began as a poem similar to the sailor ballads of *John Marr* and grew, through successive stages of revision, into a full-length manuscript, which Melville was still considering when he died in 1891.[1] Like his uncollected poems, and "Weeds and Wildings," it is a fascinating fragment. Perhaps Melville never meant to publish *Billy Budd* at all but to keep it forever, like Billy himself, a fresh untouched "juvenile" (p. 87). Yet with its resonant themes, mysterious characters, discordant and difficult language, and mature reflections on history, political conflict, law, the sea, philosophy, and words themselves, this novella has come to seem one of Melville's finest and most profound works.

Like the "Agatha" correspondence, it also contains tantalizing traces of Melville's ideas about writing. In one passage, the *Billy Budd* narrator remarks that he may lead a reader down a forbidden and transgressive trail:

> In this matter of writing, resolve as one may to keep to the main road, some by-paths have an enticement not readily to be withstood. I am going to err into such a by-path. If the reader will keep me company I shall be glad. At the least we can promise ourselves that pleasure which is wickedly said to be in sinning, for a literary sin the divergence will be. (p. 56)

In explaining how to comprehend a character as uncommon as Claggart, he directs the reader's attention to his practice as writer: "But for the adequate comprehending of Claggart by a normal nature, these hints are insufficient. To pass from a normal nature to him one must cross 'the deadly space between.' And this is best done by indirection" (p. 74). Advertising his literary transgressions, indirections, and latitudes, Melville even more brazenly announces his ambiguity: "Who in the rainbow can draw the line where the violet tint ends and the orange tint begins? Distinctly we see the difference of the colors, but where exactly does the one first blendingly enter into the other? So with sanity and insanity" (p. 102). This overt mystification of the writer's art has earned Melville the admiration of some readers and the undying frustration of others.

In *Billy Budd* we see Melville's most self-conscious application of many of the ideas he laid out in the "Agatha" correspondence. Just as each detail in Agatha's story reverberates with symbolic meaning, so every feature of character, setting, and language in *Billy Budd* conveys a world of significance. As Melville pointed out to Hawthorne, each facet of the story in Clifford's narration glistened with meaning: "The narrative from the Diary is instinct with significance. – Consider the mention of the *shawls* – & the inference derived from it. Ponder the conduct of this Robinson throughout. – Mark his trepidation & suspicion when any one called upon him. – " Objects like the shawl, the legacy of Robertson's dead second wife, mysteries like Robertson's secret motives, feelings of dread and suspicion all fascinated Melville. He found the story so "instinct with significance," deeply imbued with meaning, that one has only to refine one's own instincts slightly to apprehend it.

Like the "Agatha" story too, *Billy Budd* had it roots in an original source, one indeed that bore a personal relation to Melville's life. In 1842 Captain Alexander Slidell Mackenzie, of the naval training ship *Somers*, detected what he thought was a mutiny among his men, most of whom were young midshipmen preparing to be officers. Of the three suspected mutineers, the leader, Phillip Spencer, happened to be the son of the US Secretary of War. Although the ship was operating in a time of peace and was sailing only two days away from the Virgin Islands, Mackenzie invoked the Articles of War and had Spencer and his two supposed confederates hanged, a decision that aroused outrage back at home, particularly from friends of the elder Spencer. Mackenzie went on trial but was acquitted. His first mate and the officer who served on the drumhead court that decided the case was Guert Gansevoort, Melville's cousin, whom he represented in "Bridegroom Dick" as a hero of the Mexican War and as "Tom Tight," who never blabs a secret: " 'Gentlemen, in vain with your wassail you beset, / For the more I tipple, the tighter do I get' " (p. 275). The pun draws attention to the two ways in which Gansevoort, a probable alcoholic, is "tight," but it also suggests a well of private emotions that Melville's narrative might explore. Melville refers explicitly to the *Somers* in *Billy Budd* in characteristically oblique terms:

> Not unlikely they were brought to something more or less akin to that harassed frame of mind which in the year 1842 actuated the Commander of the U.S. brig-of-war *Somers* to resolve, under the so-called Articles of War, Articles modeled upon the English Mutiny Act, to resolve upon the execution at sea of a midshipman and two petty-officers as mutineers designing the seizure of the brig. Which resolution was carried out though in a time of peace and within not many days' of home. An act vindicated by a naval court of inquiry subsequently convened ashore. History, and here cited without comment. True, the circumstances on board the *Somers* were different from those on board the *Bellipotent*. But the urgency felt, well-warranted or otherwise, was much the same. (pp. 113–14)

Seemingly loyal to Guert, Melville nevertheless appears to question Vere's decision, here and elsewhere throughout the text. Thus, as in the "Agatha" story, he felt free to adapt his source to develop a narrative line of his own.

"Find Out the Suggestiveness for Yourself": The Reader of *Billy Budd*

Perhaps its most critical similarity with the "Agatha" story is that *Billy Budd* implies an alert reader who, like Hawthorne, must become actively involved in creating the story. Melville, of course, suggested that Hawthorne *write* the story; nothing in *Billy Budd* implies that he considers the reader a fellow-author. But he does assume a reader who knows a great number of the books Melville read, is conversant with fairly arcane matters of European military and political history, and cares about subtle arguments and fine distinctions. He seems to assume, then, a *prepared* reader, someone who, like Hawthorne, might easily pick up the narrative thread. In Hawthorne's case, Melville assumed that the author of "Wakefield" might be prepared to take on "Agatha": "And here I am reminded of your London husband; tho' the cases so rudely contrast. – Many more things might be mentioned; but I forbear; you will find out the suggestiveness for yourself; & all the better perhaps, for my not intermeddling." Although Melville floods Hawthorne with "tributary items" of interest, he leaves the task to Hawthorne, making him a generous gift of his ideas.

Such a spirit of collaboration infuses *Billy Budd* as well, although indeed the narrator pours out a flood of "tributary items" to inform and influence a reader. But like the "Agatha" story, *Billy Budd* concerns a legal case and puts the reader in the position of jury or outside observer who must judge the verdict wisely. Melville tried a similar tactic in "Bartleby," where the lawyer-narrator essentially presents himself as on trial for his treatment of his employee. The story offers testimony for the reader to consider and judge. *Billy Budd* presents a literal case, that of Billy's trial for striking a superior officer, but it also puts itself and its literary method on trial in a self-effacing surrender of the author's control of the narrative. If in "Agatha" Melville seems to be inviting Hawthorne to write the story himself, in *Billy Budd* he appears to beckon the reader into his own authorial position, to locate him at his desk and ask how, given the facts, he or she might decide this perplexing case.

Billy Budd, a "Handsome Sailor," is popular everywhere he goes, the last person one would suspect of hidden or sinister motives. His only flaw in an otherwise unsullied nature is a speech impediment that causes him to stutter when he encounters stress. The story takes place in 1797, during the war between England and France for control of the Mediterranean and Atlantic, when naval officers were in the habit of impressing, or seizing sailors from merchant vessels or onshore taverns to man their ships. It also takes place shortly after the mutinies at Spithead and the Nore, two locations on the River Thames where English sailors rebelled for higher wages and improved working conditions. A warship, the *Bellipotent*, under Captain Edward Fairfax Vere, stops a merchant ship, the *Rights of Man*, and impresses young Billy Budd, the favorite of the crew. Billy accepts his fate lightly, dashing off a jaunty farewell to his friends: "And good-by to you, old *Rights of Man!*" (p. 49). With either military severity or paranoid rigor, the presiding officer takes this statement as a subversive quip, not realizing that Billy is wholly innocent, a kind of "upright barbarian, much such perhaps as Adam presumably might have been ere the urbane Serpent wriggled himself into his company" (p. 52).

Because of his good looks, good nature, and youthful athleticism, Billy gets assigned to the foretop, where he seems to adjust well to life in the highly charged atmosphere of a naval ship. He catches the attention of John Claggart, however, the master-at-arms or officer in charge of arming, training, and disciplining the crew. To Claggart, a man of what Melville calls "Natural Depravity" (p. 75), Billy's innocence, beauty, and goodness are deeply galling. From some spirit that might be called evil, jealous, or mad, Claggart arranges various little annoyances to cause Billy to misbehave. At one point, one of his underlings approaches Billy and tries to tempt him into a conspiracy to mutiny. Billy, to whom any such suggestion is simply incomprehensible, throws him off. He confides his perplexity to a wise "Merlin" of a sailor called the "Dansker," who confounds him by saying oracularly that "Jemmy Legs [Claggart] is down on you" (p. 85). Billy can make little sense of this, having no experience of an antipathy like Claggart's, but the Dansker turns out to be right. During a brief skirmish, when the *Bellipotent* is engaged at sea, Claggart goes to Vere and tells him that he has received news of an incipient mutiny involving Billy Budd.

Vere, a moderate and cautious leader, calls Billy to the cabin to give his side of the story, with fatal and unforeseen results. Billy is so shocked by the false accusations that he cannot speak. Instead, "The next instant, quick as the flame from a discharged cannon at night, his right arm shot out, and Claggart dropped to the deck" (p. 99). Vere sees at once that, given the recent mutinies at Spithead and the Nore, he cannot treat this episode of violence lightly, even though he knows that Billy is no mutineer. He calls a drumhead court and, acting as witness, prosecutor, and judge at once, secures a guilty verdict for Billy. Billy must hang, and Vere must tell him this terrible news, in a closeted interview that Melville implies must have evoked profound emotion in both men – a kind of "sacrament" (p. 115) that must be kept from the prying eyes of the world.

In a moving and ritual finale, Vere assembles the men at dawn the next day to "witness punishment" (p. 122). Unexpectedly, at the moment just before his execution, Billy cries out " 'God bless Captain Vere!' " Melville emphasizes the natural and spiritual beauty of these words: "Syllables so unanticipated coming from one with the ignominious hemp about his neck – a conventional felon's benediction directed aft towards the quarters of honor; syllables too delivered in the clear melody of a singing-bird on the point of launching from the twig, had a phenomenal effect, not unenhanced by the rare personal beauty of the young sailor spiritualized now thro' late experiences so poignantly profound" (p. 123). But his death is followed by intimations of the ugly and ironic ravages of war. In three different endings to the narrative, Melville suggests the meaninglessness of Billy's heroic and lyrical words. In the first, Vere dies in a random engagement, having missed his chance for a fame like that of his hero Nelson, and calling Billy's name in tones that "were not the accents of remorse," an outcome suggesting that he viewed Billy's execution as necessary to his "most secret of all passions, ambition" (p. 129). In the second ending, Melville's narrator quotes an account of the events in a maritime journal, where Claggart appears as a hero and Billy an evil villain. In a third ending, Billy's shipmates preserve pieces of the mast from which he was hanged: "To them a chip of it was as a piece of the Cross" (p. 131). Their idolatry is no truer to Billy's story than Vere's final words or the newspaper's venom. In the ballad they write about him, "Billy in the Darbies," Billy is almost unrecognizable, appearing to be an older man with much more sexual and worldly experience than the innocent of the story and appearing as well to have taken part in a mutiny after all. The multiple endings ironically undermine both the character Billy Budd and the story that bears his name, raising doubts about the meaning and intentions of the text.

If Vere's rigid response to Billy's killing of a superior officer make the boy's death inevitable, Melville's rendering of the events encourages the reader to explore other possibilities, to "find out the suggestiveness for yourself." Finding out the "suggestiveness" differs markedly from knowing the significance or meaning of what happened. Melville never fully reveals his intended meaning. But he does offer abundant suggestiveness, and a reader must embrace it in order to absorb the full potential of the story.

One method for plumbing the story's suggestiveness is to make full use of its allusiveness and intertextuality. It is dense with images drawn from Greek and classical mythology and drama, the Judeo-Christian Bible, and European and American history, as well as literary authors like Plato, Montaigne, Calvin, Marvell, Ann Radcliffe, Burke, Paine, Voltaire, Hawthorne, and Carlyle. These complicate and enrich an otherwise simple plot by layering in story lines from tragedy, theology, Gothic romance, and the history of revolutions in America, France, and England. An alert reader will recognize the nuances implied by comparisons between Billy and Georgiana in Hawthorne's "The Birthmark," for example, or characters in Radcliffe's *The Mysteries of Udolpho*; by references to biblical figures like Adam and Eve, Cain and Abel, Abraham and Isaac, Jacob, Joseph, Elijah and Elisha, and Christ; by allusions to the *Iliad* and the *Oresteia*, Greek myths about Hercules, Apollo, Orpheus, Chiron, and the three Graces; and by descriptions of historical figures like Nelson, Napoleon, Titus Oates, Guy Fawkes, Tecumseh, and Captain Cook.

This dazzling array of references is not only decorative, however. It also creates narrative patterns within the story around religious, political, and ethical themes. These systems of thought, belief, and most importantly judgment implied by different allusions frequently collide, putting the text's unity and integrity at risk and making it a battleground. We can see this structure of conflicting systems in at least three common interpretations of the story.

The first might be called the Judeo-Christian reading of *Billy Budd*. In the context of allusions to Old and New Testament figures, Billy appears most often as an innocent (like Adam), a child (like Isaac or Joseph), a hero (like David), and a martyr (like Christ). He may also be something of a new prophet, like Elisha, or a martyr and sacrifice (like Abel or, potentially, Isaac). The plot may be viewed as a biblical or Miltonic conflict between good and evil, with Billy as the innocent Adam, Claggart as the evil serpent, and Vere as the righteous God in judgment on them both. In this reading, Billy may also be a Christ who is punished so that the sailors may be saved, an angel who heralds a new Messiah, or the Messiah himself, whose power is greater than that of earthly law and might. If so, then Billy's death is the logical outcome of Adam's fall and Christ's sacrifice and martyrdom. His fall is a fortunate fall, and Claggart serves a necessary purpose in making that fall occur. Billy's intentions are, as Vere affirms, of no concern, since events play themselves out according to a providential plan.

The main problem with this reading, as seductive as it is, is that in the world of Christian allegory everything that happens to produce the fortunate outcome is right and good. Thus human judgment has no power to change events, nor is it useful in any way. In any human sense, then, Billy's death is meaningless. He is by nature good, and his death shows no agency on his part. It may inspire the sailors' superstitious reverence, but Billy is a symbol, acting out his assigned part in the allegory, not asserting his will or choosing to be good in any way.

Another irony of the biblical or Miltonic framework is that it may create sympathy for a character that readers might consider a villain. Although Claggart is evil and is identified with the serpent, like Milton's Satan he is also appealingly human, far more intelligent than Billy, and instrumental to divine design in more active ways than Billy as well. Hence, the odd result of identifying Billy with Adam or Christ is to create a useful role for Claggart, to make his death a kind of sacrifice too. In associating Claggart with Saul, as he does in chapter 12, Melville implies that Claggart faces considerable competition from David/Billy, and his jealousy and anxiety might seem understandable. The effect of applying the biblical framework, then, is to raise questions about its legitimacy: just the kinds of questions theology tries to suppress.

A second set of associations in the story – allusions to the world of classical Greek drama and philosophy – locates its plot and characters in a system we might call ethical rather than theological. In the world of Greek tragedy, divine power is represented by a pantheon of gods and a concept of fate, rather than by Christian redemption. In this system, the story becomes a conflict not so much between good and evil as between right and wrong, as defined by human as well as divine laws. Ethics get worked out somewhere in the realm between politics and religion. Neither absolute nor wholly earthly, ethics require human action and compromise, and in the world of classical reference – tragedy and myth – plots focus on fallible human choices. Tragic heroes generally err, but the drama privileges their power and obligation to choose.

In the ethical universe of the story, Billy acts parts very different from those in the Christian framework. Here he is associated with the gods Apollo and Hercules, figures of beauty and strength who nevertheless commit quite human errors. He is also linked with Achilles and, through several references to Agamemnon, with both the *Iliad* and the *Oresteia*. Vere calls him a "fated boy" (p. 99), indicating that like the figures in tragedy he suffers from a fatal flaw (the stutter, perhaps, or the violence that makes him act without thinking) and must play out his destiny to its catastrophic conclusion. In this scenario, Billy is not good and perfect but flawed and violent. The ethical debate over whether he acted rightly or not in killing Claggart calls his character into question, although it also suggests that Claggart too acted wrongly.

Indeed, in the framework of classical tragedy, Billy may not even be the hero of the story, as he might be in a Christian drama. A tragic hero is traditionally a man or woman capable of reason, will, and choice. Billy seems to have none of these traits. They belong more properly to Vere, and much in the story suggests that he is the tragic hero of *Billy Budd*, in that he judges the actions of Billy and Claggart and must choose how to act in response. The fact that he chooses a fatal course creates pity (for Vere's suffering) and terror (at the forces ranged against him, forces more earthly than divine, it must be added, for he serves an earthly not a heavenly king). The most sympathetic figure in the ethical drama may well be Vere, who is himself associated with the tragic figure of Orpheus, condemned to watch his beloved die and later destroyed himself for his adherence to "forms, measured forms" (p. 128).

In a third context, that of history rather than theology or tragedy, *Billy Budd* is a story about war, revolutionary violence, and the law. Its domain is primarily political more than religious or ethical. In this context, the dominant forces are not gods or fates but human powers: governments and people. In this political drama, the story plays itself out against the backdrop of revolutions in England (the seventeenth-century revolutions of Cromwell against the Crown and the restoration of the monarchy under Charles II), France, and America (both smoldering at the time, 1797, when the story takes place). Vere fronts the conservative aristocratic forces of privilege represented by Burke and the world of Marvell's poem "On Appleton House," to which Melville refers in chapter 6. Claggart is associated with conspiratorial forces on both sides of the religious divide in England, the Protestant Titus Oates and Catholic Guy Fawkes. And Billy, identified with the rebellious sailors of the Spithead and Nore mutinies and with the American Thomas Paine, of the *Rights of Man*, seems to represent revolutionary and democratic ideologies of a new world order.

In the political context, the central conflict is not between good and evil or right and wrong but rather between winners and losers, the powerful and the powerless. The world of revolution suggests violent protest against the aristocracy Vere represents, two forces locked in dialectical conflict, one class rising up against another and being quelled in turn by another uprising class. Hence laws exist to protect the dominant class; a social compact requires that one not threaten the country's security in wartime; and the good of the whole requires the sacrifice of individual will. Vere articulates this position best in the courtroom scene, of course, when he places national security above Billy's motives and character. His political perspective bespeaks a fundamental faith in the progressive motions of history. It suggests the power and primacy of civilization, of higher forms of life (aristocratic, European, patriarchal, white), over lower ones (the mob).

As with the theological and ethical systems the story constructs, Melville indicates a central problem with this political structure. Political power is influenced and modified by history, by the actions and accidents of human beings. Those in power may not always remain in power, and a new force, not necessarily a better one, may revolt and take power instead. Vere, in fact, may be insane, or may use his authority illegitimately, as Melville suggests by including the surgeon's doubts about his behavior. As in Europe's revolutions, or the *Somers* mutiny, a force in power may not prevail, especially if it does not have right on its side.

The political plot creates a new set of associations and meanings for Melville's characters. In suggesting that Billy may be a revolutionary who sacrifices himself to maintain his comrades' safety, the story creates sympathy for his democratic and generous heroism. Vere and Claggart, representing illegitimate power from above and below, cede center stage to Billy, the man of the people. The problem with this reading, of course, is that Billy refuses to lead, rejects the invitation to mutiny, and in blessing Captain Vere supports rather than undermines his authority. In spite of his devotion to the sailors, Billy does nothing to secure the rights of men, instead appearing to assent to monarchy and tradition without protest. Nevertheless, the late nineteenth-century reader of the story would appreciate the historical irony that the world Vere defended has long since given way to the revolutionary classes from which Billy sprang. In the cycles of history, Vere's power and that of the king and nation he represented are gone.

Billy Budd constructs other structures of meaning throughout the story – those defined by aesthetics, sexuality, gender, and race come immediately to mind – and we could trace further the ways in which Melville's use of different systems of reference complicates the text. The point, however, should be clear. Since each of these systems conflicts with the others, no one interpretation of the story can hold its ground against the others. Is Billy a meek Christ or a militant Achilles? Is Vere a tragic hero or a corrupt careerist? Is Claggart a villain or a wily conspirator? Are the sailors potential revolutionaries or acquiescent sheep? And as with the characters, so with the story. The three different endings enact these problems all over again. The death of Vere, "cut off too early for the Nile and Trafalgar" (p. 129), may appear a tragic conclusion to his agony. The newspaper report making Billy a ringleader of the resentfully impressed and Claggart a brave defender of the king replays the political drama to its ironic finale. And the image of the sailors preserving splinters from Billy's mast as if they were pieces of the Cross reminds readers of the Christian allegory once more. Yet again Melville makes it clear that no one reading can prevail over the others; they are all equally wrong and in some startling way also oddly right.

Melville uses allusions in *Billy Budd* to expand the story's range of significance, and he puts competing plots in conflict with each other, forcing readers to embrace the resulting inconsistencies and ambiguities. Each of these tactics invites readers to "find out suggestiveness" through various means. Along with considering the conflict as one between good and evil, right and wrong, or victor and victim, he poses an opposition between beauty and ugliness. One might think of this essentially aesthetic problem in terms of literary art – as a choice between poetry and prose – or in terms of sexuality – as a choice between sexual vitality and impotence – or in terms of music – as a choice between natural song, like that of Orpheus or the bird, and the martial drums that beat the men to quarters. These terms all gather around the "cynosure" (p. 44) of all eyes, Billy himself. He is physically beautiful, and his beauty is associated with sailor poetry in the figure of the Handsome Sailor, who comes from a "less prosaic time" (p. 43), and with the sailors' lyric voice in the concluding ballad. If the sailors' poetry is beautiful, then the prose of naval order is harsh and ugly, and the story seems to make a romantic argument for the superiority of lyric over prose.

At the same time, Billy is sexually appealing and virile, associated with handsome Greek gods and men and with figures of homoerotic desire like David. In this reading Claggart, by contrast, represses his desire for the physical beauty and sexual naturalness of Billy; the narrator acknowledges that "he could have loved Billy, but for fate and ban" (p. 88), but Claggart refuses to do so. Vere imagines Billy as someone "who in the nude might have posed for a statue of Adam before the Fall" (p. 94), but in the end is just as repressed as Claggart; at Billy's execution, he "stood erectly rigid as a musket in the ship-armorer's rack" (p. 124). Whereas Vere maintains an erect posture but cannot discharge, and Claggart has been similarly and perpetually frustrated throughout the story, Billy seems the one figure of potentially healthy phallic energy. But at the decisive moment, his arm shoots out in an expression of deadly violence, not sexual release and joy, and on the night before his death he lies among the cannons like a small child in a cradle, not a masculine hero. One might say, then, that Melville does not create simple sexual categories in the story, such as homosexual vs. heterosexual or natural vs. repressed. All the men in the story are blocked, and Melville seems to suggest that their natural sexual functions have been subsumed into the work of the cannons, as the reproductive functions of the factory women in "Tartarus of Maids" have been absorbed into the making of blank paper.[2]

Melville associates Billy's beauty not only with lyric expressiveness and sexual pleasure but also with the text itself. In one sense the qualities assigned to Billy Budd, the character – simplicity, beauty, pleasure, music, innocence – appear polar opposites of those by which we might characterize *Billy Budd*, the text – complexity and ambiguity, harshness and discord, knowingness, subtlety, and "ragged edges" (p. 128). It is in many ways a hostile text, one that repels a reader with its "narration having less to do with fable than with fact" (p. 128). Readers might prefer a text more like Billy – an erotic text that arouses the reader, producing intimacy with the character and the writer as well. Instead Melville presents an erotic character but not an erotic text. The fate of this text is to kill its beautiful object, to kill what it has created, to take Billy's beauty and destroy it. Shakespeare's argument that the sonnet preserves the beloved's beauty is here questioned. Billy's beauty is preserved within the story by his untimely death, but its effect is spoiled by a corrosive narrative that makes us turn from the spectacle of this beauty in frustration.

In the end, the parts of *Billy Budd* do not add up to a whole. Something is always lacking, some hint always suggesting what might appear. But a reader can "find out" this suggestiveness by investing generously in the narrator and his characters. Such generous reading is the reader's gift to the author, but, in an odd way, it is also the author's gift to the receptive reader.

Afterword

"Restoring To You Your Own Property": Owning Melville

One of the most astonishing features of the "Agatha" correspondence is that Melville claimed to be making the story a gift to Hawthorne. But he offered this gift in a provocative and sophisticated way. He claims not to be instructing Hawthorne in what to write but simply returning to him what he has already written, as if, in creating "Wakefield," Hawthorne has already accomplished "Agatha": "I do not therefore, My Dear Hawthorne, at all imagine that you will think that I am so silly as to flatter myself I am giving you anything of my own. I am but restoring to you your own property – which you would quickly enough have identified for yourself – had you but been on the spot as I happened to be." In this remarkable transfer of literary property, Melville makes it seem that Hawthorne owns what Melville has made.

Who knows what Melville meant by this enigmatic maneuver? Was he being coy, coaxing Hawthorne into accepting his proposition so that, at a time when Hawthorne had moved away from the Berkshires, they could at least keep the correspondence, if not the neighborly visits, going? Was he joking in a way that flattered Hawthorne while still asserting his own authorial quickness? Melville, after all, was the one who had been "on the spot." Or was he testing a serious philo- sophical premise? These questions, along with many others that the letter raises, address the riddle of Melville's motivations as author and friend, and they are inevitably unanswerable. But they offer a remark- ably apt way to consider Melville's legacy to readers coming a century or two after him. With his clever notion of literary property, Melville invites readers to consider themselves as already in possession of what he writes. All they need to do is to acknowledge the "suggestiveness" of what he has written and make out the rest for themselves.

For some of Melville's works, readers in the twenty-first century do, in a sense, own them before they read them. With the ubiquity of *Moby-Dick*, in particular, as a name for seafood restaurants, an inspiration for *Jaws* and *Star Trek*, a story that has migrated to comic books and anime, the source for a global coffee company's name, many readers find it all too familiar before they pick up the book. Melville's statement to Hawthorne suggests that such familiarity need not breed contempt; it may in fact be a good thing. To own Melville – meaning to possess Melville but also to acknowledge him – is to recognize his writing as one's own. It is, as Melville tells Hawthorne, to receive what he gives as one's own property, that is, as something that one might do or think for oneself. Melville, then, offers his work, as Tennyson's Ulysses wrote wishfully of himself, as "a part of all that I have met." A gift of this kind breaks down the barriers raised by property laws and concepts of personal space and ownership. The author enters the reader's space as if inhabiting his or her own and invites the reader to do the same with his.

This fluid notion of reading, as if author and reader were simply borrowing each other's space for a while, seems both very new – it is hard to think of Melville, the giant of American literature, as an extension of oneself – and, in a digital age, already quite old. That is, internet communication makes it possible to own texts in ways never imagined in the past. For one thing, as I noted in the preface, they are free. For another, the boundaries between providers and users of texts have become porous in ways that invite abuse and theft but also offer opportunity, exchange, creative learning, and flexible sharing. Hence the idea of literary or creative property has come under intense scrutiny, with the result that copyright restrictions now often impede the trade in ideas that they were once designed to allow. In light of controversies over copyright law, plagiarism, fair use of the internet, and intellectual property, the ideas Melville expresses in the "Agatha" letter seem quite radical. If everyone treats what someone else has written as his or her own property, what will happen to artistic creativity?

What indeed? Perhaps the most radical implication of Melville's radical idea is that artistic creativity comes to life when the artificial boundaries determined by property rights surrender to gravity. Ideas could be loose fish in the fullest sense. It does not seem, though, as if the world is ready to give up the concept of private property. Another way to take Melville at his word, without upsetting the whole struc- ture of society, would be to "own" him in the second sense, of acknowl- edging his work fully, by putting aside one's preconceptions of his reputation and status and reading his works afresh. To do so is to rec- ognize, as Clarel does, that the "books not all have told." That is, the books that purport to tell us about Melville (including this one) cannot replace one's own direct experience of Melville's works. And Melville's books themselves have not told us all that we might learn on further reading. To "own" Melville, then, is to read and keep reading. And read some more.

Appendix

The "Agatha" Correspondence

1.　TO NATHANIEL HAWTHORNE
　　13 AUGUST 1852, PITTSFIELD

Pittsfield Aug: 13th 1852.

– While visiting Nantucket some four weeks ago, I made the acquaintance of a gentleman from New Bedford, a lawyer, who gave me considerable information upon several matters concerning which I was curious. – One night we were talking, I think, of the great patience, & endurance, & resignedness of the women of the island in submitting so uncomplainingly to the long, long abscences of their sailor husbands, when, by way of anecdote, this lawyer gave me a leaf from his professional experience. Altho' his memory was a little confused with regard to some of the items of the story, yet he told me enough to awaken the most lively interest in me; and I begged him to be sure and send me a more full account so soon as he arrived home – he having previously told me that at the time of the affair he had made a record in his books. – I heard nothing more, till a few days after arriving here at Pittsfield I received thro' the Post Office the enclosed document. – You will perceive by the gentleman's note to me that he assumed that I purposed making literary use of the story; but I had not hinted anything of the kind to him, & my first spontaneous interest in it arose from very different considerations. I confess, however, that since then I have a little turned the subject over in my mind with a view to a regular story to be founded on

From *L* 232–7, 239–40, 242, and 622–5.

these striking incidents. But, thinking again, it has occurred to me that this thing lies very much in a vein, with which you are peculiarly familiar. To be plump, I think that in this matter you would make a better hand at it than I would. – Besides the thing seems naturally to gravitate towards you (to spea[k] . . . [half a line torn] should of right belong to you. I cou[ld] . . . [half a line torn] the Steward to deliver it to you. –

The very great interest I felt in this story while narrating to me, was heightened by the emotion of the gentleman who told it, who evinced the most unaffected sympathy in it, tho' now a matter of his past. – But perhaps this great interest of mine may have been largely helped by some accidental circumstances or other; so that, possibly, to you the story may not seem to possess so much of pathos, & so much of depth. But you will see how it is. _____

In estimating the character of Robinson Charity should be allowed a liberal play. I take exception to that passage from the Diary which says that *"he must have received a portion of his punishment in this life"* – thus hinting of a future supplemental castigation. – I do not at all suppose that his desertion of his wife was a premeditated thing. If it had been so, he would have changed his name, probably, after quitting her. – No: he was a weak man, & his temptations (tho' we know little of them) were strong. The whole sin stole upon him insensibly – so that it would perhaps have been hard for him to settle upon the exact day when he could say to himself, *"Now* I have deserted my wife["]; unless, indeed upon the day he wedded the Alexandran lady. – And here I am reminded of your *London husband*; tho' the cases so rudely contrast. – Many more things might be mentioned; but I forbear; you will find out the suggestiveness for yourself; & all the better perhaps, for my not intermeddling. _____

If you should be sufficiently interested, to engage upon a regular story founded on this narration; then I consider you but fairly entitled to the following tributary items, collected by me, by chance, during my strolls thro the islands; & which – as you will perceive – seem legitimately to belong to the story, in its rounded & beautified & thoroughly developed state; – but of all this you must of course be your own judge – I but submit matter to you – I dont decide.

Supposing the story to open with the wreck – then there must be a storm; & it were well if some faint shadow of the preceding *calm* were thrown forth to lead the whole. – Now imagine a high cliff over-hanging the sea & crowned with a pasture for sheep; a little way off – higher up, – a light-house, where resides the father of the future Mrs Robinson the First. The afternoon is mild & warm. The sea with an air of solemn deliberation, with an elaborate deliberation, ceremoniously rolls upon the beach. The air is suppressedly charged with the sound of long lines of surf. There is no land over against this cliff short of Europe & the West Indies. Young Agatha (but you must give her some other name) comes wandering along the cliff. She marks how the continual assaults of the sea have undermined it; so that the fences fall over, & have need of many shiftings inland. The sea has encroached also upon that part where their dwelling-house stands near the light-house. – Filled with meditations, she reclines along the edge of the cliff & gazes out seaward. She marks a handful of cloud on the horizon, presaging a storm thro' all this quietude. (Of a maratime family & always dwelling on the coast, she is learned in these matters[.]) This again gives food for thought. Suddenly she catches the long shadow of the cliff cast upon the beach 100 feet beneath her; and now she notes a shadow moving along the shadow. It is cast by a sheep from the pasture. It has advanced to the very edge of the cliff, & is sending a mild innocent glance far out upon the water. There, in strange & beautiful contrast, we have the innocence of the land placidly eyeing the malignity of the sea. (All this having poetic reference to Agatha & her sea-lover, who is coming in the storm: the storm carries her lover to her; she catches a dim distant glimpse of his ship ere quitting the cliff.) ⸺ P.S. It were well, if from her knowledge of the deep miseries produced to wives by marrying seafaring men, Agatha should have formed a young determination never to marry a sailor; which resolve in her, however, is afterwards overborne by the omnipotence of Love. – P.S. No 2. Agatha should be active during the wreck, & should, in some way, be made the saviour of young Robinson. He should be the only survivor. He should be ministered to by Agatha at the house during the illness ensuing upon his injuries from the wreck.⸺Now this wrecked ship was driven over the shoals, & driven upon the beach where she goes to pieces, all but her stem-part. This in course of time becomes embedded in the sand – after the lapse of some years showing nothing but the sturdy stem (or, prow-bone) projecting some two feet at low water. All the rest is filled & packed down with the sand. – So that after her husband has disappeared the sad Agatha every day sees this melancholy monument, with all its remindings. _____

After a sufficient lapse of time – when Agatha has become alarmed about the protracted abscence of her young husband & is feverishly expecting a letter from him – then we must introduce the mail-post – no, that phrase wont' do, but here is the *thing*. – Owing to the remoteness of the lighthouse from any settled place no regular mail reaches it. But some mile or so distant there is a road leading between two post-towns. And at the junction of what we shall call the Light-House road with this Post Rode, there stands a post surmounted with a little rude wood box with a lid to it & a leather hinge. Into this box the Post boy drops all letters for the people of the light house & that vicinity of fisher-men. To this post they must come for their letters. And, of course, daily young Agatha goes – for seventeen years she goes thither daily[.] As her hopes gradually decay in her, so does the post itself & the little box decay. The post rots in the ground at last. Owing to its being little used – hardly used at all – grass grows rankly about it. At last a little bird nests in it. At last the post falls.

_____

The father of Agatha must be an old widower – a man of the sea, but early driven away from it by repeated disasters. Hence, is he subdued & quiet & wise in his life. And now he tends a light house, to warn people from those very perils, from which he himself has suffered.

_____

Some few other items occur to me – but nothing material – and I fear to weary you, if not, make you smile at my strange impertinent officiousness. – And it would be so, were it not that these things do, in my mind, seem legitimately to belong to the story; for they were visably suggested to me by scenes I actually beheld while on the very coast where the story of Agatha occurred. – I do not therefore, My Dear Hawthorne, at all imagine that you will think that I am so silly as to flatter myself I am giving you anything of my own. I am but restoring to you your own property – which you would quickly enough have identified for yourself – had you but been on the spot as I happened to be.

Let me conclude by saying that it seems to me that with your great power in these things, you can construct a story of remarkable interest out of this material furnished by the New Bedford lawyer. – You have a skeleton of actual reality to build about with fulness & veins & beauty. And if I thought I could do it as well as you, why, I should not let you have it. – The narrative from the Diary is instinct with significance. – Consider the mention of the *shawls* – & the inference derived from it. Ponder the conduct of this Robinson throughout. – Mark his trepidation & suspicion when any one called upon him. – But why prate so – you will mark it all & mark it deeper than I would, perhaps.

I have written all this in a great hurry; so you must spell it out the best way you may.

[Enclosure: John Henry Clifford's story of Agatha, from his legal diary]

May 28th 1842 Saturday. I have just returned from a visit to Falmouth with a M[r] Janney of M[o] on one of the most interesting and romantic cases I ever expect to be engaged in. – The gentle-man from Missouri M[r] Janney came to my house last Sunday evening and related to myself and partner that he had married the daughter of a M[rs] Irvin formerly of Pittsburgh Pa. and that M[rs] Irvin had married a second husband by the name of Robertson. The latter deceased about two years since. He was appointed Adm[r] to his Estate which amounted to $20 000 – about 15 months afterwards M[rs] Robertson also died and in the meantime the Adm[r] had been engaged in looking up heirs to the Estate – He learned that Robertson was an Englishman whose original name was Shinn – that he resided at Alexandria D.C. where he had two nephews – He also wrote to England and had ascertained the history and genealogy of the family with much accuracy, when on going to the Post Office one day he found a letter directed to James Robertson the deceased, post marked Falmouth Mass[tts] – On opening it he found it from a person signing herself Rebecca A. Gifford and addressing him as "Father." The existence of this girl had been known before by M[rs] Robertson and her husband had pronounced her to be illegitimate[.] The Adm[r] then addressed a letter to M[rs] Gifford informing her of the decease of her father. He was surprized soon after by the appearance in S[t] Louis of a shrewd Quaker from Falmouth named Dillingham with full powers and fortified by letters and affidavits shewing the existence of a wife in Falmouth whom Robertson married in 1807 at Pembroke M[a]ss & the legitimacy of the daughter who had married a M[r] Gifford and laying strong claims to the entire property.

The Adm[r] and heirs having strong doubts arising from the declarations of Robertson during his lifetime & the peculiar expressions

contained in the letters exhibited, as to the validity of the marriage &
the claim based upon it, determined to resist and legal proceedings
were at once commenced. The object of the visit of Mr Janney was to
attend the taking of depositions, upon a notice from the claimants –
The Minister Town Clerk and Witnesses present at the ceremony
established the fact of a legal marriage and the birth of a child in
wedlock, beyond all cavil or controversy all of the witnesses were of
the highest respectability and the widow and daughter interested me
very much.

It appeared that Robertson was wrecked on the coast of Pembroke
where this girl, then Miss Agatha Hatch was living – that he was hospitably entertained and cared for, and that within a year after, he
married her, in due form of law – that he went two short voyages to
sea. About two years after the marriage, leaving his wife *enciente* [*sic*]
he started off in search of employment and from that time until *Seventeen* years afterwards she never heard from him in any way whatsoever, directly or indirectly, not even a word. Being poor she went
out nursing for her daily bread and yet contrived out of her small
earnings to give her daughter a first rate education. Having become
connected with the Society of Friends she sent her to their most celebrated boarding school and when I saw her I found she had profited
by all her advantages beyond most females. In the meantime Robertson had gone to Alexandria D.C. where he had entered into a successful and profitable business and married a second wife. At the expiration
of this long period of 17 years which for the poor forsaken wife, had
glided wearily away, while she was engaged away from home, her
Father rode up in a gig and informed her that her husband had
returned and wished to see her and her child – but if she would not
see him, to see her child at all events – They all returned together and
encountered him on the way coming to meet them about half a mile
from her father's house. This meeting was described to me by the
mother and daughter – Every incident seemed branded upon the
memories of both. He excused himself as well as he could for his long
absence and silence, appeared very affectionate refused to tell where
he was living and persuaded them not to make any inquiries, gave
them a handsome sum of money, promised to return for good and left
the next day – He appeared again in about a year, just on the eve of
his daughter's marriage & gave her a bridal present. It was not long
after this that his wife in Alexandria died – He then wrote to his

son-in-law to come there – He did so – remained 2 days and brought back a gold watch and three handsome shawls which had been previously worn by some person – They all admitted that they had suspicions then & from this circumstance that he had been a second time married.

Soon after this he visited Falmouth again & as it proved for the last time – He announced his intention of removing to Missouri & urged the whole family to go with him, promising money land and other assistance to his son-in-law. The offer was not accepted He shed tears when he bade them farewell – From the time of his return to Missouri till the time of his death a constant correspondence was kept up money was remitted by him annually and he announced to them his marriage with Mrs Irvin – He had no children by either of his last two wives.

Mr Janney was entirely disappointed in the character of the evidence and the character of the claimants. He considered them, when he first came, as parties to the imposition practised upon Mrs Irvin & her children. But I was satisfied and I think he was, that their motives in keeping silence were high and pure, creditable in every way to the true Mrs Robertson.
She stated the causes with a simplicity & pathos which carried that conviction irresistibly to my mind. The only good(?) it could have done to expose him would have been to drive Robertson away and forever disgrace him & it would certainly have made Mrs Irvin & her children wretched for the rest of their days – "I had no wish" said the wife "to make either of them unhappy, notwithstanding all I had suffered on his account" – It was to me a most striking instance of long continued & uncomplaining submission to wrong and anguish on the part of a wife, which made her in my eyes a heroine.

Janney informed me that R. and his last wife did not live very happily together and particularly that he seemed to be a very jealous suspicious man – that when a person called at his house he would never enter the room till he knew who it was & "all about him.["] He must have recieved a portion of his punishment in this life. The fact came out in the course of examination that they had agreed to give Dillingham one half of what he might obtain deducting the expenses from his half – After the strength of the evidence became known Mr Janney commenced the making of serious efforts to effect a compromise of the claim. What the result will be time will shew – This is, I suspect, the end of my connexion with the case –

[Note from John Henry Clifford with the enclosure above]
                                    New Bedford July 14th 1852

Herman Melville
Dr Sir
        Above I send you the little story I promised you –
                                        Respectfully Yours

[Melville's note]
        P.S. The business was settled in a few weeks afterwards, in a most amicable & honorable manner, by a division of the property. I think Mrs. Robinson & her family refused to claim or recieve anything that really belonged to Mrs. Irwin, or which Robinson had derived through her. –

2.   TO NATHANIEL HAWTHORNE
        25 OCTOBER 1852, PITTSFIELD

                                    Monday Morning
                                    25th Oct: 1852.

My Dear Hawthorne –
    If you thought it worth while to write the story of Agatha, and should you be engaged upon it; then I have a little idea touching it, which however trifling, may not be entirely out of place. Perhaps, tho', the idea has occurred to yourself. – The probable facility with which Robinson first leaves his wife & then takes another, may, possibly, be ascribed to the peculiarly latitudinarian notions, which most sailors have of all tender obligations of that sort. In his previous sailor life Robinson had found a wife (for a night) in every port. The sense of the obligation of the marriage-vow to Agatha had little weight with him at first. *It* was only when some years of life ashore had passed that his moral sense on that point became developed. And hence his subsequent conduct – Remorse &c. Turn this over in your mind & see if it is right. If not – make it so yourself.
    If you come across a little book called "Taughconic" – look into it and divert yourself with it. Among others, you figure in it, & I also. But you are the most honored, being the most abused, and having the greatest space allotted you. – It is a "Guide Book" to Berkshire.

I dont know when I shall see you. I shall lay eyes on you one of these days however. Keep some Champagne or Gin for me.

My respects and best remembrances to Mrs: Hawthorne & a reminder to the children.

H Melville

If you find any *sand* in this letter, regard it as so many sands of my life, which run out as I was writing it.

3.   TO NATHANIEL HAWTHORNE
        BETWEEN 3 AND 13 DECEMBER 1852, BOSTON

My dear Hawthorne, – The other day, at Concord, you expressed uncertainty concerning your undertaking the story of Agatha, and, in the end, you urged *me* to write it. I have decided to do so, and shall begin it immediately upon reaching home; and so far as in me lies, I shall endeavor to do justice to so interesting a story of reality. Will you therefore enclose the whole affair to me; and if anything of your own has occurred to you in your random thinking, won't you note it down for me on the same page with my memorandum? I wish I had come to this determination at Concord, for then we might have more fully and closely talked over the story, and so struck out new light. Make amends for this, though, as much as you conveniently can. With your permission I shall make use of the "Isle of Shoals," as far as the name goes at least. I shall also introduce the old Nantucket seaman, in the way I spoke to you about. I invoke your blessing upon my endeavors; and breathe a fair wind upon me. I greatly enjoyed my visit to you, and hope that you reaped some corresponding pleasure.

H. Melville

Julian, Una, and Rose, – my salutations to them.

Notes

Chapter 1

1 Jay Leyda, ed., *The Melville Log: A Documentary Life of Herman Melville, 1819–1891* (1st pub. 1951, in 2 vols.; New York: Gordian Press, 1969), 1: 43.

2 Some scholars, however, disagree. See Mary K. Bercaw Edwards, "Was Herman Melville Ever Really in the Typee Valley?" (paper delivered at the Melville and the Pacific Conference, Lahaina, Maui, June 3, 2003). *ESQ: A Journal of the American Renaissance* published a special issue on this question, titled "Melville in the Marquesas: Actuality of Place in *Typee* and Other Island Writings" (vol. 51, 2006). Scholars G. R. Thompson, Robert C. Suggs, Ruth M. Blair, T. Walter Herbert, Vanessa Smith, Alex Calder, Lee Quinby, Geoffrey Sanborn, John Bryant, and Samuel Otter conducted a spirited debate on the topic of Melville's travels in the Marquesas.

Chapter 2

1 I am grateful to Mary K. Bercaw Edwards for pointing out this feature of Melville's scenic descriptions of Nantucket.

2 See Robert K. Wallace, *Melville and Turner: Spheres of Love and Fright* (Athens: University of Georgia Press, 1992), and his essay, " 'Unlike Things Must Meet and Mate': Melville and the Visual Arts," in Wyn Kelley, ed., *A Companion to Herman Melville* (Oxford: Blackwell Publishing, 2006), 342–61.

3 For further information about Melville's views on slavery, see John Stauffer, "Melville, Slavery, and the American Dilemma," in Kelley, ed., *Companion*,

214–30. For a dissenting view and a comprehensive comparison between Melville's views and those of abolitionist Lydia Maria Child, see Carolyn Karcher, "The Moderate and the Radical: Melville and Child on the Civil War and Reconstruction," *ESQ* 45 (1999), 187–257.

Chapter 3

1   Examples include Charles R. Anderson, *Melville in the South Seas* (New York: Columbia University Press, 1939); Merrill R. Davis, *Melville's* Mardi: *A Chartless Voyage* (New Haven: Yale University Press, 1952); William H. Gilman, *Melville's Early Life and* Redburn (New York: New York University Press, 1951); Wilson Heflin, *Melville's Whaling Years*, ed. Thomas Farel Heffernan and Mary K. Bercaw Edwards (Nashville: Vanderbilt University Press, 2004); and Howard Vincent, *The Tailoring of* White-Jacket (Evanston: Northwestern University Press, 1970).

2   Examples of such studies include T. Walter Herbert, *Marquesan Encounters: Melville and the Meaning of Civilization* (Cambridge, MA: Harvard University Press, 1980), and Geoffrey Sanborn, *The Sign of the Cannibal: Melville and the Making of a Postcolonial Reader* (Durham: Duke University Press, 1998).

3   On race and class see Cindy Weinstein, *The Literature of Labor and the Labors of Literature: Allegory in Nineteenth-Century American Fiction* (Cambridge and New York: Cambridge University Press, 1995), and Carol Colatrella, *Literature and Moral Reform: Melville and the Discipline of Reading* (Gainesville: University Press of Florida, 2002).

4   For two recent examples, see John Bryant, "'A Work I Have Never Happened to Meet': Melville's Versions of Porter in *Typee*" (83–97) and Bryan Short, "Plagiarizing Polynesia: Decolonization in Melville's *Omoo* Borrowings" (98–110), both in Jill Barnum, Wyn Kelley, and Christopher Sten, eds., *"Whole Oceans Away": Melville and the Pacific* (Kent, OH: Kent State University Press, 2007).

5   For social and sexual themes see Caleb Crain, "Lovers of Human Flesh: Homosexuality and Cannibalism in Melville's Novels," *American Literature* 66 (1994), 25–53; Samuel Otter, *Melville's Anatomies: Bodies, Discourse, and Ideology in Antebellum America* (Berkeley: University of California Press, 1998); and Sanborn, *The Sign of the Cannibal*.

6   For a reading of this passage in relation to the themes of sacrifices and victims in *Typee*, see Giorgio Mariani, "'Chiefly Known by His Rod': The Book of Jonah, Mapple's Sermon, and Scapegoating," in John Bryant, Mary K. Bercaw Edwards, and Timothy Marr, eds., *"Ungraspable Phantom"*:

Essays on Moby-Dick (Kent, OH: Kent State University Press, 2006), 46–9.

7 See Mary K. Bercaw, *Melville's Sources* (Evanston: Northwestern University Press, 1987); Bryant, "A Work," in Barnum, Kelley, and Sten, eds., *"Whole Oceans Away"*; Herbert, *Marquesan Encounters*; Sanborn, *The Sign of the Cannibal*; Short, "Plagiarizing," in Barnum, Kelley, and Sten, eds., *"Whole Oceans Away"*.

8 See Bryant, "A Work," and Mary K. Bercaw Edwards's forthcoming *Cannibal Old Me: Oral Sources of Melville's Narrative Voice* (Kent, OH: Kent State University Press, 2008).

9 For a reading of *Typee* as tattoo, see Martin Kevorkian, Stanley Orr, and Matt Rollins, "Lines of Dissent: Oceanic Tattoo and the Colonial Contest," in Barnum, Kelley, and Sten, eds., *"Whole Oceans Away,"* 291–304.

Chapter 4

1 See Elizabeth Renker, *Strike Through the Mask: Herman Melville and the Scene of Writing* (Baltimore: Johns Hopkins University Press, 1996).

2 See Wai-chee Dimock, *Empire for Liberty: Melville and the Poetics of Individualism* (Princeton: Princeton University Press, 1989); Paul Lyons, *American Pacifism: Oceania in the U.S. Imagination* (New York: Routledge, 2006); Renker, *Strike Through the Mask*; and Sanborn, *The Sign of the Cannibal*.

3 See Colatrella, *Literature and Moral Reform*.

4 See Vincent, *The Tailoring of* White-Jacket; Weinstein, *The Literature of Labor*; and Renker, *Strike Through the Mask*.

Chapter 5

1 See Dennis Berthold, "Class Acts: The Astor Place Riots and Melville's 'The Two Temples,'" *American Literature* 71 (1999), 429–61.

2 See Paul Lauter, "Melville Climbs the Canon," *American Literature* 66 (March 1994), 1–24; F. O. Matthiesson, *American Renaissance: Art and Expression in the Age of Emerson and Whitman* (New York: Oxford University Press, 1941); Donald E. Pease, *"Moby-Dick* and the Cold War," in Walter Benn Michaels and Donald E. Pease, eds., *The American Renaissance Reconsidered* (Baltimore: Johns Hopkins University Press, 1985), 113–55; Clare Spark, *Hunting Captain Ahab: Psychological Warfare and the Melville Revival* (Kent, OH: Kent State, 2001).

3   See Harrison Hayford, "Unnecessary Duplicates: A Key to the Writing of *Moby-Dick*," in his *Melville's Prisoners* (Evanston: Northwestern University Press, 2003).

Chapter 6

1   See Caroline Levander, "The Female Subject in *Pierre* and *The Piazza Tales*," in Kelley, ed., *Companion*, 423–34; Wyn Kelley, "Pierre's Domestic Ambiguities," in Robert S. Levine, ed., *The Cambridge Companion to Herman Melville* (Cambridge and New York: Cambridge University Press, 1998), 91–113; and Cindy Weinstein, *Family, Kinship, and Sympathy in Nineteenth-Century American Literature* (Cambridge and New York: Cambridge University Press, 2004).
2   For different treatments of Pierre's passions, see James Creech, *Closet Writing/Gay Reading: The Case of Melville's* Pierre (Chicago: University of Chicago Press, 1993), who argues that Pierre's love of Isabel masks a homoerotic attraction to his father; and Christopher Castiglia, "Pierre's Bad Associations: Public Life in the Institutional Nation," in Kelley, ed., *Companion*, 197–213, who shows how Pierre's emotions are manipulated by the rise of institutionalism in America.

Chapter 7

1   See Marvin Fisher, *Going Under: Melville's Short Fiction and the American 1850s* (Baton Rouge: Louisiana State University Press, 1977); William B. Dillingham, *Melville's Short Fiction, 1853–1856* (Athens: University of Georgia Press, 1977).
2   See Sheila Post-Lauria, *Correspondent Colorings: Melville in the Marketplace* (Amherst: University of Massachusetts Press, 1996).
3   See John Evelev, *Tolerable Entertainment: Herman Melville and Professionalism in Antebellum New York* (Amherst and Boston: University of Massachusetts Press, 2006).
4   See Wyn Kelley, "Hawthorne and Melville in the Shoals: 'Agatha,' the Trials of Authorship, and the Dream of Collaboration," in Jana Argersinger and Leland S. Person, eds., *Hawthorne and Melville: Writing a Relationship* (Athens, GA: University of Georgia Press, 2008).
5   All references to Melville's stories come from this volume.
6   See Leland S. Person, "Gender and Sexuality," in Kelley, ed., *Companion*, 231–46.

7 See Christopher Sten, " 'Facts . . . Picked Up in the Pacific': Fragmentation, Deformation, and the (Cultural) Uses of Enchantment in *The Encantadas*," in Barnum, Kelley, and Sten, eds., *"Whole Oceans Away,"* 213–23.

8 See Hester Blum, "Douglass's and Melville's 'Alphabets of the Blind'," in Robert S. Levine and Samuel Otter, eds., *Frederick Douglass and Herman Melville: Essays in Relation* (Chapel Hill: University of North Carolina Press, 2008).

9 See Robert K. Wallace, *Douglass and Melville: Anchored Together in Neighborly Style* (New Bedford: Spinner Publications, 2005).

Chapter 8

1 See Hester Blum, "Atlantic Trade," in Kelley, ed. *Companion*, 113–28.

2 See also Gale Temple, "Fluid Identity in *Israel Potter* and *The Confidence-Man*," in Kelley, ed. *Companion*, 451–66.

Chapter 9

1 See Robin Grey, *The Complicity of Imagination: The American Renaissance, Contests of Authority, and Seventeenth-Century English Culture* (Cambridge and New York: Cambridge University Press, 1997); Walter E. Bezanson, "Melville's Reading of Arnold's Poetry," *PMLA* 69/3 (1954), 365–91; and Peter Norberg, "Finding an Audience for *Clarel* in Matthew Arnold's *Essays in Criticism*," *Leviathan: A Journal of Melville Studies* 6/1 (2004), 35–54.

2 See Bryant, "Melville's Rose Poems: As They Fell," *Arizona Quarterly* 52 (1996), 49–84; Samuel Otter, "How *Clarel* Works," in Kelley, ed., *Companion*, 467–81; Elizabeth Renker "Melville's Poetic Singe," *Leviathan: A Journal of Melville Studies* 2/2 (Oct. 2000), 13–31; Renker, "Melville the Realist Poet," in Kelley, ed., *Companion*, 482–96; Douglas Robillard, "Introduction," in his edition of *The Poems of Herman Melville* (Kent, OH: Kent State University Press, 2000), 1–49; William C. Spengemann, "Melville the Poet," *American Literary History* 11 (1999), 569–609.

3 See Edgar A. Dryden, *Monumental Melville: The Formation of a Literary Career* (Stanford: Stanford University Press, 2004).

4 See Stanton Garner, *The Civil War World of Herman Melville* (Lawrence: University Press of Kansas, 1993).

5 Paul M. Dowling, "Robert E. Lee and Melville's Politics in *Battle-Pieces and Aspects of the War*." *Melville Society Extracts* 128 (Feb. 2005), 1–2, 18–23.

6   See Edgar A. Dryden, "Death and Literature: Melville and the Epitaph," in Kelley, ed. *Companion*, 299–312, which frames my discussion of the elegies in *Battle-Pieces*.

7   On the nature imagery in *Clarel*, including the palm, see Basem Ra'ad, "Ancient Lands," in Kelley, ed., *Companion*, 129–45.

8   Robert Milder, *Exiled Royalties: Melville and the Life We Imagine* (Oxford: Oxford University Press, 2006), 192.

9   See Warren Rosenberg, "Poem as Palm: Polynesia and Melville's Turn to Poetry," in Barnum, Kelley, and Sten, eds., *"Whole Oceans Away,"* 239–52.

Chapter 10

1   See Douglas Robillard, "Introduction," to *John Marr and Other Sailors, With Some Sea-Pieces, By Herman Melville: A Facsimile Edition* (Kent, OH: Kent State University Press, 2006), 1–12.

2   See R. D. Madison, "Literature of Exploration and the Sea," in Kelley, ed., *Companion*, 282–98.

3   Milder, *Exiled Royalties*, 145.

4   See John Bryant, ed., *Tales, Poems, and Other Writings: Herman Melville* (New York: Modern Library, 2001).

5   Laurie Robertson-Lorant, *Melville: A Biography* (New York: Clarkson Potter, 1996); John Bryant, "Melville's Rose Poems: As They Fell," *Arizona Quarterly* 52 (1996), 49–84.

6   See Robert Milder, *Exiled Royalties*, 221–3, and Renker, "Melville the Realist Poet."

7   The manuscript is in the Houghton Library at Harvard University.

Chapter 11

1   See Harrison Hayford and Merton M. Sealts Jr.'s introduction to their edition of *Billy Budd*.

2   See Eve Sedgwick, "Billy Budd: After the Homosexual," in Myra Jehlen, ed., *Herman Melville: A Collection of Critical Essays* (Englewood Cliffs, NJ: Prentice-Hall, 1994), 217–34; and Robert K. Martin, "Melville and Sexuality," in Levine, ed., *Cambridge Companion*, 186–201.

Bibliography

General

Adler, Joyce. *War in Melville's Imagination*. New York: New York University Press, 1981.

Argersinger, Jana, and Leland S. Person, eds. *Hawthorne and Melville: Writing a Relationship*. Athens, GA: University of Georgia Press, 2008.

Barnum, Jill, Wyn Kelley, and Christopher Sten, eds. *"Whole Oceans Away": Melville and the Pacific*. Kent, OH: Kent State University Press, 2007.

Baym, Nina. "Melville's Quarrel with Fiction." *PMLA* 94 (1979), 25–52.

Bercaw, Mary K. *Melville's Sources*. Evanston: Northwestern University Press, 1987.

Bergmann, Hans. *God in the Street: New York Writing from the Penny Press to Melville*. Philadelphia: Temple University Press, 1995.

Berthoff, Werner. *The Example of Melville*. Princeton: Princeton University Press, 1962.

Bryant, John. *Melville and Repose: The Rhetoric of Humor in the American Renaissance*. New York: Oxford University Press, 1993.

Bryant, John, ed. *A Companion to Melville Studies*. Westport, CT: Greenwood Press, 1986.

Bryant, John, and Robert Milder, eds. *Melville's Evermoving Dawn: Centennial Essays*. Kent, OH: Kent State University Press, 1997.

Coffler, Gail. *Melville's Allusions to Religion: A Comprehensive Index and Glossary*. Westport, CT: Greenwood Press, 2004.

—— *Melville's Classical Allusions: A Comprehensive Index and Glossary*. Westport, CT: Greenwood Press, 1987.

Colatrella, Carol. *Literature and Moral Reform: Melville and the Discipline of Reading*. Gainesville: University Press of Florida, 2002.

Cowan, Walker. *Melville's Marginalia.* Diss. Harvard University, 1965.

Delbanco, Andrew. *Melville: His World and Work.* New York: Knopf, 2005.

Dillingham, William B. *Melville and His Circle: The Last Years.* Athens: University of Georgia Press, 1996.

—— *Melville's Later Novels.* Athens: University of Georgia Press, 1986.

Dimock, Wai-chee. *Empire for Liberty: Melville and the Poetics of Individualism.* Princeton: Princeton University Press, 1989.

Douglas, Ann. *The Feminization of American Culture.* New York: Alfred A. Knopf, 1977.

Dryden, Edgar A. *Melville's Thematics of Form: The Great Art of Telling the Truth.* Baltimore: Johns Hopkins University Press, 1968.

—— *Monumental Melville: The Formation of a Literary Career.* Stanford: Stanford University Press, 2004.

Duban, James. *Melville's Major Fiction: Politics, Theology, and Imagination.* DeKalb: University of Illinois Press, 1983.

Evelev, John. *Tolerable Entertainment: Herman Melville and Professionalism in Antebellum New York.* Amherst and Boston: University of Massachusetts Press, 2006.

Franchot, Jenny. *Roads to Rome: The Antebellum Protestant Encounter with Catholicism.* Berkeley: University of California Press, 1994.

Franklin, Bruce. *In the Wake of the Gods: Melville's Mythology.* Stanford: Stanford University Press, 1963.

Fredericks, Nancy. *Melville's Art of Democracy.* Athens: University of Georgia Press, 1995.

Gidmark, Jill B. *Melville Sea Dictionary: A Glossed Concordance and Analysis of the Sea Language in Melville's Nautical Novels.* Westport, CT: Greenwood Press, 1982.

Gilmore, Michael. *American Romanticism and the Marketplace.* Chicago: University of Chicago Press, 1985.

Grey, Robin. *The Complicity of Imagination: The American Renaissance, Contests of Authority, and Seventeenth-Century English Culture.* Cambridge and New York: Cambridge University Press, 1997.

Grey, Robin, ed. *Melville and Milton: An Edition and Analysis of Melville's Annotations of Milton's Poetry.* Pittsburgh: Duquesne University Press, 2004.

Harvey, Bruce. *American Geographics: U.S. National Narratives and the Representation of the Non-European World, 1830–1865.* Stanford: Stanford University Press, 2001.

Hayford, Harrison. *Melville's Prisoners.* Evanston: Northwestern University Press, 2003.

Higgins, Brian, and Hershel Parker, eds. *Herman Melville: The Contemporary Reviews.* Cambridge and New York: Cambridge University Press, 1995.

Irwin, John T. *American Hieroglyphics: The Symbol of Egyptian Hieroglyphics in the American Renaissance*. Baltimore: Johns Hopkins University Press, 1980.

Jehlen, Myra, ed. *Herman Melville: A Collection of Critical Essays*. Englewood Cliffs, NJ: Prentice-Hall, 1994.

Karcher, Carolyn. *Shadow Over the Promised Land: Slavery, Race, and Violence in Melville's America*. Baton Rouge: Louisiana State University Press, 1980.

Kelley, Wyn. *Melville's City: Urban and Literary Form in Nineteenth-Century New York*. Cambridge and New York: Cambridge University Press, 1996.

Kelley, Wyn, ed. *A Companion to Herman Melville*. Oxford: Blackwell Publishing, 2006.

Kier, Kathleen E. *A Melville Encyclopedia*: *The Novels*. Troy, NY: Whitson, 1994.

Lauter, Paul. "Melville Climbs the Canon." *American Literature* 66 (March 1994), 1–24.

Lee, A. Robert, ed. *Herman Melville: Critical Assessments*. 4 vols. Robertsbridge, Sussex: Helm Information Ltd, 2001.

—— *Herman Melville: Reassessments*. London: Barnes and Noble, 1984.

Levin, Harry. *The Power of Blackness*: *Poe, Hawthorne, Melville*. New York: Alfred A. Knopf, 1958.

Levine, Robert S., ed. *The Cambridge Companion to Herman Melville*. Cambridge and New York: Cambridge University Press, 1998.

Leyda, Jay, ed. *The Melville Log: A Documentary Life of Herman Melville, 1819–1891*. 1st pub. 1951, in 2 vols. New York: Gordian Press, 1969.

Marovitz, Sanford, and A. C. Christodoulou, eds. *Melville "Among the Nations."* Kent, OH: Kent State University Press, 2002.

Marr, Timothy. *The Cultural Roots of American Islamicism*. Cambridge and New York: Cambridge University Press, 2006.

Martin, Robert K. *Hero, Captain, and Stranger: Male Friendship, Social Critique, and Literary Form in the Sea Novels of Herman Melville*. Chapel Hill: University of North Carolina Press, 1986.

McWilliams, John. *Hawthorne, Melville, and the American Character: A Looking-Glass Business*. Cambridge and New York: Cambridge University Press, 1984.

Milder, Robert. *Exiled Royalties*: *Melville and the Life We Imagine*. Oxford: Oxford University Press, 2006.

Miller, Perry. *The Raven and the Whale: The War of Words and Wits in the Era of Poe and Melville*. New York: Harcourt, Brace & World, 1964.

Nelson, Dana. *The Word in Black and White: Reading "Race" in American Literature, 1638–1867*. New York: Oxford University Press, 1922.

Otter, Samuel. *Melville's Anatomies: Bodies, Discourse, and Ideology in Antebellum America*. Berkeley: University of California Press, 1998.

Parker, Hershel. *Herman Melville: A Biography*, vol. 1: *1819–1851*. Baltimore: Johns Hopkins University Press, 1996; vol. 2: *1851–1891*. Baltimore: Johns Hopkins University Press, 2002.

Pease, Donald E. *Visionary Compacts: American Renaissance Writings in Cultural Context*. Madison: University of Wisconsin Press, 1987.

Person, Leland S. *Aesthetic Headaches: Women and a Masculine Poetics in Poe, Melville, and Hawthorne*. Athens: University of Georgia Press, 1988.

Pullin, Faith, ed. *New Perspectives on Melville*. Kent, OH: Kent State University Press, 1978.

Renker, Elizabeth. *Strike Through the Mask: Herman Melville and the Scene of Writing*. Baltimore: Johns Hopkins University Press, 1996.

Reynolds, David S. *Beneath the American Renaissance: The Subversive Imagination in the Age of Emerson and Melville*. New York: Alfred A. Knopf, 1988.

Reynolds, Larry. *European Revolutions and the American Literary Renaissance*. New Haven: Yale University Press, 1988.

Robertson-Lorant, Laurie. *Melville: A Biography*. New York: Clarkson Potter, 1996.

Robillard, Douglas. *Melville and the Visual Arts: Ionian Form, Venetian Tint*. Kent, OH: Kent State University Press, 1997.

Rogin, Michael. *Subversive Genealogy: The Politics and Art of Herman Melville*. New York: Alfred A. Knopf, 1983.

Rowe, John Carlos. *Through the Custom-House: Nineteenth-Century American Fiction and Modern Theory*. Baltimore: Johns Hopkins University Press, 1982.

Ruttenburg, Nancy. *Democratic Personality: Popular Voice and the Trial of American Authorship*. Stanford: Stanford University Press, 1998.

Ryan, Robert C. Introduction: "'Weeds and Wildings, Chiefly: With a Rose or Two,' by Herman Melville: Genetic and Reading Text." Ph.D. Diss. Northwestern University, 1967.

Samson, John. *White Lies: Melville's Narrative of Facts*. Ithaca: Cornell University Press, 1989.

Sanborn, Geoffrey. *The Sign of the Cannibal: Melville and the Making of a Postcolonial Reader*. Durham: Duke University Press, 1998.

Schultz, Elizabeth, and Haskell Springer, eds. *Melville and Women*. Kent, OH: Kent State University Press, 2006.

Sealts, Merton M., Jr. *Melville's Reading*. Revised edn. Columbia: University of South Carolina Press, 1988.

—— *Pursuing Melville, 1940–1980*. Madison: University of Wisconsin Press, 1982.

Seelye, John. *Melville: The Ironic Diagram*. Evanston: Northwestern University Press, 1971.

Short, Bryan. *Cast By Means of Figures: Herman Melville's Rhetorical Development*. Amherst: University of Massachusetts Press, 1992.

Sten, Christopher. *The Weaver-God, He Weaves: Melville and the Poetics of the Novel.* Kent, OH: Kent State University Press, 1996.

Sten, Christopher, ed. *Savage Eye: Melville and the Visual Arts.* Kent, OH: Kent State University Press, 1991.

Stern, Milton R. *The Fine Hammered Steel of Herman Melville.* Urbana: University of Illinois Press, 1957.

Stuckey, Sterling. *Going Through the Storm: The Influence of African-American Art in History.* New York: Oxford University Press, 1994.

Sundquist, Eric J. *To Wake the Nations: Race and the Making of American Literature.* Cambridge, MA: Harvard University Press, 1993.

Thompson, Lawrance R. *Melville's Quarrel with God.* Princeton: Princeton University Press, 1951.

Tolchin, Neal L. *Mourning, Gender, and Creativity in the Art of Herman Melville.* New Haven: Yale University Press, 1988.

Wald, Priscilla. *Constituting Americans: Cultural Anxiety and Narrative Form.* Durham: Duke University Press, 1995.

Wallace, Robert K. *Douglass and Melville: Anchored Together in Neighborly Style.* New Bedford: Spinner Publications, 2005.

—— *Melville and Turner: Spheres of Love and Fright.* Athens: University of Georgia Press, 1992.

Weinstein, Cindy. *Family, Kinship, and Sympathy in Nineteenth-Century American Literature.* Cambridge and New York: Cambridge University Press, 2004.

—— *The Literature of Labor and the Labors of Literature: Allegory in Nineteenth-Century American Fiction.* Cambridge and New York: Cambridge University Press, 1995.

Wenke, John. *Melville's Muse: Literary Creation and the Forms of Philosophical Fiction.* Kent, OH: Kent State University Press, 1995.

Wright, Nathalia. *Melville's Use of the Bible.* Durham: Duke University Press, 1949.

Chapter 1

Arvin, Newton. *Herman Melville.* New York: William Sloane, 1950.

Chase, Richard. *Herman Melville: A Critical Study.* New York: Macmillan, 1949.

Cohen, Hennig, and Donald Yannella. *Herman Melville's Malcolm Letter: "Man's Final Lore."* New York: Fordham University Press and the New York Public Library, 1992.

Feidelson, Charles. *Symbolism and American Literature.* Chicago: University of Chicago Press, 1953.

Fiedler, Leslie. *Love and Death in the American Novel.* New York: Criterion Books, 1960.

Howard, Leon. *Herman Melville: A Biography*. Berkeley: University of California Press, 1951.

Lawrence, D. H. *Studies in Classic American Literature*. 1923. New York: Penguin Books, 1977.

Lewis, R. W. B. *The American Adam: Innocence, Tragedy, and Tradition in the Nineteenth Century*. Chicago: University of Chicago Press, 1955.

Marx, Leo. *The Machine in the Garden: Technology and the Pastoral Ideal in America*. New York: Oxford University Press, 1964.

Matthiesson, F. O. *American Renaissance: Art and Expression in the Age of Emerson and Whitman*. New York: Oxford University Press, 1941.

Metcalf, Eleanor Melville. *Herman Melville: Cycle and Epicycle*. Cambridge: Harvard University Press, 1953.

Miller, Edwin Haviland. *Herman Melville: A Biography*. New York: Braziller, 1975.

Mumford, Lewis. *Herman Melville*. New York: Harcourt, Brace & Company, 1929.

Olson, Charles. *Call Me Ishmael: A Study of Melville*. San Francisco: City Lights Books, 1947.

Parker, Hershel, ed. *The Recognition of Herman Melville*. Ann Arbor: University of Michigan Press, 1967.

Weaver, Raymond. *Herman Melville*. New York: Doran, 1921.

Chapter 2

Kelley, Wyn. "Hawthorne and Melville in the Shoals: 'Agatha,' the Trials of Authorship, and the Dream of Collaboration." In Jana Argersinger and Leland S. Person, eds., *Hawthorne and Melville: Writing a Relationship*. Athens, GA: University of Georgia Press, 2008.

Parker, Hershel. "Herman Melville's *The Isle of the Cross*: A Survey and a Chronology." *American Literature* 62/1 (1990), 1–16.

Chapter 3

Anderson, Charles R. *Melville in the South Seas*. New York: Columbia University Press, 1939.

Bryant, John. *Melville Unfolding: Sexuality, Politics, and Versions of* Typee. Ann Arbor: University of Michigan Press, 2007.

Crain, Caleb. "Lovers of Human Flesh: Homosexuality and Cannibalism in Melville's Novels." *American Literature* 66 (1994), 25–53.

Dillingham, William B. *An Artist in the Rigging: The Early Work of Herman Melville*. Athens: University of Georgia Press, 1972.

Heflin, Wilson. *Melville's Whaling Years*, ed. Thomas Farel Heffernan and Mary K. Bercaw Edwards. Nashville: Vanderbilt University Press, 2004.

Herbert, T. Walter. *Marquesan Encounters: Melville and the Meaning of Civilization*. Cambridge, MA: Harvard University Press, 1980.

Lyons, Paul. *American Pacifism: Oceania in the U.S. Imagination*. New York: Routledge, 2006.

Chapter 4

Davis, Merrill R. *Melville's* Mardi: *A Chartless Voyage*. New Haven: Yale University Press, 1952.

Gilman, William H. *Melville's Early Life and* Redburn. New York: New York University Press, 1951.

Vincent, Howard. *The Tailoring of* White-Jacket. Evanston: Northwestern University Press, 1970.

Chapter 5

Brodhead, Richard. *New Essays on* Moby-Dick. Cambridge and New York: Cambridge University Press, 1991.

Bryant, John, Mary K. Bercaw Edwards, and Timothy Marr, eds. *"Ungraspable Phantom": Essays on* Moby-Dick. Kent, OH: Kent State University Press, 2006.

Frank, Stuart. *Herman Melville's Picture Gallery: Sources and Types of the "Pictorial Chapters" of* Moby-Dick. Fairhaven, MA: Edward J. Lefkowicz, 1986.

Heimert, Alan. *"Moby-Dick and American Political Symbolism." American Quarterly* 15 (1963), 498–534.

Herbert, T. Walter. Moby-Dick *and Calvinism: A World Dismantled*. New Brunswick, NJ: Rutgers University Press, 1977.

Higgins, Brian, and Hershel Parker, eds. *Critical Essays on Melville's* Moby-Dick. New York: G. K. Hall, 1992.

James, C. L. R. *Mariners, Renegades, and Castaways: The Story of Herman Melville and the World We Live In*. London: Allison & Busby, 1985.

Levine, Lawrence W. *Highbrow/Lowbrow: The Emergence of Cultural Hierarchy in America*. Cambridge, MA: Harvard University Press, 1988.

Makino, Arimichi. *White Phantom Over the World: Melville and American Ideology*. Tokyo: Nanundo, 1996.

Markels, Julian. *Melville and the Politics of Identity: From* King Lear *to* Moby-Dick. Urbana: University of Illinois Press, 1993.

Morrison, Toni. "Unspeakable Things Unspoken: The Afro-American Presence in American Literature." *Michigan Quarterly Review* 28 (1989), 1–34.

Parker, Hershel, and Harrison Hayford, eds. Moby-Dick *as Doubloon: Essays and Extracts (1851–1970)*. New York: Norton, 1970.

Pease, Donald E. "*Moby-Dick* and the Cold War." In Walter Benn Michaels and Donald E. Pease, eds., *The American Renaissance Reconsidered*. Baltimore: Johns Hopkins University Press, 1985, 113–55.

Person, Leland S. "Melville's Cassock: Putting on Masculinity in *Moby-Dick*." *ESQ* 40 (1994), 1–26.

Said, Edward. "Introduction to *Moby-Dick*." In *Reflections on Exile and Other Essays*. Cambridge, MA: Harvard University Press, 2000.

Schultz, Elizabeth. *Unpainted to the Last:* Moby-Dick *and Twentieth-Century Art*. Lawrence: University Press of Kansas, 1995.

Spanos, William V. *The Errant Art of* Moby-Dick*: The Canon, the Cold War, and the Struggle for American Studies*. Durham: Duke University Press, 1995.

Spark, Clare. *Hunting Captain Ahab: Psychological Warfare and the Melville Revival*. Kent, OH: Kent State University Press, 2001.

Stallybrass, Peter. "Books and Scrolls: Navigating the Bible." In Jennifer Andersen and Elizabeth Sauer, eds. *Books and Readers in Early Modern England*. Philadelphia: University of Pennsylvania Press, 2002, 42–79.

Sten, Christopher. *Sounding the Whale:* Moby-Dick *as Epic Novel*. Kent, OH: Kent State University Press, 1996.

Vincent, Howard. *The Trying Out of* Moby-Dick. Kent, OH: Kent State University Press, 1980.

Chapter 6

Avallone, Charlene. "Calculations for Popularity: Melville's *Pierre* and *Holden's Dollar Magazine*." *Nineteenth-Century Literature* 43 (1988), 82–110.

Creech, James. *Closet Writing/Gay Reading: The Case of Melville's* Pierre. Chicago: University of Chicago Press, 1993.

Higgins, Brian, and Hershel Parker, eds. *Critical Essays on* Pierre. Boston: G. K. Hall, 1983.

Silverman, Gillian. "Textual Sentimentalism: Incest and Authorship in Melville's *Pierre*." *American Literature* 74/2 (2002), 345–72.

Chapter 7

Berthold, Dennis. "Class Acts: The Astor Place Riots and Melville's 'The Two Temples.'" *American Literature* 71 (1999), 429–61.

Bickley, R. Bruce, Jr. *The Method of Melville's Short Fiction*. Durham: Duke University Press, 1975.

Blum, Hester. "Douglass's and Melville's 'Alphabets of the Blind.'" In Robert S. Levine and Samuel Otter, eds. *Frederick Douglass and Herman Melville: Essays in Relation*. Chapel Hill: University of North Carolina Press, 2008.

Burkholder, Robert, ed. *Critical Essays on Herman Melville's "Benito Cereno."* New York: G. K. Hall, 1992.

Dillingham, William B. *Melville's Short Fiction, 1853–1856*. Athens: University of Georgia Press, 1977.

Fisher, Marvin. *Going Under: Melville's Short Fiction and the American 1850s*. Baton Rouge: Louisiana State University Press, 1977.

Fliegelman, Jay, ed. Herman Melville. *Benito Cereno*. Bedford Cultural Edition. Boston: Bedford/St. Martin's, 2008.

Kelley, Wyn, ed. Herman Melville. *Benito Cereno*. Bedford College Edition. Boston: Bedford/St. Martin's, 2008.

Levine, Robert S. *Conspiracy and Romance: Studies in Brockden Brown, Cooper, Hawthorne, and Melville*. Cambridge and New York: Cambridge University Press, 1989.

McCall, Dan. *The Silence of Bartleby*. Ithaca: Cornell University Press, 1989.

Newman, Lea. *A Reader's Guide to the Short Stories of Herman Melville*. Old Tappan, NY: Macmillan, 1986.

Post-Lauria, Sheila. *Correspondent Colorings: Melville in the Marketplace*. Amherst: University of Massachusetts Press, 1996.

Ra'ad, Basem L. "'The Encantadas' and 'The Isle of the Cross': Melvillean Dubieties." *American Literature* 63 (1991), 316–23.

Robbins, Sarah. "Gendering the History of the Antislavery Narrative: Juxtaposing *Uncle Tom's Cabin* and *Benito Cereno, Beloved* and *Middle Passage*." *American Quarterly* 49/3 (1997), 531–73.

Wiegman, Robin. "Melville's Geography of Gender." *American Literary History* 1 (1989), 735–53.

Chapter 8

Cook, Jonathan. *Satirical Apocalypse: An Anatomy of Melville's* The Confidence-Man. Westport, CT: Greenwood Press, 1996.

Quirk, Tom. *Melville's Confidence Man: From Knave to Knight*. Columbia: University of Missouri Press, 1982.

Rampersad, Arnold. *Melville's* Israel Potter: *A Pilgrimage and a Progress*. Bowling Green, OH: Bowling Green University Popular Press, 1969.

Trimpi, Helen P. *Melville's Confidence Men and American Politics of the 1850s*. Hamden, CT: Archon Books, 1987.

Chapter 9

Bezanson, Walter E. "Historical and Critical Note." *Clarel: A Poem and Pilgrimage in the Holy Land*. 1876, in vol. 12 of *The Writings of Herman Melville*, ed. Harrison Hayford, Alma A. MacDougall, Hershel Parker, and G. Thomas Tanselle. Evanston and Chicago: Northwestern University Press and the Newberry Library, 1991, 505–637.

—— "Melville's Reading of Arnold's Poetry." *PMLA* 69/3 (1954), 365–91.

Dowling, Paul M. "Robert E. Lee and Melville's Politics in *Battle-Pieces and Aspects of the War*." *Melville Society Extracts* 128 (Feb. 2005), 1–2, 18–23.

Finkelstein, Dorothy Metlitsky. *Melville's Orienda*. New Haven: Yale University Press, 1961.

Garner, Stanton. *The Civil War World of Herman Melville*. Lawrence: University Press of Kansas, 1993.

Goldman, Stan. *Melville's Protest Theism: The Hidden and Silent God in* Clarel. DeKalb: Northern Illinois University Press, 1993.

Kenny, Vincent. *Herman Melville's* Clarel: *A Spiritual Autobiography*. Hamden, CT: Shoe String Press, 1973.

Knapp, Joseph G. *Tortured Synthesis: The Meaning of Melville's* Clarel. New York: Philosophical Library, 1971.

Norberg, Peter. "Finding an Audience for *Clarel* in Matthew Arnold's *Essays in Criticism*." *Leviathan: A Journal of Melville Studies* 6/1 (2004), 35–54.

Obenzinger, Hilton. *American Palestine: Melville, Twain, and the Holy Land Mania*. Princeton: Princeton University Press, 1999.

Potter, William. *Melville's* Clarel *and the Intersympathy of Creeds*. Kent, OH: Kent State University Press, 2004.

Warren, Robert Penn. "Melville the Poet." *Kenyon Review* 8 (1946), 208–23.

Warren, Rosanna. "Dark Knowledge: Melville's Poems of the Civil War." In James M. McPherson, Richard H. Cox, and Paul M. Dowling, eds. *Battle-Pieces and Aspects of the War: Civil War Poems*. Amherst, NY: Prometheus, 2001, 269–93.

Chapter 10

Renker, Elizabeth. "Melville's Poetic Singe." *Leviathan: A Journal of Melville Studies* 2/2 (Oct. 2000), 13–31.

Robillard, Douglas, "Introduction." In *The Poems of Herman Melville*, ed. Robillard. Kent, OH: Kent State University Press, 2000, 1–49.

Shurr, William. *The Mystery of Iniquity: Melville as Poet, 1857–1891*. Lexington: University Press of Kentucky, 1972.

Stein, William Bysshe. *The Poetry of Melville's Late Years: Time, History, Myth, and Religion*. Albany: State University of New York Press, 1970.

Chapter 11

Johnson, Barbara. *The Critical Difference: Essays in the Contemporary Rhetoric of Reading*. Baltimore: Johns Hopkins University Press, 1980.

Martin, Robert K. "Melville and Sexuality." In Robert Levine, ed. *The Cambridge Companion to Melville*. Cambridge and New York: Cambridge University Press, 1998, 186–201.

Milder, Robert, ed. *Critical Essays on Melville's* Billy Budd, Sailor. Boston: G. K. Hall, 1989.

Parker, Hershel. *Reading* Billy Budd. Evanston: Northwestern University Press, 1990.

Sedgwick, Eve. "Billy Budd: After the Homosexual." In Myra Jehlen, ed. *Herman Melville: A Collection of Critical Essays*. Englewood Cliffs, NJ: Prentice-Hall, 1994, 217–34.

Yannella, Donald, ed. *New Essays on* Billy Budd. Cambridge and New York: Cambridge University Press, 2002.

Index

Page numbers in **bold** refer to major discussions of works; page numbers in *italics* refer to illustrations